The Indian Association of Alberta

Laurie Meijer Drees

The Indian Association of Alberta: A History of Political Action

UBC Press · Vancouver · Toronto

15 14 13 12 11 10 09 08 07 06 5 4 3 2

Printed in Canada on acid-free paper

Library and Archives Canada Cataloguing in Publication

Meijer Drees, Laurie, 1965-
The Indian Association of Alberta

Includes bibliographical references and index.
ISBN-13: 978-0-7748-0876-7 (bound); 978-0-7748-0877-4 (pbk.)
ISBN-10: 0-7748-0876-4 (bound); 0-7748-0877-2 (pbk.)

1. Indian Association of Alberta – History. 2. Indians of North America – Alberta – Politics and government. 3. Indians of North America – Canada – Government relations. I. Title.

E78.A34M43 2002 971.23'00497 C2002-910094-1

Canada

UBC Press acknowledges the financial support of the Government of Canada through the Book Publishing Industry Development Program (BPIDP) for our publishing activities, as well as the support of the Canada Council for the Arts and the British Columbia Arts Council.

This book has been published with the help of a grant from the Humanities and Social Sciences Federation of Canada, using funds provided by the Social Sciences and Humanities Research Council of Canada.

UBC Press
The University of British Columbia
2029 West Mall
Vancouver, BC V6T 1Z2
(604) 822-5959 / Fax: (604) 822-6083
www.ubcpress.ca

In memory of Frank Laurie Barron, 1942-2000

Contents

Illustrations

Acknowledgments

I am pleased to acknowledge many different people who helped me during the research and writing of this book. Working on a monograph was a great learning experience for me, and I hope the completed product is readable and interesting to those wanting to know more about Canadian Native peoples and politics in the mid-twentieth century. Various institutions assisted me in the completion of this work. I am indebted to the staff at the Glenbow Archives, Calgary, who organized and maintained the various papers related to the Indian Association of Alberta (IAA). They graciously allowed me to use their records freely, including some still-uncatalogued materials. This book is an extension of my dissertation research, which was originally concluded at the University of Calgary, under the supervision of Dr. D.B. Smith. The staff at UBC Press encouraged me to rework the original dissertation, and their comments, as well as those of the anonymous reviewers, were most helpful.

Writing the history of Native political activity from a locally rooted perspective is a task hindered by the fact that many of the related documents and recollections are not easily accessible. In the case of the IAA's history, important papers and photographs revealing the early years of its activity are still held privately. Luckily, a few important individuals were willing to contribute their personal recollections, documents, and photographs. I am very grateful to Stan Cuthand, Hugh Dempsey, Pauline Dempsey, Murray Dobbin, William Norris, Gordon Crowchild, Ruth Gorman, Dorothy Gowan, Cynthia Downe, Muriel Manywounds, Harold Cardinal, Sheldon Cardinal, Jim Tootoosis, and Neal McLeod, all of whom provided me with oral history related to various apsects of the IAA and the history of Indian political activity on the prairies. I hold none of them responsible for any errors I might have made in the interpretation of that information. Their contributions were invaluable to this research, augmenting the dry historical documents with stories representing a very significant human element. I am also indebted to Hugh and Pauline Dempsey, who both worked for the organization at varying times, for giving me access to their private collections of related documents and photographs. Dr. Dempsey's patience and generosity contributed immeasurabley to my understanding of the IAA.

I would also like to thank my colleagues and friends at the University of Saskatchewan and the Saskatchewan Indian Federated College who assisted me with proofreading and who also offered patient conversations on the ideas that are embodied in this book. Thanks to Brenda Macdougall, Ron Laliberte, Winona Wheeler, and Frank Tough. At critical moments, Neal Mcleod and Lesley McBain helped me with specific research questions on oral history and the Department of Indian Affairs.

Last, I must give special thanks to individuals for whose assistance and encouragement I am especially grateful. I am indebted to Maria Campbell, who supported my efforts and work when my mentor and friend, Dr. F.L. Barron, died. Dr. Barron was a significant influence on my development as a scholar, and he encouraged my research on this subject from the start. My family, and Michael, never doubted the project and were there for me to the end.

Introduction

After the Second World War, Indian leaders and their associates across western Canada were active in political unions. Although they were unpaid, the time and effort they invested was extensive. Their aim: to gain the ear of Canadian governments and citizens. From British Columbia to Saskatchewan men and women gathered and worked to achieve that goal. For example, on the Northwest Coast Peter Kelly and Frank Calder planned the meetings of the Native Brotherhood of British Columbia; in Alberta, John Laurie spent evenings typing out minutes of Indian Association of Alberta conferences; in Saskatchewan, John Tootoosis rode the dirt roads of reserves to the many meetings of the Union of Saskatchewan Indians (USI). Sadly, despite the significant impact of Aboriginal peoples on Canada's political structure and system, few of their actions are recognized in the general Canadian historical record. The history of Aboriginal political action in Canada is long, and, in the mid-twentieth century, leaders across the west began to gain momentum in their drive to have their voices heard outside their own, often isolated, reserve communities.

In Alberta the IAA came to represent treaty Indian people's interests. Officially founded in 1939 by John (Johnny) Callihoo and Métis leader Malcolm Norris, the IAA derived in part from the League of Indians of Western Canada, which had been operating out of Saskatchewan since 1928. The founding of the IAA, however, represented a deliberate break with the league. The IAA's existence presented a new direction for Indian politics in the Prairie provinces – a move towards provincial organization. Although the IAA is perhaps best known for its role in spearheading the protest against the 1969 White Paper on Indian Affairs, and publishing the Red Paper soon after, its early history reveals much about First Nations perspectives concerning the place of Indian peoples in Canada before the civil rights movements and large-scale federal funding of Aboriginal organizations changed Canadian politics and society.

From its inauspicious beginnings in 1939 to its operation as a full-fledged political association by the late 1950s, the IAA came to represent a large body of treaty Indian peoples across the province. Most important, the association shaped their collective identity within Alberta and made their concerns and demands known to both the federal government and the provincial government. During its first twenty years of operation, the IAA initiated and sustained dialogue between Indian Affairs officials and local representatives of various reserve communities. It agitated for the reform of the Indian Act and for changes in Indian education and health care. It also created awareness of the condition of Alberta's Indian peoples among the non-Indian community and fought to protect its members' treaty rights.

My purpose in this book is to investigate the first three decades of the IAA's existence. I seek to provide a much-needed narrative based on significant events in Canadian First Nations political history. In doing so I identify and describe significant factors – social, political, and economic – that contributed to the founding and growth of the IAA. I examine how the IAA functioned and seek to create an understanding of the role of non-Indian peoples in its activities. During this time period the IAA received a great deal of assistance from its non-Native secretary John Laurie, Opposition politicians, and citizens groups, especially the Edmonton-based Friends of the Indians Society. Finally, I attempt to characterize the relationship between the IAA and the state, that is, the provincial and federal governments.

The overall picture of the IAA that emerges in these decades is of an innately flexible organization that was a direct response to the poor social and economic conditions experienced by many Alberta reserve communities. It was also an organization that was concerned, on an everyday level, with treaty rights. It was not a singular product of war veterans or other "outsiders" but, rather, a movement that ebbed and flowed as a result of the interaction between Indian leaders and outside forces. The IAA lost much of its influence after its first generation of leaders died, limping on until the late 1960s saw its rejuvenation. From the beginning, the Canadian state appears to have responded relatively positively to the IAA. This may have been due to the desire of non-Native politicians to enhance their own image as liberal-minded citizens as much as to their desire to assist treaty Indians in their struggle to improve their position.

A subtle yet significant internal tension characterized the history of the IAA in the first decades of its operation. This tension derived from the differing views of the IAA held by Secretary John Laurie and First Nations peoples. On the one hand, it seems that IAA members perceived the association as an instrument for asserting their treaty rights and special status within Canada, for reaffirming their separateness from the state. On the other hand, Laurie saw the IAA as a vehicle for drawing Indian peoples into Canadian society by encouraging their engagement with the Canadian state. Indian peoples saw the IAA as a protective or distinctive institution; Laurie saw it as a modernizing institution – one that represented redemption for Indian peoples, a chance for them to regain their freedom within the Canadian state through the exercise of democracy. As a result of the IAA's internal tension, during the first decade of its operation its policies vacillated between striving for distinct Aboriginal status and equal rights within Canadian society. The IAA certainly never presented a harmonized vision of the political, social, and economic change necessary to meet the needs of Indian peoples until it confronted the White Paper of 1969; rather, it asserted treaty rights while simultaneously seeking a closer relationship between Indian peoples and the Canadian state. By June 1970, however, the IAA's conflicted position was clear: it found itself integrated into the Canadian political system and in pursuit of treaty rights in the hyphenated form of "citizens-plus." The IAA's position was presented that month to Prime Minister Pierre Trudeau and his Cabinet in the form of a document that became known as the Red Paper. This document, drafted by the Alberta Native leaders with assistance from Preston and Ernest Manning's consulting firm (and borrowing heavily from the Hawthorn Report), launched Aboriginal politics in Canada in a new direction. Rather than focusing upon the social issues of the past, Native politicians began to focus upon reasserting a conversation about treaties and rights – a conversation that their forerunners had last attempted to initiate in the 1940s.

The main questions that I pursue throughout this book derive from themes established in the older literature pertaining to the history of Indian political activity. Over the past forty years, academic analyses of Canadian Aboriginal political activity – at both national and provincial levels – have been produced only sporadically. From Phillip Drucker's work on the Native Brotherhood of British Columbia to more recent writings (including biographies of Aboriginal leaders and surveys of Aboriginal political associations), existing works represent a disparate and relatively small body of literature. Even more significantly, historians have virtually ignored the intellectual structures grounding Indian political activity in the twentieth century.

In his work *Tribal Secrets* (1995), Native American scholar Robert Allen Warrior emphasizes the importance of investigating how American Indian intellectuals write and speak to each other in their social, political, economic, cultural, and spiritual struggle for an American Indian future.[1] The history of Indian political activity in Canada consists of more than scattered and reactionary "protest movements" or homogeneous "Pan-Indian" movements.[2] The philosophies driving Indian political action, such as those expressed by Prairie Indian leaders in the early and mid-twentieth century, were complex and varied. Native American scholar

Elizabeth Cook-Lynn recognizes this when she writes of the American experience: "It is as though the American Indian has no intellectual voice with which to enter into America's important dialogues."[3]

The situation is much the same in Canadian writing: First Nations in Canada's history have rarely had their intellectual voices heard or recognized. This book represents the first application of Cook-Lynn's idea to the treatment of First Nations leaders in academic writing. An inquiry into the nature of Indian political thought and action in this interwar/postwar period provides insight into a political culture intertwined with belief systems, expressive symbols, and a unique historical experience particular to specific Prairie First Nations cultures and communities. In fact, as Cook-Lynn notes, Native American intellectualism distinguishes itself through its focus on tribal indigenousness and sovereignty. This claim is applicable to the Canadian context as well.[4] My history of the IAA seeks to reveal what being treaty Indians meant to Native leaders in western Canada.

As a non-Aboriginal scholar, I came to this topic circuitously, and it has taken time for me to understand my own limitations. Despite my efforts, this work represents a superficial sketch of main trends in IAA history, from the perspective of an observer both culturally and generationally removed from the events described. I recognize that it is my own voice that has been added to those documents and accounts that make up the IAA's history. I also emphasize that much more oral history needs to be done on this subject. Cook-Lynn notes that, ideally, these stories and this type of research need to be generated from within the culture rather than from "the outside looking in."[5] Superficially, I agree with this ideal. However, I also believe that any scholar willing to discuss the political and intellectual heritage of First Nations communities in Canada should be willing to take up the challenges inherent in this topic. Multiple perspectives on these subjects are sorely needed if adequate intellectual discussions are to be held. And in Canada today these discussions need to begin.

I also believe that writing histories such as this one is a more complex business than Cook-Lynn's model of "outsider"/"insider" suggests. The IAA and its members represent a heterogeneous history with no true outsiders or insiders; instead, there were those in the centre and those on the periphery. By implication, there were also many between those extremes. All those lives affected by the IAA between 1939 and the 1960s were somehow connected – and not always by culture or language. Similarly, writers of this history are either closer to or more removed from the topic, depending upon their various personal characteristics. By extension, although the history of the IAA is not related directly to my own community, it is indirectly linked to my own family. The Norris and Downe family histories, prominent in the story of the IAA, are intertwined with mine, and these intersections indicate to me the extent to which this history – of reserve communities and their political, social, and economic aspirations – is far more wide-ranging than are the boundaries of those communities, both geographic and social. It is for these reasons that I chose to tackle the difficult task of trying to present my own version of IAA history.

Over time my interest in the subject has deepened beyond the preliminary research this narrative represents. After investigating the activities and goals of the IAA, I became increasingly intrigued with the lives and ideas of Prairie Aboriginal leaders. For example, the more I read and heard about John Callihoo, the first president of the IAA, the more obvious it became to me that he promoted and symbolized a specific set of ideas and ideals. As I studied the history of the IAA's actions and interactions I began to hear a particular language of citizenship and sovereignty in tones and metaphors that I had not encountered elsewhere in the academic literature. Reflection on these texts led me to conclude that First Nations political unions in twentieth-century Canada are the embodiments of historically rooted visions – visions as diverse as any coming from Canada's many non-Aboriginal political leaders.

Identifying, documenting, and studying the politics and visions of Native leaders in Canada's west after the Second World War is a task that presents some special challenges to academics trained in documentary approaches to history. First, the existing literature is thin. Few published sources document historical Native politics from Aboriginal perspectives. Second, correspondence, speeches, and other standard unpublished primary documentary sources frequently used by intellectual historians to sketch political histories are equally scarce for many Indian leaders, including those of the IAA. This can be explained in part by the fact that most leaders were orators who spoke frequently and eloquently in their Aboriginal languages rather than from prepared written speeches. And those who did produce writings often kept their papers within their communities or families. As a result, the material is not easily available to outsiders. It is imperative that scholars interested in the historical development of Aboriginal political activity understand that oral history and community-based research are vital avenues to providing insight into the political history of Prairie First Nations communities. The truth of this history is in the people and so it is they who must be consulted.

This book follows the chronological history of the IAA. Chapters 1 to 3 investigate the origins and early years of the IAA. In its first twenty years of operation, the association assumed and expanded its role as the voice of treaty Indian peoples throughout the province. Initially, the IAA primarily represented people in the Edmonton, Saddle Lake, and Hobbema Agencies,[6] but gradually it recruited members in the southern and far northern regions of the province. By 1946 the IAA had formed a local on the Blood reserve, and by the 1950s it involved communities in the Athabasca region. During this period the IAA's elected executive established its basic policies and practices, and standardized its meetings and agendas.

An examination of the IAA's origins raises a number of ancillary questions. Who were the individuals who created the first constitution of the IAA, and what were their intentions? What issues, both inside and outside Indian communities, spurred IAA founders to create a political association? Since the IAA experienced a period of "dormancy" during the Second World War, to what extent did the re-founded association continue with its original mandate? How was the IAA structured? What was the role of women in the IAA? To date, most studies of Indian political associations have emphasized the impact of the Second World War on their origins. It is commonly held that the overseas experiences of Indian war veterans during the Second World War contributed to Prairie Indian politicization by directly causing the former to assert their citizenship rights upon their return home.[7] The history of the IAA challenges this notion. In Alberta, Indian war veterans did not pursue local issues and treaty rights. In fact, few veterans had had much experience in the residential schools. Furthermore, the issues that concerned the IAA membership predated the Second World War.

Chapter 4 concerns itself with the role of non-Indians in the IAA. In its early decades of operation the IAA executive appears to have been heavily influenced by one individual, John Laurie, a non-Native high school teacher who served as IAA secretary and advisor until his death in 1959. The writings and actions of John Laurie indicate that he saw the IAA as a vehicle for helping Indian peoples integrate into non-Indian society. Through the IAA, Laurie, far from being the impartial secretary he held himself out to be, promoted specific issues and a certain political ideology. Though he often spoke on behalf of the IAA, Laurie's liberal democratic views tended to obscure (or sometimes redirect) the issues that concerned the IAA membership. It was only with his death in 1959 that his influence truly ended, and a new generation of leaders could begin to make their mark on the IAA.

Chapters 5 through 7 concentrate on describing the relationship between the IAA and the federal Indian Affairs administration. Again, John Laurie had a strong hand in directing IAA relations with the government. Laurie was well connected to both politicians and social reformers across Alberta, and he used these connections to support IAA interaction with the government. Interestingly, despite official reticence to facilitate Indian political activity, after the Second World War the IAA became one of the first unions to be officially recognized by the federal government. IAA influence in federal circles was partially a result of its successful presentations to the Special Joint Committee of the Senate and House of Commons, which was empowered to investigate the Indian Act and Indian administration. By the 1950s the association was prominent in the House of Commons and had forged a relationship with Alberta's provincial government. Over the course of the 1940s and 1950s the IAA moved from being on the fringes of the Canadian political system to participating within it.

Chapter 8 looks at the end of the IAA in the 1960s. Although the IAA lost much of its momentum in the mid-1960s, it did experience a revival in 1968, when it attained federal funding and new leadership. From that moment on, Aboriginal politics entered the modern era, were fully integrated into Canada's political machine, and were subject to a new set of conflicting interests. When it challenged the infamous 1969 White Paper, devised by the Liberal government of the day and aimed at eliminating the Indian Act, the IAA successfully pushed a new vision of the position of registered Indian peoples in Canada at the national level. The IAA had changed Aboriginal politics in Canada.

In Chapter 9, in moving from the specifics of IAA history to the level of political leadership, I attempt to refine and specify the discussion on changing political visions in Canadian Aboriginal communities. This chapter pioneers an attempt at comparing and contrasting the leadership of IAA president Johnny Callihoo with that of his Saskatchewan contemporary, John Tootoosis. The Union of Saskatchewan Indians, headed for many years by John Tootoosis, initially had a close relationship with the IAA, although their respective leaders considered each other "enemies." The provincial border was an open one in terms of the flow of political ideas, but Indian leaders in Saskatchewan and Alberta interpreted their roles in different ways. Although Chapter 9 does not fit the chronology underlying the rest of the work, I think that it is fitting that it close the history of the IAA because it poses larger philosophical questions about Aboriginal political thought and intellectual history.

Finally, Chapter 10 summarizes the general trends in IAA history between 1939 and the late 1960s as I view them. The contemporary landscape of Aboriginal politics in Canada at both national and provincial levels has been so strongly influenced by the IAA and its members that our connection to this past must be emphasized.

Obviously, the IAA story suggests many complex questions that are beyond the scope of this investigation. For example, I would suggest that there be further study of the role of the Church in the IAA. Archival evidence suggests that Roman Catholic and Protestant clergy supported the association from its early days through the 1950s. The clergy did influence Indian political activity at the grassroots level; however, the extent of their influence on the IAA is as yet unclear. The history of the IAA also raises questions about the interaction between the provincial government and Indian communities. The Social Credit government in Alberta, officially reluctant to concern itself with Indian matters, did make policy and legislative decisions that affected Indian communities. Furthermore, the history of the IAA presents very interesting material relating to the role of women in Indian politics. Although I have noted the role of women in the IAA, I have not analyzed gender influence on IAA actions and agendas. And, of course, the political philosophies of First Nations leaders such as Tootoosis and Callihoo, as well as interaction between the IAA and the USI, are subjects deserving of more attention than I am able to provide in this work. In fact, students of Aboriginal history in Canada will find that comparisons of different Aboriginal political movements are in order.

The story of the IAA is rich in questions and themes, many of which are related to current issues in Aboriginal politics. Much oral history and community-based research can and should be done as this would shed additional light on Aboriginal views of the IAA and the role it played in Aboriginal politics in postwar Canada.

Theoretical Perspectives and Sources

This analysis of the IAA derives its perspective from anthropologists such as Jean and John Comaroff, and Pierre Clastres as well as from historians such as Natalie Zemon Davis, Lynn Hunt, and Robert Darnton. These authors have focused on wide-ranging issues related to processes extended through time: relationships between history and culture, social movements, state formation and power, and questions of identity and social change. Rather than presupposing or creating unity and coherence in historical events, what has been labelled by academic historians as the "new" history seeks to chronicle and identify intentions, contingencies, and relationships among people through time.[8] This new history emphasizes discontinuity, ambiguities, and the fractured nature of events. French philosopher Michel Foucault initiated this trend in historical investigation as early as 1972 when he stated: "the problem is no longer one of tradition, of tracing a line, but one of division, of limits; it is no longer one of lasting foundations, but one of transformations that serve as new foundations."[9] While older works describing the history of Indian political activity emphasize the great continuities in, and developmental nature of, that activity, this work favours the disjunctures.

The writing of John and Jean Comaroff stimulated me to think critically about previous writings related to Indian political action. In *Ethnography and the Historical Imagination,* these authors develop the idea that the history of colonized peoples is not reducible to a series of cataclysmic events and ruptures that redirected their otherwise static social systems towards modernity or some assimilated state.[10] They emphasize that historical social movements are presented to the historian post facto as dispersed fragments within unbounded fields rather than as a chain of clear-cut events. The function of the historian, in turn, is to restore the scattered shards of past events to a world of meaningful connections; these historical happenings "have to be anchored in the processes of their production, in the orbits of connection and influence that gave them life and force."[11] If one takes these ideas to heart, then it seems obvious that, in order to reconstruct the history of the IAA, one has to anchor the swirling cross-currents of social activity to a larger context without denying the ambiguity and disunity of the events that constituted that organization. Thus I attempt to link the quotidian roots of the IAA to a larger Prairie and Canadian history. The founding of the IAA neither marked the "beginning" of Indian political activity nor constituted a sign of Indian peoples' realization that they could now assert some form of public power; rather, the IAA simply represented a new forum within which reserve communities could voice some of their concerns. The IAA was not First Nations peoples' only source of political power or collective identity; it was merely one they found most useful between 1939 and the late 1960s. The IAA may have been a new institution, but the ideas and collectivity it represented had a long-standing history.

Archival sources related to the IAA's history are limited, but they do include the business papers of the early association as well as the personal papers of several of its prominent members. Former archivist of the Glenbow Archives in Calgary, Hugh Dempsey (John Laurie's successor as secretary of the IAA), did much to save and preserve these valuable records. As a result, the John Laurie Papers, the James Gladstone Papers, the IAA business papers, and scattered documents deriving from other IAA supporters housed in the Glenbow Archives represent the largest collection of material on the IAA's early years. These papers document the history of the IAA from 1939 through the late 1950s and are very revealing of John Laurie's involvement in the association. I must acknowledge and emphasize that, when I conducted this research, some of those papers were not yet catalogued. Some of them were still in private hands, and others had not yet been filed. These papers derive from the private collections of Hugh Dempsey and Murray Dobbin and are documented as such in this work. Although I hold photocopies of these papers, they are now incorporated into the various Glenbow collections.

In addition, the National Archives of Canada Record Group 10 (RG 10) also contains a significant collection of government policy statements and Indian Affairs correspondence related to the IAA. The record in the National Archives primarily represents the Indian Affairs' correspondence with the IAA, and it gives a good picture of the response of Ottawa bureaucrats to an Aboriginal association that demanded Indian Affairs' accountability. Unfortunately, this federal record of government-IAA interaction thins out remarkably after 1964. It is not clear whether the IAA's activities slowed so much that the paper trail in Ottawa was reduced or whether the records have simply not yet made it to publicly accessible files.

Two other archives were relevant to my research into IAA history. The Saskatchewan Archives Board's Historical Records Section contains oral histories of Saskatchewan leaders who knew IAA leaders and who were willing to share their memories of them. In turn, The University of Alberta Archives contain the Reta Rowan Papers, which relate to the activities of the IAA at the provincial level. Reta Rowan was an important figure in the group known as the Friends of the Indians Society, which operated out of Edmonton, and her personal papers contain many interesting photographs of IAA members and IAA meetings. In addition, they contain the meeting minutes of the Friends of the Indians Society. These papers offer a non-Aboriginal perspective on the activities of the IAA into the 1950s.

Only a small, albeit very significant, fragment of the archival material informing this history derived from private collections. As is true for most investigations into any aspect of twentieth-century Aboriginal history in Canada, Aboriginal families have a substantive cache of information. In some cases, families allow researchers to make use of this material; however, much of it is not widely available. In my case, I am immensely grateful for two personal collections of papers that were made available to me. Other extensive private collections have not yet been opened to researchers, although they are known to exist and will remain unnamed out of respect for the privacy of the families that hold them. I hope that, one day, they will be used to highlight the significance of Aboriginal political history to the evolution of the Canadian state.

Last, but not least, a rich yet underutilized source of information on IAA history lies in the memories of those who participated in the organization in its early years. Gordon Crowchild, Muriel Manywounds, Harold Cardinal, William Norris, Ruth Gorman, Cynthia Downe, Hugh Dempsey, Maria Campbell, Stan Cuthand, and Pauline Dempsey were among those who generously shared with me their recollections of the IAA. Although far from comprehensive, these accounts acknowledge the importance of the undocumented, unpublished, unarchived sources and the significance of sharing them with a larger audience. Unfortunately, many of the major and original contributors to the IAA – such as Malcolm Norris, Johnny Callihoo, Albert Lightning, Clarence McHugh, and others – have died, leaving their memories of the IAA unrecorded. Conversely, there are many individuals who can still contribute to a deeper understanding of the IAA.

Photographs also serve as a significant source of information on the IAA. In the 1940s and 1950s, several IAA members and their supporters were avid photographers who enjoyed capturing friends and family on film at various IAA-related functions. Collectively, these images can reveal a great deal about the personal and intimate side of IAA history. They also provide insight into many details of the IAA that are missing in the written record. Simple questions such as "Who attended the IAA meetings?" or "Where were the meetings held?" are more easily answered when photographs of the period are consulted. Most interestingly, the photographs of John Laurie reveal a highly personal view of Prairie Indian politics and social activity, often featuring Laurie's closest friends and favourite activities. These photographs are held in the Glenbow Archives. Reta Rowan's photos of her IAA adventures focus on a very different subject matter than did John Laurie's: women. Rowan spent time with the Aboriginal women she met in reserve communities and always seemed eager to take snapshots of them. Although women's participation in the IAA is not always obvious from the written records, it is clear from Rowan's photographs. These photographs are held in the University of Alberta Archives.

Despite the availability of some very interesting source material on the IAA, after 1966 much of the association's history is difficult to document. Time may reveal that more documents are available through the regional Indian Affairs offices or through private collections; however, at the time of writing, documentary sources pertaining to the mid- to late 1960s were extremely thin. No record of IAA meeting minutes are readily available for the period after 1966. The tables and text presented here pertaining to this period are based on archival material.

Names of reserve communities and Indian bands used in this work are those that were in use from the 1930s through the 1950s. Recently, many bands and communities in Alberta have changed their names to better reflect their First Nation status and the use of indigenous languages. However, in the interest of clarity and accuracy, I use the older names – including Blackfoot, Sarcee, Blood, Stoney, and others. It is these names that both permeate the records and reflect contemporary usage. Because the IAA was concerned with representing "Indians," in this book I refer to the First Nations residents of Alberta as "Indian" or "Indian peoples." The federal and provincial governments engaged in Aboriginal affairs according to the definition of "Indian" contained within the Indian Act. Time and practice will change and clarify the usage of terms such as "Indian," "Native," "First Nations," and "Aboriginal"; however, when dealing with this transitional period it is difficult to be both historically and politically correct at all times for all peoples. In this case, it is the historical record that primarily determines my use of names and terms. All views presented in this work are derived strictly from my own interpretation of the papers that I studied and the conversations in which I participated. I humbly accept responsibility for them all and acknowledge that some of my views may, unwittingly, be in error.

The Indian Association of Alberta

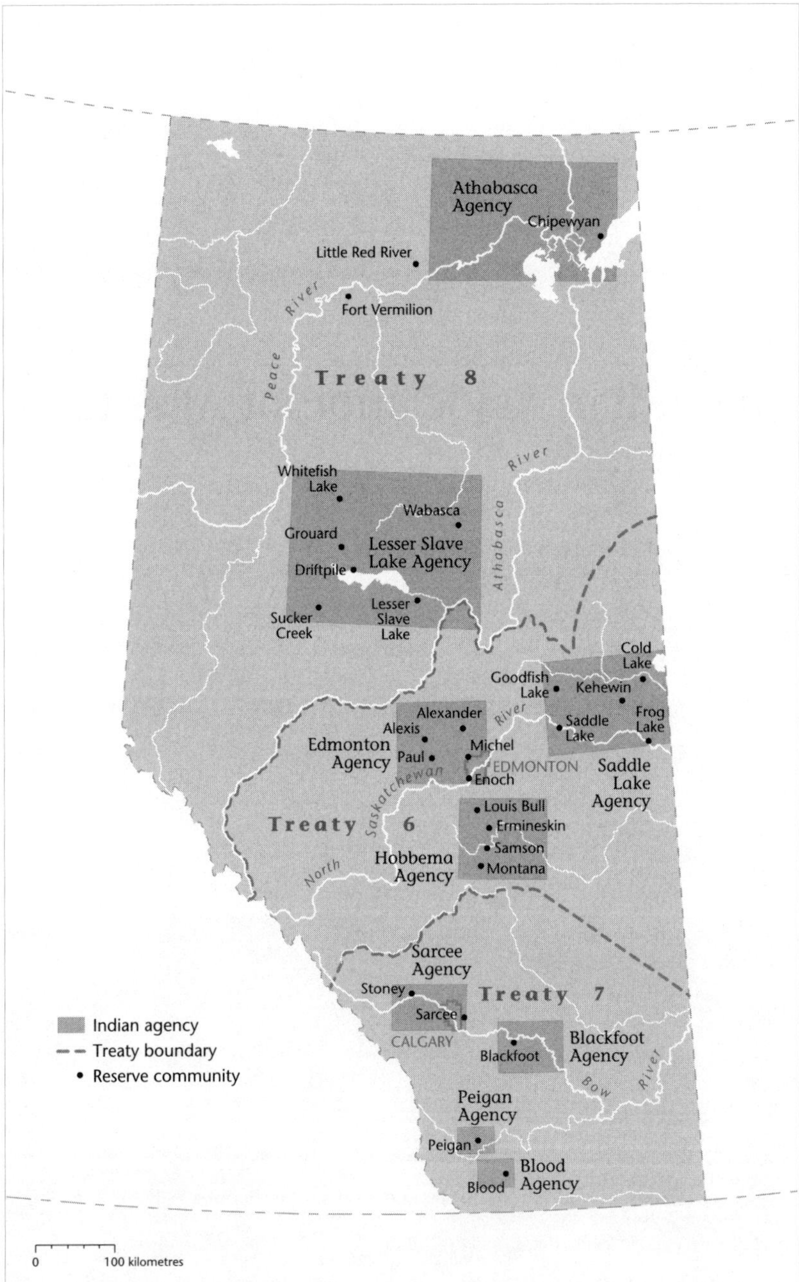

Map of Alberta showing treaty boundaries, selected reserve communities, and general location of Alberta Indian agencies.

1
A General Setting

During the years between its founding in 1939 and the late 1960s, the Indian Association of Alberta (IAA) functioned within a complex tapestry of events and people. Many factors influenced its actions and historical moves, and these factors formed the weft and warp within which the IAA was enmeshed. Federal policies, provincial economic development, the existence of other Aboriginal political organizations, and public sentiment are all woven into the fabric of IAA history. A central event of the period between 1939 and the 1960s affecting IAA history was Canada's involvement in the Second World War. Although the war is usually discussed in terms of minority rights and their effects on federal Indian policy,[1] the social and economic impact of the war on Canada strongly affected Prairie Indian peoples within their own home communities. The industrialization of the Canadian economy and the subsequent urbanization of the nation's population, for example, changed the relationship between Indian communities (which remained rural and agrarian) and the rest of Canadian society. The postwar era also saw an extension of federal government involvement in the nation's social realm. Again, these social welfare policies affected both Indian and non-Indian communities but in different ways.

The effect of the war on Canadian demographics and economics is significant to the social history of Alberta Indian people. Canadian historians have extensively described how the nation's involvement in the European war brought it out of its deep economic depression.[2] The massive growth of agricultural production, manufacturing, and industry associated with the war caused a dramatic increase in employment and urbanization following the depression years. As early as 1940, Canada was called upon to produce war materials not only for its own troops, but also for Britain; and, by 1941, Canadian production of munitions, small arms, chemicals, ships, and military vehicles was in full swing.[3] The Canadian west also benefited from the war production program. Local factories in Winnipeg, Edmonton, and Regina began working on war orders by late 1941, and this small boom helped relieve unemployment on the Prairies, as it did elsewhere.[4] Ultimately, this war-induced industrialization encouraged large numbers of people to relocate to regional cities in order to take advantage of new jobs.

As the war affected industry, it also affected agriculture. Although wheat prices did not increase as dramatically during the war as was initially expected, government subsidies encouraged Canadian farmers to diversify their production for the export markets. Overall, between 1939 and 1944, Prairie farmers saw their total cash incomes increase by approximately 200 percent.[5] Interestingly, much as industrial growth in Canada contributed to urbanization, so, indirectly, did changes in agricultural practice. During the war the shortage of farm labour and the rising income of farmers encouraged the mechanization of farming. The result of this trend was larger farms run with fewer people. Historians Howard and Tamara Palmer have indicated that, in the case of Alberta, small farmers soon found themselves unable to compete with the larger, more mechanized farms and were forced to sell out. By 1951 the majority of the population of Alberta had become urban.[6]

Indian peoples in Canada, and especially in the Prairies, were affected by this wartime industrialization and urbanization. For those who remained on the home front, the shortage of workers on rural farms and the growth of Canada's resource industries created many new jobs both on and off reserves. As Harold McGill, director of the Indian Affairs Branch of the Department of Mines and Resources, reported in 1941, "greater opportunities for employment have become available to Indians coincident with the increased demands for labour caused by the war."[7] McGill pointed out how wartime industries absorbed Indian peoples into the building trades, ranching, logging, and mining. Other areas where Indian peoples found temporary employment in these years of economic expansion were in road building, farming, and the sugar beet industry.[8] Despite this boom in wage employment, however, reserve economies based on farming faltered. Mechanization gradually decreased the need for Indian labour,[9] and Indian farmers, unable to expand their farms or to mechanize, soon found themselves unable to compete with their non-Indian neighbours. The urbanization and industrialization of both farm and city life in Canada after the Second World War did little to benefit Indian reserve communities.

Another significant development during this period was the expansion of the federal government's role in Canadian society. Following Canada's declaration of war on Germany, the federal government set about mobilizing its economic resources through the War Measures Act. Out of the government's expanded participation in the Canadian war economy came increased federal involvement in the area of social security. An initial development in social security legislation, beyond the initiation of pension legislation in 1927, occurred with the Unemployment Insurance Act, 1940. Soon after, the Family Allowance Act, 1944, created universal family allowances. These two acts paved the way for increased government involvement in public welfare during the postwar years, when reconstruction of Canadian society was seen as a top priority.[10] By the mid-1940s, social policy theorists as well as Canadian politicians had reached a consensus on the importance of comprehensive social security; the only question that remained was how social security measures could best be financed and implemented.

Just as changes in the economy affected Indian communities, so did the government's new social welfare orientation. Strangely, despite growing government involvement in social security, initially Indian peoples did not receive the same social security benefits as did non-Indians. The original Old Age Pensions Act, 1927, which made Canadians eligible for a means-tested pension, explicitly excluded Indians from its provisions.[11] Only by the late 1940s did the Department of Indian Affairs (DIA) begin to extend some pension benefits to the registered Indian population, paying individuals who received incomes of under $400 per month a pension of eight dollars per month. In 1950 the amount of pension moneys to eligible Indians was increased slightly; however, over time, strict requirements and documentary procedures proved prohibitive for many Indian applicants. As a result, few of the pension benefits reached Indian peoples.[12] Only in 1951 was the former Old Age Pensions Act finally replaced by two new pieces of legislation: the Old Age Security Act, which officially and universally extended pensions to Indian peoples, and the Old Age Assistance Act, which maintained the older residual pattern of granting aid.[13]

Between 1935 and 1957, the Mackenzie King and Louis St. Laurent governments established what some historians have labelled "the age of bureaucracy" and "the age of welfare." During these decades of Liberal majority rule, Canada enjoyed growing economic prosperity based on the internal postwar "reconstruction" of the nation.[14] According to political scientist Reg Whitaker, the postwar years supported strong, centralized action on the part of the federal government in re-engineering postwar Canadian society.[15] In combination, economic prosperity and collectivist sentiments resulted in a federalist Liberal government policy focused upon national development, full employment, immigration, and improved living conditions for the general Canadian population.[16] Between 1939 and 1957 "bureaucracy" and "social welfare" came to characterize the Liberal federal government's priorities. During these years, Canada's Indian population was affected by the federal Liberal agenda as much as were other Canadians. Federal Indian policies of the 1940s and 1950s reveal that

Indian peoples, like non-Indian peoples, were to be recipients of Liberal attempts to smooth away regional differences and to promote national prosperity. Canadian national development was the government priority, and all segments of the population were to be drawn into this plan. In reality, however, the inclusion of status Indian peoples in a new economy and welfare state did not necessarily progress in the same manner as did the inclusion of other Canadians. This was an issue that concerned the IAA over a long period of time.

At the provincial level, Indian communities faced numerous circumstances that influenced their political activities. Within Alberta the political climate was very different from that in Ottawa; the social welfare sentiment that became part of Liberal ideology did not consistently prevail at the provincial level. Between 1939 and the late 1950s, Alberta politics was dominated by the Social Credit party. Swept to power in 1935 under the leadership of fundamentalist Christian William Aberhart, the Social Credit party presented itself as a reform-oriented party, attracting working-class support and promising radical changes to the monetary system, redistribution of income, price controls, medicare, and even some state control over industry. Much of the popularity enjoyed by the Social Credit party was rooted in the hardship suffered by Albertans during the Great Depression as well as in growing public disillusionment with the other political parties in the province, including the United Farmers of Alberta and the Labour party.[17] Historians Howard and Tamara Palmer suggest that Alberta experienced a phase of political radicalism between 1939 and 1949, when Albertans embraced a new politics emphasizing collective action and socialist ideals.[18] This collectivist intellectual climate within Alberta contributed to the founding of the IAA in 1939. Many Indian leaders supported left-wing ideals and believed that their involvement in this kind of politics would benefit their communities.

Despite its superficial socialism, however, the politics of the Social Credit party shifted to the right. After the Second World War, large-scale agriculture and mineral resource development created dramatic prosperity in Alberta. The result of this prosperity was that, where once the Social Credit provincial government championed a social welfare ideology, after the war it came to see socialists as its chief opposition.[19] Within a short period of time, Indian peoples found themselves devoid of support within provincial politics. In addition, they also found themselves gradually excluded from the provincial economy. The development of oil and gas resources in Alberta, beginning in 1947 with the Leduc fields, for example, played a negligible role in Indian communities, and the contrast between Indian and non-Indian economic status was amplified despite the development of mineral resources on some southern reserves.[20] Furthermore, the oil industry created demands for skilled workers, and small-scale agriculture as practised on reserves decreased in economic significance.[21] The oil boom, which benefited some sectors of Alberta's population, neatly side-stepped its Indian population.[22] Overall, to the IAA, the post-war conservatism of the Alberta government represented a substantive hurdle to the achievement of social justice for Indian peoples. In fact, direct provincial government initiatives to assist the Aboriginal population of the province were not taken until 1964.[23]

The IAA also operated in a time when Native organizations, although not numerous, were certainly making their mark on Canada's political landscape. In western Canada Aboriginal communities had long been active, particularly in British Columbia, where leaders were primarily interested in having their claims to their ancestral lands recognized by the colonizing governments. Groups such as the Allied Tribes of British Columbia were founded as early as 1915, to be followed by other BC organizations, including the Native Brotherhood of British Columbia (1931) – an extension of the Alaska Native Brotherhood and one of BC's most influential Indian organizations. On the West Coast, these organizations worked for more than just land rights, and the Brotherhood did much to promote the rights of fishers and cannery workers. On the Prairies, residents of reserve communities rallied around several smaller organizations that appeared to operate successfully for a few years and then dissipate. Before the Second World War political union-style meetings were pioneered by the League of Indians of Canada (a group very successful on the Prairies in the 1920s and a forerunner of the League of Indians in Western Canada), the Association of Western Allied Tribes (1925), and even the Métis Association of Alberta. After the war, the number of small associations expanded to include the Manitoba Indian Brotherhood (1946), Saskatchewan's Queen Victoria Treaty Protective Association (1947), and the Union of Saskatchewan Indians (1946) to name the most obvious.[24] Not all survived or thrived; however, all contributed to the publicizing of Aboriginal claims. By the late 1960s the road pioneered by the early associations had been well trodden by the many unions that sprang up following the implementation of government funding for Aboriginal organizations.

Within this context the work of the IAA was clearly significant: it represented one of the few Prairie organizations to maintain a presence on the political scene over the long term. It was not alone in its works, and its leaders had experience with other organizations as well; however, its longevity and tenacity set it apart from other similar unions founded on the Prairies at the same time. The IAA leaders and its membership generated enough momentum to carry their group through an ever-changing political wilderness. The details of its founding and workings bear witness to its relative effectiveness.

In the most general sense, even before one considers the intricate details of the IAA, it can be seen that the history of this association played itself out within the context of multiple local and national forces. Its story is part of the demographic changes taking place in Canadian society, including the thrust towards urbanization and industrialization following the Second World War. The IAA was a product of federal Liberal government policies – both Indian policy and social welfare policy; it was an effect of and a reaction to the new prosperity of Alberta, and the way in which that prosperity was managed by the Social Credit government in the postwar years; and it was also the product of a long history of Indian political activity in Canada. The IAA represented Indian peoples' views of their place within Canadian society during a particular era, and the process of articulating those views in the face of national and provincial political and economic developments helped them to forge a distinctive collective consciousness.

2
The Origins of the Indian Association of Alberta

> The Indian Association of Alberta, as you know, is a Democratic organization ... for the betterment of [Indian] social and economic conditions as promised under Proclamation and Treaties made with them by the representatives of his Majesty's governments.
>
> – Malcolm Norris to Ben Calfrobe, 1944[1]

To date, Canadian historians writing about Native political activity have emphasized the significance of forces external to Native communities as triggers for political action within those communities. Paul Tennant, for example, in his discussion of British Columbia Indian political activity between 1900 and 1969, portrays Aboriginal political actions as a direct response to internal colonialism within the Canadian state.[2] Similarly, James Pitsula suggests that the presence of a Co-operative Commonwealth Federation (CCF) government in Saskatchewan, a premier concerned with minority rights, and the experiences of Native war veterans who served overseas drove Indian peoples to take initiatives on the political front. He claims that the war experience gave Indian leaders "a greater degree of worldliness and sophistication than they would otherwise have had" and that these two factors were central to the founding of the Union of Saskatchewan Indians.[3] Brian Titley's work follows a similar line of argument, emphasizing the importance of the world wars in instigating action within Indian communities. In his view, "the war [Second World War] had brought Indians from many parts of Canada into contact with one another for the first time and sowed the seeds of pan-Indian consciousness. It created an awareness of common grievances which led naturally to a perceived need for political action."[4]

Informative as these interpretations of historical Indian political activity are, they do not provide insight into how local events and daily experiences within Indian communities shaped First Nations internal political history.[5] Within the existing literature, "just cause" for the evolution of political movements within Aboriginal communities is generally interpreted as coming from outside them.[6]

The origins and early history of one Indian political union, the Indian Association of Alberta, suggests that, in fact, local interests strongly influenced the founding of the group. Naturally, Indian leaders were also concerned with, and affected by, outside government policies, and some had widened their political viewpoint as a result of their war experiences. But Native leaders were also focused upon the daily problems plaguing reserve communities, and, in Alberta, many of these leaders were farmers who had never left the province. The history of the IAA has been little studied, and an investigation into its origins provides important insights into twentieth-century Aboriginal political movements and leaders.

The IAA was officially formed in 1939 by several bands located in central Alberta. They created the IAA because they were unhappy with the way the system of reserve land use affected band membership as well as farming, hunting, and fishing rights; they also hoped to improve the poor social and economic situation on their reserves. In addition, they wanted more information on their treaty rights and the Indian Act. Reserve leadership had long-standing concerns over treaty rights, and the IAA represented a new avenue for expressing these concerns to Indian Affairs. Finally, many were unable, or unaware of how, to voice their concerns to the federal government. The IAA was a product of strong regional and specific community interests rather than national or pan-Indian interests.[7]

Although local issues played a prime role in the founding of the IAA, the association was undeniably linked to older political movements. In membership, spirit, and action, it had direct links to the League of Indians of Western Canada, a union founded by Fred Loft in the 1920s. The Métis Association of Alberta also influenced the IAA. Organized in 1932, the Métis union assisted the IAA with strategic planning and the drafting of its constitution. Finally, as some IAA members were also members of the Social Credit party and provincial farm unions,[8] they were familiar with the social reform politics that were prominent in the Prairies during the 1930s.

Alberta Indian Reserve Communities during the Interwar Years

In Alberta, reserve communities are largely located in remote parts of the province, away from major urban centres. Historically, their isolation discouraged the development of any collective identity or political movements as communication between communities was difficult. Reserves in the southern part of the province include the Blood (Kainai), Blackfoot (Siksika), Sarcee (Tsuu T'ina), and Stony (Nakoda). The bands in this region adhered to Treaty 7, which was signed at Blackfoot Crossing in 1877. At an early date they developed economies based on ranching, some farming, and logging.

In the central part of Alberta, reserve communities were created at Hobbema (between Calgary and Edmonton), at Saddle Lake, Kehewin, Cold Lake, Frog Lake, and near the Saskatchewan border east of Edmonton. Several were also clustered near Edmonton, including the Alexis, Paul, Alexander, Michel, and Stony Plain reserves. The bands in these communities adhered to Treaty 6, which was signed at Fort Carlton in 1876. From the earliest reserve years, the economies of these bands were based on a combination of mixed farming, hunting, trapping, and fishing in local lakes.

The Indian groups in the northern regions moved from the land to government-created settlements much more slowly than did those in the southern regions. Bands around and north of Lesser Slave Lake continued to live on the land, hunting, trapping, and fishing as they had for generations, only gradually settling into reserve-based communities following the signing of Treaty 8 in 1899. In fact, the government did not begin seriously surveying the Athabasca region until 1913, and then it did so only to mark the places bands used for camping and permanent dwelling sites.[9] Reserves were located in the Peace River District, near Lesser Slave Lake, at Cold Lake, and at Lake Athabasca. The Cree and Athapaskan groups in northern Alberta, aside from their historic involvement with Europeans in the fur trade, were quite isolated from the changes brought on by European settlement in the agricultural belt. They remained so until the middle north opened to non-Native trappers and prospectors in the early decades of the twentieth century.

During the 1920s and 1930s, individual Alberta reserve communities faced a variety of challenges, some shared, some unique. First, these communities fell under the jurisdiction of the Indian Act, a formidable piece of federal legislation that outlined the special legal rights and restrictions faced by registered Indian peoples across Canada. The Indian Act, first formulated in 1876 and periodically amended, regulated the existence of Indian peoples in various ways. It defined who could be considered an "Indian" and, thus, who could live on reserves. It also controlled band membership; regulated the education of Indian children, the use of reserve lands, and the sale of agricultural products and other resources produced on reserve; outlined the activities of local governing band councils; and regulated the movements of Indian peoples. In short, the Indian Act controlled virtually every aspect of reserve life. Throughout the province many reserve residents viewed the act as both restrictive and incomprehensible.

Over the decades the Indian Act evolved into an extensive and complex statute. With each revision, it acquired provisions that further undermined, or sought to control, the social, political, and economic activities of reserve communities. For example, in the 1880s the act contained amendments controlling the consumption of liquor by Indians, forbidding the holding of traditional ceremonies and gatherings (including the potlatch), and allowing Indian Affairs administration to over-ride band council decisions. In the 1920s, further oppressive measures were inserted into the act, including Section 141 (1927), which explicitly forbade bands to attempt to raise funds for the purpose of pursuing claims against the government. As Paul Tennant points out, although these sections did not directly outlaw the organization of political groups in Indian communities, they did lead to a general understanding among Indian leaders that political activity was not well received by the government.[10] These provisions and amendments to the act all contributed to discouraging Indian communities from gathering for political purposes, from attempting to assert band decisions in the face of government opposition, and from soliciting paid assistance in making their claims to the government.[11]

The terms of treaties signed between local Indian leaders and Dominion government representatives in the late nineteenth century also influenced life in Alberta reserve communities. Generally, the treaties promised Indian peoples rights to hunt and fish, land for reserves, European-style schools and education, assistance with agriculture, and a payment of annuities and gratuities. Treaties 6 and 7 resembled each other, although, in the latter, bands disposed to engage in pastoral rather than in agricultural pursuits were given cattle instead of farming implements.[12] The terms of Treaty 8 followed the general outline of the previous treaties, except that, due to the widespread opposition to the reserve system in the middle north, the appointed treaty commissioners were authorized to exercise a larger degree of discretion in negotiating reserves than was the case with the earlier treaties.[13] Of the three treaties, only Treaty 6 contained a clause that provided a promise of medical assistance to its adherents. The treaties promised reserve communities assistance with the development of a new agricultural economy as well as some protection for the traditional hunting and fishing economy.

The leaders of the bands who signed the agreements imbued the oral and written promises made by the treaty commissioners with great significance. Cree historian Stan Cuthand suggests that the promises were viewed as "sacred," although not in the European sense of the word. According to Cuthand, those who signed Treaty 6 believed that its promises were based on goodwill and trust, that they would be dealt with wisely and cautiously, and that the treaty was forever binding in sacred, or in what he refers to as "mythological," terms.[14] For Indian peoples across Alberta, treaty promises were viewed as the foundation of the relationship between Indian peoples and the Canadian government. Treaties were perceived to have been concluded in good faith, and it was expected that each of their terms would be fulfilled. The southern bands viewed the promise of short-term assistance and the protection of their resources and lands from the encroachment of settlers as centrally important,[15] while the northern bands viewed the protection of their traditional economies as of paramount significance.[16]

To Indian leaders of the 1920s and 1930s, the treaties and the Indian Act appeared, in many ways, to be in conflict with one another. The act controlled and regulated Indian life, while the treaties promised a relationship based on mutual respect between government and Indian groups. At the same time, many people in Alberta reserve communities viewed the act as protecting treaty promises.[17] Since both the treaties and the Indian Act determined life in reserve communities – one by establishing the relationship with government and providing some of the basics of community life (including reserve lands, education, and monetary assistance), the other by regulating everyday affairs – both were of daily significance.

During the interwar years Alberta reserve communities lacked an impartial forum within which to present their grievances. The Indian Agent, a federal civil servant appointed to manage reserve affairs, was the only individual sanctioned to deal with Indian complaints. This proved frustrating for many Indian communities as the Agent was often unwilling to deal with their complaints. For example, in the 1930s the Native community at the Saddle Lake reserve perceived Indian Agent Gullion to be "all powerful" and extremely difficult to approach. Typically, when band council members brought complaints to his office, he limited his meeting times with them and was generally unsupportive.[18] Cree writer Joseph Dion notes that, in the Depression years on the Kehiwin reserve in the Saddle Lake Agency, "the agent was chief ruler of our lives."[19] The almost total dependence of the reserve community and its local band council on the Indian Agent drove the people to seek other means of having their concerns addressed.

Practical challenges also loomed large in the daily life of members of Alberta's reserve communities. Throughout the 1920s and 1930s the reserve economies in Alberta generally fared poorly. In the southern and central parts of the province, farming and ranching proved difficult and only marginally sustainable. On the Peigan reserve – where stock-raising and farming were the primary basis of the economy – the severe winter of 1919-20 destroyed a large part of the cattle herd. In the following summers conditions were extremely dry, and crop failures and shortages of pasturage and water for stock further checked any agriculture advances.[20] Pastures were completely grazed off, and the cattle meant to serve as rations for the community were in a poor state.[21] The increased mechanization of farming after the First World War also conspired against the Peigan farmers, who were limited in their ability to acquire modern equipment and, therefore, could not cultivate larger acreages.[22] On the large Blood reserve, the situation was similar. Ranchers from the community noticed a decline in their herds, and crop failures were common. Looking back on these years, some Blood commented "that they didn't even realize there was a Depression outside the reserve."[23]

Even in the Edmonton Agency area, where drought was not a major factor, it was nonetheless impossible to provide for community needs through farming. Elk meat was imported from the national parks to feed the destitute, and families were encouraged to fish, hunt, and garden in order to supplement their diets.[24] Muriel Manywounds, whose father Ralph Steinhauer farmed on the Saddle Lake reserve beginning in the 1920s, recalls that not all the reserve land in that community was ideal for agriculture. Her father, one of the successful farmers, was forced to supplement his income with lumbering and labouring during the 1930s.[25] Many others in the Edmonton Agency, who were less successful with agriculture on the reserve, sought income off reserve either by working for non-Indian farmers, by cutting wood, or by moving into urban centres and applying to civic authorities for relief.[26] The migration of people off reserve in search of work or relief on other reserves became relatively common in Alberta in the 1930s, and it was enough of a problem to irritate Indian Agents.[27] On more distant reserves, such as the one at Sucker Creek near Lesser Slave Lake, poor farming conditions drove the destitute to snare rabbits and catch fish for their survival.[28]

In northern Alberta the trapping, hunting, and fishing economy was similarly challenged and undermined by the Great Depression. In the early 1920s, non-Indians were moving to the bush in large numbers, seeking to benefit from relatively high prices for furs and a strong fur industry economy.[29] Indian peoples, in contrast, failed to benefit from this brief upswing in the fur economy because they were being displaced from prime trapping lands by non-Indians.[30] With the Great Depression, trapping would be increasingly important to the survival of Aboriginal economies.

Yet provincial regulations and conservation practices in the interwar years made it even more difficult for reserve communities to acquire any degree of economic freedom through hunting, fishing, and trapping. The Natural Resources Transfer Act, 1930, recognized Indian treaty rights to hunt, trap, and fish on all unoccupied Crown lands and other lands to which they might have the right of access, but only for their own consumption. Many reserve residents perceived this to be an infringement of the original treaty promise that hunting and fishing would continue as before the signing of the treaties. On Edmonton Agency reserves, for example, after 1930 fishing was suddenly limited by a host of regulations, all of which were supposed to be communicated to the reserve population by the Indian Agent. In the late 1930s the issue of fishing permits still troubled reserve residents and agents alike.[31] Problems arising out of the fishing restrictions varied. On Lake Wabamun, near Edmonton, Indians from the adjacent reserve were allowed to fish only on a small section of the lake when new regulations were instituted in 1938 to protect spawning fish.[32] At Saddle Lake, the agent noted community concerns about restrictions placed on the "rat" hunt.[33] Further north, in turn, Indian fishers found themselves engaged in altercations with conservationists who posed as provincial Game Guardians.[34] This state of affairs left the northern, non-farming reserve communities with few alternative sources of food and income, and it worried them greatly. As one individual testified to the Indian Agent at Portage La Loche:

> I will tell you about your Indians from Whitefish. They have not even killed fish as they have been forbidden to do so. When it was fishing time they were stopped by a Game Guardian ... We would like you very much to come here and make arrangements for us to continue getting our living here as before. We are becoming very miserable over this if you do not do something yourself you will have to feed us all because we have no fish, the way it looks now we can only trap on the reserve. When the people are not sick they are not scared to get meat to live on, now, now we have no fish and we cannot let the lake remain idle.[35]

Ultimately, Indians in the northern regions of the province could do little to affect this turn of events. In the central and northern parts of the province, where access to fish and game was still possible, these resources were slowly being denied to reserve communities.

In addition to these problems, Alberta reserve communities faced the alienation of reserve lands – a process that had begun before the First World War. The Soldier Settlement Act, 1917, which provided lands for soldiers returning from the First World War, facilitated the alienation of substantive reserve property. Later, the revised Soldier Settlement Act, 1919, gave the government the power to purchase reserve lands for soldiers under terms established in the Indian Act.[36] The government also alienated lands from reserves prior to the Great War, when Indian populations were viewed as declining and when settlers clamoured for additional lands on the Prairies. The period between 1910 and 1935 probably witnessed the greatest loss of reserve lands in Alberta in the twentieth century.[37]

Up to 1930, the agencies located in the province's prime farming regions were subject to reserve land surrenders and leases, sometimes of substantive size. In particular, the Edmonton Agency reserves (including Michel, Alexander, and Enoch reserves) saw their original reserves reduced in size by an average of 44 percent between the time of their establishment and 1930. The Hobbema Agency, in central Alberta's prime agricultural region, was similarly subjected to the process of reserve land alienation, the Montana, Ermineskin, and Louis Bull reserves being those most affected.[38] Northern reserves, located outside the prime agricultural regions of the province, suffered virtually no loss of reserve lands prior to 1930.

Of all Alberta reserves, the Peigan and Blackfoot Agencies endured the largest sale of original reserve lands. The Blackfoot band council agreed to the sale of approximately 125,000 acres of its 300,800-acre reserve in 1910, and, in 1911 and 1918, these lands were sold to the public. According to newspaper reports at the time, the reason for the land sale was that "the Indians have been rapidly dying of late years until now there are only about 700 on the reserve, and naturally they do not require so much land as formerly."[39] According to Indian Agent George Gooderham, prior to this sale the Blackfoot were quite poor, having only a few cattle and not engaging in any farming. The sale of the land provided the band with substantive funds, which were to ensure that every member of the band receive food, clothing, and shelter.[40] Following the land sale, the Blackfoot band was deemed to be self-sufficient.

The Peigan reserve was also greatly reduced by land sales; however, unlike the case with the Blackfoot, the Peigan surrenders were largely completed without band consent. In 1909, contrary to the procedures outlined in the Indian Act,[41] the Peigan Agent forced the sale of the lands. Unlike the Blackfoot band, the Peigan band was, in addition, made the mortgagor of the land. It was forced to accept time payments from purchasers, many of whom defaulted.[42] As a result of this financial situation, unlike the Blackfoot, the Peigan were unable to use the proceeds from the sales for their own development. Through the 1920s, the IAB continued to offer Peigan reserve lands for sale.[43] By 1930, the Peigan reserve was reduced by 23,102 acres, or 20 percent of its original size. The sale of these reserve lands did little to benefit the reserve community and served only to undermine its agricultural economy.

Alberta reserve communities faced many similar challenges despite the differences in their locations, sizes, economies, governing agents, and treaty rights. In almost every community, the daily pursuits of individuals were hampered in some way, either by restrictions imposed through the Indian Act, by new provincial regulations and legislation, or by Indian Affairs staff (such as the Indian Agent). In a small number of communities, losses of reserve lands undercut the local economy. Although many reserve residents were only vaguely aware of the events in the "outside" world during these decades, leaders within the reserve communities keenly felt the restrictions placed on their peoples. And, in response to this, they sought opportunities on and off the reserve to have their grievances addressed.

External Influences on Alberta Reserve Communities

Throughout the interwar years, Alberta's reserve populations were neither unique nor isolated from the rest of the provincial population. Interaction between reserve communities and non-Indian communities was common because they shared the same agricultural economy. In fact, the position of Alberta's reserve communities during this period was in keeping with the general demographics of Alberta. Before the Second World War, Alberta's population was primarily rural and personal incomes were largely derived from agriculture. The provincial population did not change much during the interwar years. Alberta's population remained relatively stagnant, at about 700,000 between 1930 and 1939, and the province even experienced some degree of population loss as the severe droughts and consistently poor grain prices drove farmers elsewhere.[44] Before the war, small-scale farming was the foundation of life in most parts of southern and central Alberta, as it was in reserve communities. Farming provided not only an economic, but also a philosophical foundation to Prairie life. As Roger Gibbins notes for this period, farming "was more than a business; it was a different way of life with its own mores, patterns of community organization, and institutional forms. Mutual aid and cooperation were fundamental ingredients ... extended beyond the local community through the creation of countless cooperative organizations."[45] Some of the cooperative ideals that existed in non-Indian farming communities carried over into reserve farming communities.

During the interwar years, a handful of leaders in Alberta reserve communities sought to improve the social and economic conditions on their reserves by joining cooperative organizations. Because the Indian Act, as amended in 1927, strictly forbade bands to hire lawyers to investigate any claims against the government,[46] some Aboriginal leaders turned to other off-reserve political groups, including the United Farmers of Alberta, the Métis Association of Alberta, and the League of Indian Nations of North America (an international organization headed by one Lawrence Two Axe). The attraction of Indian farmers to farm unions such as the United Farmers of Alberta is not surprising as these populist groups battled the problems of small-scale farmers, promoted cooperation among farmers, and emphasized the improvement of community life in the areas of women's rights, health, welfare, and education. Indian Affairs officially discouraged the political organization of Indian peoples on reserve before the Second World War, but it did little to openly stop meetings held in communities during the 1920s. As a result, leaders of reserve communities supported an organization that grew directly out of the grievances of eastern Canadian Indian groups: the League of Indians of Canada. Together, these organizations shaped the daily grievances of Indian peoples into a political agenda that eventually became the basis for the IAA.

Although Indian peoples in Alberta participated in a number of other political associations, the most prominent was the League of Indians of Canada.[47] The league originated in eastern Canada through the efforts of Frederick Ogilvie Loft, a member of the Six Nations and a veteran of the First World War. According to one biographer, Loft's experiences as a war veteran and his desire to see Indian war veterans receive similar benefits to non-Indian veterans, motivated him to organize a political union. In addition, the Great War brought Indians from different parts of Canada together for the first time, sowing the seeds of a pan-Indian consciousness and creating awareness of common grievances.[48] Loft held a founding convention at Ohsweken in the Six Nations territory in the winter of 1918, at which time he attempted to organize an association to help Indian peoples present their wishes and concerns to the government.[49]

From Ontario the league branched out to Manitoba, Saskatchewan, and Alberta, where organizational meetings were held in 1920, 1921, and 1922, respectively.[50] In Alberta, the league had a strong presence in the Treaty 6 regions near Edmonton and St. Paul, and, to a lesser extent, in southern Alberta.[51] Throughout the 1920s and 1930s, the league operated in Alberta and Saskatchewan in 1932. These branches continued holding combined meetings for both Alberta and Saskatchewan league members as all shared a common interest in Treaty 6, which covered areas in both provinces.[52]

Through its activities, the league provided Indian communities in Alberta with a structure and insight into their common grievances. Not surprisingly, the types of resolutions made at league meetings in Alberta reflected the daily problems faced by reserve communities. For example, resolutions passed in 1931 at Saddle Lake called for a halt to reserve land surrenders; for the preservation of hunting, trapping, and fishing rights; and for an increase in economic assistance to bands.[53] The league operated sporadically over the interwar years but generated a class of committed leaders interested in keeping its ideals alive.

The United Farmers of Alberta (UFA) contributed less directly to the politicization of Alberta reserve communities. Formed in 1909 in Edmonton, one of the central goals of the UFA was to protect and advance farmers' interests in the face of low prices for farm products.[54] Tremendously popular from the start, within the first year of its existence this union established over 2,000 members in 122 locals.[55] Besides protecting farmers' commercial interests, the UFA also aimed to improve the standard of living for rural peoples; and its women's auxiliary strove to improve rural health, education, social services, and economic security for farmers. Essentially, the UFA was a socially oriented organization aiming for the betterment of rural living; among its central goals were the attainment of "Equity" and an "increase [in the] the strength of the common people."[56] Women played a prominent role in this union.[57]

Not surprisingly, successful Indian farmers in reserve communities joined farmers unions. The ideals of social change, mutual aid, education, health, and increasing the power of the farmer were all compatible with the ideals of reserve farmers. It is also conceivable that Indian Agents would find membership in a farm union more acceptable for their Indian wards than membership in an Indian political group; Indian farmers themselves found the UFA appealing because its meetings and activities accommodated seasonal farming activities.[58] Although it is extremely difficult to trace the membership of Indian farmers in the UFA, it is known that several did join. Ralph Steinhauer and his wife, of Saddle Lake, were active in the UFA and its women's auxiliary, the United Farm Women of Alberba (UFWA); Johnny Callihoo of the Michel reserve was a member of the Alberta Farmers Union; Malcolm Norris of Edmonton actively participated in the CCF; and Frank Cardinal of Sucker Creek was also a member of farm groups. In fact, those who remember the founding of the IAA are quick to recall that "it was really a farmer's group."[59] Clearly, the radical agrarian politics dominating Alberta in the interwar years made an impression on these people, and the ideals of the farmers unions transferred easily to Indian political initiatives.

The Métis Association of Alberta (MAA) influenced the IAA at both personal and ideological levels. In 1932 L'Association des Métis d'Alberta et des Territoires du Nord Ouest, a formal Métis political organization, was created in Alberta to provide for the economic, educational, and medical needs of the Métis people in the region and to gain a land base for them.[60] Prominent leaders in this group included Malcolm Norris, a highly educated Métis from Edmonton; Joe Dion, a Cree schoolteacher from Gurneyville; and Jim Brady, a labourer from St. Paul.[61]

Individually, these leaders were "progressive" in the sense that they valued western European forms of education and the application of government-sponsored social welfare measures to their communities. Norris, for example, was broadly educated, came from a prominent Métis family in St. Albert, and spent part of his young adulthood as a trapper and trader in northern Alberta. Then, at age thirty, he began to take courses in geology at the University of Alberta in order to satisfy his interest in prospecting. There he was introduced to a circle of intellectuals who embraced socialism, and, gradually, his interest in social justice and politics expanded.[62] In addition to his academic and political interests, Norris's fluency in English and Cree served him well in his involvement with Aboriginal political movements.

Like Norris, Brady's background included wealth and education. His grandfather was closely involved with Louis Riel in 1885 and collected considerable wealth through the fur trade.[63] Dion, in turn, also possessed a progressive orientation, and he was also well connected in the Indian communities of northern Alberta. Dion's family came from the Kehewin reserve in the Saddle Lake Agency, and he was the nephew of Big Bear, one of the great Cree leaders who challenged the federal government in 1885. Though Dion gave up his treaty status, he served as teacher for his reserve and was concerned with the social conditions of the people in that community – Indian and Métis alike.[64] Each of these individuals came from a privileged background, which encouraged them to assume positions of leadership within their community.

Collectively, these leaders strove, through the MAA, to petition Alberta's legislature to address the issues facing Métis peoples. They aimed to achieve change by pressuring politicians in a non-political and non-religious manner.[65] Like the farmers unions, the MAA was based on a network of locals, each reporting to an executive whose role it was to communicate directly with government. Métis leaders believed that this arrangement gave unity to an otherwise divided Métis voice.[66]

Between 1932 and 1938, the MAA proved remarkably successful. In 1934 it managed to press the UFA government to set up the Ewing Commission to investigate "the condition of the Half-Breed population of Alberta, keeping particularly in mind the health, education, relief and general welfare of such population."[67] Norris and Brady both made presentations to the Ewing Commission, and each emphasized the importance of self-determination for the Métis people. In addition, when appearing before the commission, both voiced their concern over the state of Métis health care and education. Norris and Brady struggled to improve the daily life of the Métis peoples, and their efforts contributed to the passage of Alberta's Métis Betterment Act, 1938.

The ideas Norris and Brady promoted for the improvement of the impoverished Métis community in Alberta were just as valid to Indian reserve communities. In Alberta's reserve communities, self-determination, better education, and improved health services were all priorities during the 1930s. Since the MAA was prominent in the Edmonton area in the early 1930s, it is not surprising that some of its ideas carried over to members of the area's reserve communities, where links between Métis and Indian communities were common. Most significantly, the MAA contributed to the IAA the notion that the voice of a community had to be unified in order to be politically effective. Norris and Brady believed that a strong union executive was key to establishing a unified voice and a credible body that would communicate directly with the government. As a later organizer of the Saskatchewan Métis Association said when recalling Norris: "the Indians knew that whoever was in control had the power and the say and they could do what they want to do and it was really a political threat over their head at all times. And the only way they could do away with that is by unifying. Malcolm told them [that] time and time again."[68] Not surprisingly, when the IAA formed in 1939 it also adopted this principle.

At the personal level, the connection between the MAA and the IAA was direct: Norris and Brady encouraged Johnny Callihoo of the Michel reserve to fight for a united Indian-based political association. When the IAA leader drafted the first constitution of the new Indian-oriented union, Norris was personally on hand to assist. Indian communities in the Edmonton area recognized Norris's experience in politics, and his input was welcomed by some Indian leaders. Contrary to claims that Norris restricted his political activity to the Métis question during the 1930s, he was directly involved in both Métis and Indian politics throughout this decade.[69]

Southern Alberta reserve communities, in contrast to those located in central Alberta, were slower to organize themselves into political unions. Political gatherings in southern Alberta reserve communities were sporadic and unorganized. Meetings were held at Fort Macleod in the 1910s and 1920s in response to various issues, particularly the alienation of southern Alberta reserve lands to non-Indian farmers, but to little avail.[70] In the winter of 1924, for example, over 100 individuals, including leaders from Peigan, Blood, and Blackfoot reserves, met, with the assistance of the local chamber of commerce, to organize and share their concerns before presenting them to the Indian Affairs. From the Blood reserve community, Mike Mountain Horse – a veteran of the First World War and former student at the Calgary Industrial School – acted as an organizer to defend the promises outlined in Treaty 7. Although Mountain Horse never became prominent as a political activist within a formal organization, his actions do reveal that southern communities felt that they had to take action in order to protect their treaty rights. Leaders who attended the meeting spoke eloquently in defence of their treaty promises and complained about the constraints the Indian Act placed upon their communities. Reserve lands figured prominently in the discussions, as comments by Many Chiefs, a delegate to the meeting, reveal: "Our treaty was for us to hold lands. They cannot be sold or leased unless we consent. We have not consented, but they are leased. Why is this?"[71] Other comments echoed his concerns. In a petition to the government following the meeting, Mountain Horse, who acted as secretary, wrote: "we the Indians assembled in convention do hereby petition the Federal government to repeal section 90 of the Indian Act at the next session of Parliament and give back our right in having a controlling voice in the disposition of our lands."[72]

Much attention was given to the meeting by the local press, but the DIA minimized its impact. The non-Indian supporters of the meeting were labelled self-interested. The final ruling on this protest movement was: "It is not the intention to give support to this gathering."[73] These events indicate that southern Alberta reserves were also organizing, albeit in a less unified and systematic manner than were their counterparts in central and northern Alberta. As a result, the actions of the former were more easily minimized by the Indian Affairs bureaucrats than were those of the latter.

Together, the three organizations most influential in reserve communities in the interwar years – the League of Indians of Western Canada, the UFA and its auxiliaries, and the MAA – all contributed to the politicization of Indian reserve communities. Only in the southern and northern extremes of the province was political action still informal, although concerns were similar and there was a search for outside assistance. Unions provided reserve community leaders with a forum within which to voice their grievances, encouraged collective action, promoted goals and ideals compatible with the needs and values of reserve communities, and allowed Indian members to realize the commonality of their problems. These events and organizations indicate that, prior to the Second World War,

Indian peoples in Alberta were consistently politically active, both inside and outside their communities. The daily experiences and challenges faced by reserve residents were enough to encourage their leaders to seek out opportunities and organizations to improve their community life. In fact, it is not clear that Indian war veterans formed an identifiable, primary driving force behind any form of political activity in Alberta.

The Founding of the IAA

Initially, the founding of the IAA was a response to the interests and needs of Indian peoples living on reserves in the Edmonton and Saddle Lake Agencies. The League of Indians of Western Canada had been prominent in this area throughout the interwar years; however, by the late Depression years some leaders felt that a more locally rooted organization would better serve the Alberta reserve populations. Callihoo, a successful farmer and band councillor on the Michel reserve, had been involved in the league for a number of years. In 1933, he went on to participate in the founding of a separate and independent IAA. Callihoo personified a direct link between the league, the MAA, the UFA, and the IAA.

In the 1930s the Edmonton Agency consisted of Michel, Alexander, Alexis, Paul, and Enoch reserves. Members of these communities had been actively involved in the league through meetings at Saddle Lake, Enoch, and Paul reserves in the 1930s.[74] Joe Dion recalls that, in the early days of political meetings, people would travel great distances by wagon to attend such conferences.[75] Over time, however, members of the reserve communities near Edmonton were finding it increasingly difficult to attend league meetings held as far away as Saddle Lake (and vice versa).[76] When it came to financing trips to league meetings, it was found that the Depression had undermined the resources of Indian peoples as much as it had those of non-Indians. Augustine Steinhauer, a farmer from Saddle Lake and himself a former president of the league in Alberta, wrote to Callihoo to apologize for not attending a league meeting: "its pretty hard to get money down here we have no money at all ... will you be so kind to send me the minutes of the meeting so that I'll know when our general meeting is going to be?"[77] Similarly, for members from the northern regions of Alberta, attending meetings on other reserves was particularly expensive as distances were particularly vast. As Peter Gladu indicated to Johnny Callihoo in 1937: "I can not go [to the league meeting in Saddle Lake] this year for I have no money ... I am depending on you to do the best you can for us. We have nothing."[78]

Conflict amongst the leadership also undermined the strength of the League of Indians in western Canada in general and in Alberta in particular. Specifically, Johnny Callihoo, elected as president of the Alberta Branch in March 1937, clashed with John Tootoosis, leader of the Saskatchewan

Branch since 1932.[79] Tootoosis, also a Cree leader, was from the Poundmaker reserve in Saskatchewan. Throughout the 1930s he travelled widely in both Alberta and Saskatchewan, promoting the League of Indians of Western Canada and attempting to organize reserve communities into a united political organization that would challenge Indian Affairs.[80] An indefatigable politician, Tootoosis travelled a circuit around the reserves neighbouring Poundmaker; he went into Alberta as far as Duffield, Edmonton, Hobbema, and even Lesser Slave Lake in order to press Indian leaders to fight for their treaty rights. Tootoosis had a great deal of influence in some communities.

According to Hugh Dempsey, a terrible jealousy developed between Callihoo and Tootoosis. Dempsey believes the problem arose over their struggle for political control of the Saddle Lake area of northeastern Alberta, which had its Indian agency office in Saskatchewan. Both Callihoo and Tootoosis claimed the agency for their branch of the league, and, in 1937, a confrontation between the two men at a Battleford meeting led to a permanent break.[81] The official biographers of Tootoosis claim that he offended Callihoo in a meeting by asking the latter to speak only English during a speech rather than his usual patois of Cree and English. According to Sluman and Goodwill: "The meeting then carried on but again Callihoo, through sheer contrariness, a wish to attract attention or a desire to challenge John's role as Chairman was on his feet, speaking in the same way. Thoroughly exasperated by this disrupting performance, John stopped him again ... Callihoo was silent after that but he apparently felt that he had been publicly humiliated by the Saskatchewan leader."[82]

If these accounts of the rivalry between Callihoo and Tootoosis seem trivial, they are nonetheless important because they reveal the local and very specific nature of leadership and reserve concerns. Tootoosis was struggling to establish a larger national-level Indian movement based on the league, while Callihoo was more interested in addressing the issues that frustrated the communities he represented by working within the existing state system. The Alberta leaders were much more conservative in their approach, and Callihoo was concerned with Métis issues as much as he was with Indian rights; Tootoosis, on the other hand, demanded that Indian self-determination and sovereignty be accepted by Indian Affairs and was less concerned with non-status peoples.[83]

Callihoo's focus on community issues and his conservative approach to treaty rights can be related directly to his own background. Born in 1882, for one year he attended the Dunbow Industrial School, an Indian residential school near Calgary, and then went to school in St. Albert. Despite his limited formal schooling, Johnny Callihoo was an avid reader and was essentially self-taught. After spending his youthful years travelling through northern Alberta as a freighter, he finally settled down, becoming one of the first to start farming in his community of the Michel reserve, twenty-six kilometres (sixteen miles) from Edmonton. This reserve community, unlike those surrounding it, was composed of families descended from the Iroquois voyageurs who worked for the North West Company in the nineteenth century. The large Callihoo family traced its descent from the original Callihoo, one of the first Iroquois to venture west from Kahnawake, Quebec.[84] Because of their French roots and connections, many families from the Michel reserve were closely intertwined with the other local French Métis communities near Edmonton.[85]

Although he worried about his own inadequate education, Callihoo contended that education was fundamentally important to the advancement of Indian peoples, and he involved himself in non-Aboriginal movements such as the United Farmers of Alberta. In addition, he also threw himself behind the MAA. Callihoo's family was intimately connected with the local Métis community, and, as a freighter in Alberta, Callihoo himself had worked closely with Métis peoples. In 1932 his brother, Dick Callihoo, worked to establish the MAA – a union fundamentally concerned with Métis health, education, and general welfare. In fact, Callihoo's brother was married to the half-sister of MAA founder Malcolm Norris. During the interwar years, the Callihoos, Brady, Tomkins, and Dion all met regularly to hammer out political ideas around the Norrises' kitchen table in Edmonton;[86] thus, connections between status and non-status members of the community were close and familial.[87] The link between the Michel reserve community and the reform politics that pervaded Alberta in the interwar years clearly affected Callihoo and his family and informed their political ideals.

The IAA was officially formed with the drafting of its constitution in 1939. In that year, Malcolm Norris and Johnny Callihoo worked together to create an organization that would represent Indian peoples in Alberta and protect their unique rights and interests.[88] Norris made the MAA's constitution available to Callihoo as a model for the new Indian Association.[89]

Initially, the emergence of an independent IAA in 1939 was not clear to all. People from reserve communities continued attending meetings, simply assuming they were part of the league – a natural confusion as, in many communities, meetings were frequent and informal.[90] Moreover, the IAA looked at issues similar to those considered by the Alberta branch of the league between 1937 and 1939. Issues carrying over directly from the league to the IAA included the need for additional assistance for agriculture on reserves; protecting Indian fishing, hunting, and trapping rights; protecting Indian reserve lands from expropriation; concerns with Indian Agents; medical care; and education.[91] Despite the unofficial similarities between the league and the IAA, the 1939 creation of the latter officially signalled that Alberta reserve communities were acting independently from their Saskatchewan counterparts and that they were reacting to different influences.

The first official meeting of the IAA was held in late July 1939 on the Paul reserve.[92] In its prewar state, the IAA was a product of initiatives taken by leaders from the Edmonton, Hobbema, and, to a lesser extent, Saddle Lake Agencies. Delegates to this first meeting included individuals from Hobbema, Saddle Lake, Goodfish Lake, Cold Lake, Kehewin, Michel, Enoch, Paul, Alexander, and Lesser Slave Lake.[93] Johnny Callihoo, Malcolm Norris, and Peter Burnstick (a trapper from Paul reserve) were among the key organizers of the new and independent provincial-level organization. This meeting elected Callihoo as the IAA's first president and Joe Dion as its first vice-president.[94] Callihoo was a natural choice for this position because of his experience as president for the Alberta branch of the league. Interestingly, Métis individuals had a prominent hand in the founding of this treaty-Indian focused organization.

From the start, the IAA sought to provide a solid organizational structure for the older, rather loose-knit political groups functioning in the various reserve communities. Neither the league nor the other smaller organizations provided enough support to those who were committed to asserting Indian treaty rights and improving the social and economic conditions of reserve communities.[95] In a 1945 letter to Joe Dion, Malcolm Norris expressed the following view of the IAA: "For many years in the past, Treaty Indians of Alberta and Saskatchewan would gather together periodically for the purpose of discussing their mutual problems and to seek for ways and means of adjustment to their many real grievances. Throughout these years, nothing tangible was accomplished: their meetings became more Pow-Wows, primarily because of their lack of organization and discipline among them."[96] In his view, the IAA represented an opportunity to provide solid, consistent leadership and a democratic approach where, previously, these had been lacking. Significantly, he felt that the IAA also offered a chance for non-Indians to come to the assistance of Indian communities: "Our Association is democratic in nature and principle. Again I feel it necessary to point out that we should be thankful for the OUTSIDE HELP that has been freely accorded our Association, for without same, we would never [have] progressed to the stage of organization and discipline that is so necessary to any movement."[97]

The issue of getting "outside help," of gaining assistance from non-Indians to support the cause of Indian peoples, appears as a second founding goal of the IAA. At an early date, organizer Malcolm Norris recognized that Indian peoples were at a political disadvantage because of their minority status within Canada. As a result, he felt that the IAA could benefit from appealing to non-Indian organizations. This position on the use of "outsiders" was not popular with all Indian political leaders, particularly John B. Tootoosis. In a letter to Tootoosis in 1944, Norris found himself defending the IAA's position on outside help:

> The last census revealed that the population of Canada is more than eleven million of which the Indian people are merely some 120,000 or less than 2% ... This is a very small group when you consider the Canadian picture. It is therefore necessary to seek support from outside Indian groups themselves ... All the efforts of the Indian Association of Alberta have been towards developing a better understanding among various groups of people, of seeking and GETTING SUPPORT of the various progressive groups ... This policy has been justified.[98]

Norris's conviction apparently stemmed from his experience in the Second World War. His two sons fought overseas, and one, Russell, was killed in Germany. Malcolm Norris was all too painfully aware of the politics inherent in conflict: "All history points to this – Fascism in Europe began with the segregating of small groups and the appeal to local spirit ... no group can live for itself and by itself without being pushed to the wall and left defenseless. The need for cooperation against the growth of Fascist tendencies in Canada is very urgent. This can only be achieved by meeting other groups and merging our objectives with this larger, saner, world movement."[99]

Early IAA documents reveal additional goals that the leadership set for itself.[100] Many of these issues derived directly from the league. As president of the Alberta branch of the league, for example, Johnny Callihoo was called upon to address issues ranging from concerns with Indian Agents and Indian schools, to rations for the elderly; from enfranchisement, to the Indian Act. Treaty rights and treaty promises were also brought to Callihoo's attention during his tenure as league president in Alberta.[101] The goals related to improving social and economic conditions on reserves and lobbying government could also be connected to the aims of the farmers unions.

The IAA's objectives were both practical and idealistic. In a very practical way, the IAA set out to establish and to maintain funds for legal guidance and protection for treaty Indians and their treaty rights. It also worked to educate Indian peoples concerning their rights and to advise the government regarding measures needed to ensure the welfare of treaty Indians. Clearly, the practical issue of the treaties and their maintenance figured prominently on the list of concerns in reserve communities. Norris emphasized this position in a 1944 letter to members on the Blackfoot reserve, stating that the purpose of the IAA was "the betterment of their [Indian members] social and economic conditions as promised under the Proclamation and Treaties."[102]

On a more idealistic note, the IAA sought to foster social fellowship and unity, "friendly relations between the various Red Races," "to engage in scientific study of all phases regarding the Red Race," to honour great Indian leaders, and, finally, to "Love and Help thy Brother."[103] The IAA's operations were based in the village of Villeneuve, near Edmonton, and the Michel reserve.[104] Interestingly, membership in the IAA, which was devised to struggle for treaty rights, was open to "any Treaty, non-Treaty, mixed Indian-White" individual.[105]

Generally speaking, the desire of Indian leaders to organize and to help their communities during this period met with some opposition. In 1938 the Reverend E.J. Staley, the United Church missionary on the Stoney reserve, was reported by the press to have said that he was "leery" of any Indian organization in the west. According to a newspaper account, "There is no question that the Indian people in the west have all the rights ever promised to them" and that "they have been dealt with fully and very fairly on the basis of any treaty rights."[106] Outside reserve communities in Alberta few knew about – or, if they did, supported – the concept of treaty rights.

The IAA was formed to address the daily concerns of Indian people living on reserves in central Alberta. These communities had prior experience with political activity through the League of Indians of Western Canada, the farmers unions, and the MAA. The interaction between the reserve leadership and the various political groups, coupled with the economic situation brought about by the Depression, stimulated the founding of a new, locally controlled Indian association. The impetus behind the IAA was based on the underlying contrast between living conditions of non-Indians and those of Indian peoples (both status and non-status) in the province. Focusing upon this contrast gave the IAA leadership an early mandate for action, and working with this contrast allowed it to express a vision of how life should be for the Indian peoples of Alberta.

3
The Structure and Expansion of the Early Indian Association of Alberta

> Every Treaty Indian Band in the province should be a member to the Association ... We need an organization like this very bad.
>
> – John Callihoo to Chris Shade, March 1944[1]

In order to make a more complete break with the old League of Indians of Western Canada and to strengthen the new association, the Indian Association of Alberta leaders quickly set about restructuring their organization.[2] The new IAA was constructed on the basis of a network of locals, which were governed by a set of by-laws and which reported to a provincial executive. This was similar to the United Farmers of Alberta (UFA) and the Métis Association of Alberta (MAA). It was decided that a minimum of ten active association members constituted a local, which would be headed by an elected executive. Locals functioned to "promote the objects and interests of the Association, particularly matters of local import, and [to] encourage the presentation of addresses on subjects of interest to the Association."[3] At the local level community concerns could be noted, and educational seminars could be held for its members. The provincial executive, in turn, which consisted of a "head chief" (or president), an "assistant chief" (or vice-president), a treasurer, a secretary, a provincial organizer, and three councillors, controlled and managed the business and affairs of the IAA. Low membership fees of twenty-five cents covered operating costs, and the provincial executive was unpaid.[4] It was felt that an unpaid executive would be more devoted. As non-Indian provincial secretary John Laurie later stated: "This ensures an executive of responsible, unselfish and devoted men."[5]

Although the original reserve communities involved in the IAA were located primarily in the Edmonton region, the IAA soon extended its reach. Gradually, members enlisted from reserve communities beyond the Edmonton Agency, first in the northern regions of the province, later in the southern regions. In 1941, for example, members of the Cold Lake Indian reserve, under the jurisdiction of the Onion Lake Indian Agency, hosted a large two-day meeting to discuss issues facing Indian peoples of that region. At this meeting, attended by members of the Kehewin, Frog Lake, Saddle Lake, and Big Island Lake communities, it was resolved that the reserves east of Edmonton should be organized and join the IAA. In his memoirs, Joe Dion recalled:

> Among several resolutions which were thoroughly thrashed out, one was to send a letter to Johnny Callihoo ... We asked him to lead the way and we promised to send delegates to his next meeting the following year. Thus it can truthfully be said that the Chipewyan played a big part into [sic] bringing about the birth of the Indian Association of Alberta ... In the meantime, we in the east worked diligently, holding large meetings on various reserves ... The results of these gatherings were most gratifying and the Indian movement grew steadily.[6]

The IAA's activities slowed during the war years, but the association itself did not falter. Although documentation remains scarce, the IAA continued to meet. Throughout the early 1940s these gatherings, many of them informal, were held in the northern part of Alberta: in 1940, Saddle Lake; in 1941, Cold Lake; in 1942, Kehewin; in 1943, Frog Lake.[7] As early as 1940, the IAA sent a list of resolutions and grievances to Ottawa.[8] In 1941, Callihoo forwarded a petition directly to the Indian Affairs Branch outlining several issues that concerned the communities of the Edmonton Agency. Among other things, it protested the Indian Affairs practice of accepting band funds as War Fund contributions. The petition also levelled complaints against a farm instructor for interfering with IAA and band meetings.[9] The issues discussed at early IAA meetings were primarily local and represented daily concerns.

During these years IAA member communities that could not send representatives to meetings worked and studied in order to educate themselves about their rights. Callihoo, for example, received requests for the Indian Act: "Dear Sir, I would like you to send the papers of the Indian Act. We are going to have a meeting in here and we are needing them papers bad."[10] Member reserves sometimes asked Callihoo to travel to visit them and to discuss local problems; sometimes they even offered travel money for this purpose.[11]

Despite the commonly held notion that the Indian Affairs Branch disapproved of political activities on reserve, there is little indication the government actively discouraged or disrupted IAA meetings. At the same time, it is not clear that the Indian Affairs Branch ever directly addressed the problems identified by the IAA. According to Joe Dion, the Indian Agent for the Onion Lake Agency "usually attended and supported the meetings," although he admitted "that some of the Indian Agents were not in favour of meetings being held in their reserves that is the reserves they were in charge of."[12] Similarly, Indian Agent Lewis of the Hobbema Agency noted political meetings of the league and of the IAA on his reserve in his daily journals; however, he never attempted to stop them. The Indian Affairs Branch responded to petitions sent by IAA president Callihoo to Ottawa but continued to direct complaints by communities to the local Indian Agent. In these cases, the Branch response was painfully slow, and some problems still awaited Branch consideration up to one year following the receipt of a petition.

Clearly, the enormous size of the province made the IAA organizers' task of creating a provincial union formidable. Travel between reserves during the war years was usually by car, sometimes by bus or train. Although gasoline rationing and the expense of maintaining automobiles discouraged extensive contact between reserves during the war years, it did not completely halt travel. People continued to carpool and to travel over the dirt roads connecting their communities. Members were even encouraged to bring their ration cards to meetings – an indication of the cooperative effort that went into maintaining the IAA during the war years.

Off-reserve employment during the war, like the insurmountable travel distances, also hampered the expansion and functioning of the IAA to some extent. During the early 1940s, labour demands were high across the province, and the Indian Affairs Branch directed Indian workers to the National Selective Service offices to be placed where labour was most needed. Consequently, many Indian workers, mostly men, spent long periods away from their home communities working either in northern lumber camps, in sawmills, or on threshing crews around the province.[13] The absence of this segment of the reserve population made it difficult for the IAA to organize and to hold regular meetings, since women rarely openly engaged in political activity during these years. Despite these kinds of difficulties, the IAA increased its membership during the war years, even enlisting members from the southern, non-Cree reserves.

A critical turning point for the young IAA did occur during the war, and this event gave the association greater momentum than ever. In 1944 the IAA leadership rallied to reorganize and strengthen its base in preparation to battle the Indian Affairs Branch. What provided the impetus behind the expansion of the IAA was an immediate problem based at the local level rather than any lofty ideals related to a pan-Indian cause.

At their 1944 spring convention, IAA leaders met quietly at the Hobbema Garage in the central Alberta Hobbema Agency. Specifically, they were to discuss recent attempts by the Indian Affairs Branch to remove non-status Indians from the Ermineskin and Samson reserves. Leaders from the Stoney and Blackfoot reserves and the Hobbema, Edmonton, and Saddle Lake Agencies attended, although the Blackfoot leaders were not yet IAA members. The meeting caused little concern for Indian Affairs at the time, and, the day before (24 May 1944), Agent Lewis of Hobbema reported as follows in his daily journal: "Office all day. General office routine. Sports were held for Indian children on Samson Reserve sports grounds. Indians here from Morley and Blackfoot ready for a meeting to be held tomorrow. Weather Cloudy Cool and Showers."[14] No actions were taken to stop the meeting.

The crisis was precipitated when the Branch sought to have three individuals and their families removed from the reserve. Under the Indian Act, individuals whose families had accepted scrip rather than signing on to treaty were deemed to be non-treaty and non-status and, therefore, unable to reside on reserve as wards of the federal government.[15] Over the years, in an attempt to reduce costs associated with maintaining larger reserve populations and to encourage assimilation, the cost-conscious Indian Affairs Branch had excluded many families from reserves across the province on this basis, much to the dismay of some status reserve residents who were related to these families.[16] Throughout the 1930s in the Edmonton Agency, for example, the local Indian Agent was still on alert to locate and remove any non-status individuals identified by the Branch.[17] Sometimes the families were successfully excluded, but often they returned to the reserve and their other relatives.[18] The haphazard workings of the expulsion policy were obvious to all and greatly distressed some IAA members.

At Hobbema, those faced with expulsion included James Ward, Fred Hodgson, and Albert Lightning. Both Ward and Lightning were active members of the IAA. Sometime in 1943 the Branch probed the band membership of Hodgson and Ward. The investigation concluded that the men and their families were "half-breeds" whose ancestors had received scrip. Their families were, therefore, deemed "non-status" and ineligible to reside on the reserve or to share in band benefits. Apparently, a former female member of the Ermineskin band, who had married a non-Indian (thereby losing her status), had drawn the "half-breed" background of the two men to the Branch's attention. When the woman requested that she, her husband, and her children be admitted to band membership, she argued that her family had the same rights to membership as did Hodgson and Ward.[19] Although the men had been voted unanimously into band membership by the band councils eight years previously, the investigation into the status of Hodgson and Ward led, in January 1944, to the serving of notice of their expulsion from the reserve.[20] This expulsion issue united several reserves against the Branch.

The 1944 Hobbema meeting was also important because it introduced new reserve communities beyond Edmonton to the IAA and led to a reorganization and revitalization of the union following the hard war years. Ben Calf Robe and two others from the Blackfoot reserve attended an IAA meeting for the first time in Hobbema, acting as interpreters and trying to find out what the IAA had to offer. The Hobbema meeting also confirmed that the IAA was a union whose influence extended beyond its Edmonton base. The Stoney people made an impressive showing at Hobbema; in fact, that same year the Stoney bands at Morley had the highest total number of IAA members of any area in the province (252 – 314 if one includes the Stoney at Nordegg).[21]

Significantly, at this 1944 meeting the IAA reorganized and expanded its executive. Where previously there had existed only one vice-president and three provincial councillors, after 1944 there were two vice-presidents and five provincial councillors. This was in order to give better representation to all reserves in the province as the IAA was clearly growing.[22] The new executive was promptly voted in, with Johnny Callihoo retaining his position as president, Joe House and Joe Dion taking seats as vice-presidents, and Sam Minde assuming the position of treasurer. Malcolm Norris remained Provincial Organizer, a position that allowed him to recruit for the IAA around the province. Interestingly, although the revised constitution stated that "every member of the Provincial or Executive Council must be of Indian Ancestry and of good moral character, to be eligible to office in this Association," non-Indian Calgary high school teacher John Laurie became secretary by acclamation. According to Albert Lightning, one of the Hobbema individuals ear-marked by the Indian Affairs Branch for expulsion from the reserve, "I was the one who asked John Laurie to come in."[23] Laurie became a key figure in the IAA in subsequent years and realized its aim of recruiting "outside help" to the cause.

The result of the 1944 meeting was the creation of the resolve to form a larger and more effective Indian organization. Overall, the Hobbema discussions emphasized treaty rights and the social and economic condition of Indian communities. Following the meeting, several chiefs and councillors approached Hobbema agent Lewis to discuss sending John Bear and John Crier, both IAA delegates, to Ottawa for the purpose of communicating IAA resolutions in person. According to the agent's journal: "I read circular letter re: deputations going to Ottawa to them. They decided to wait until later."[24] Ultimately, Secretary Laurie compiled the resolutions in a memorial on Indian affairs and submitted them to both the Branch and to MPs. This act marked the first official interaction between the IAA and the federal government.

Despite the high hopes raised by the Hobbema meeting, recruiting southern reserves into the IAA still proved difficult. Although the Blackfoot community showed an initial interest in the IAA, in 1944 Blackfoot, Blood, Peigan, and Sarcee communities remained suspicious of the association because of its Cree origins.[25] Historically, a sense of hostility existed between peoples in the south and the Cree of the north, and this was not easily overcome. According to Gordon Crowchild, son of early IAA supporter David Crowchild, the Blood were rich and proud and, therefore, suspicious of any movement spearheaded by poorer reserves.[26]

The Blood community had little reason to be interested in the IAA.

Unlike other reserve communities in the province, Blood leaders had established other political contacts to serve their needs. Specifically, they had connected with John Blackmore, the Social Credit MP for southern Alberta, in an attempt to benefit from Canada's postwar reconstruction plans. Early in 1944 Blackmore met with Jim White Bull and other members of the community and encouraged them to hold meetings on reserve to discuss how he might contribute to their advancement. White Bull subsequently organized several meetings and asked Blackmore to investigate treaty rights as well as the status of leases existing on the Blood reserve. On the Blood reserve, land and agricultural issues were most prominent in the minds of the community's leadership. In addition, White Bull repeated Blackmore's offer for help to the Peigan reserve. As they already had a politician's support, the Blood's and Peigan's need for assistance from the IAA seemed less pressing than it might otherwise have been. The Blood had successfully bypassed the Indian Agent and communicated their needs directly to Ottawa.[27] According to White Bull, "you be the first white man ever stand up for the Indians since white came within our country at one time."[28] Significantly, White Bull himself already had political experience. The Blood farmer held membership in the Social Credit party, and this factor may have deterred him from becoming involved in the leftist-oriented IAA.[29]

Bringing an IAA local to the Blood reserve was difficult for the IAA leaders. Only after Blood farmer Chris Shade met with John Laurie and Malcolm Norris in Calgary did members of the Blood reserve first attempt to organize an IAA local. Unfortunately, this first attempt ended in failure. Even before he was IAA secretary, John Laurie hosted young Indian guests in his home in order to enable them to attend high school in Calgary. Gerald Tailfeathers, a young man from the Blood reserve, boarded with Laurie for some time. Fellow Blood band member Chris Shade would visit Tailfeathers at Laurie's home in Calgary. On one of these visits, conversation turned to politics. Laurie supplied Shade with an IAA constitution, and Shade proceeded home to the Blood reserve with the inspiration to create an IAA local. In addition, he invited IAA president Callihoo to visit the Blood reserve to assist him with the organizing process. Excited at the prospect of having southern reserves join the movement, Callihoo wrote Shade: "Every Treaty Indian Band in the province should be a member to the Association ... We need an organization like this very bad."[30]

Although Callihoo made the trip to the south to recruit IAA members on the Blood reserve, the Blood chief and council took offence at his visit. Since the IAA shared concerns with local band councils, the need to communicate with these councils was crucial. Unfortunately for the IAA, as soon as members of the tribal council heard that a Cree had been on the reserve to organize the Blood without the permission of the chief, they immediately concluded that the group was being organized to oppose the council.[31] Contact with the IAA ceased. Only after another member of the Blood reserve, successful rancher and farmer Jim Gladstone, met with Laurie at an Anglican church diocese meeting a year later was contact with the IAA renewed. The result of this contact was that Gladstone attended an IAA annual convention at Seebe in 1945.[32] Personal contacts and the etiquette of reserve politics played a powerful role in determining whether or not a reserve might become involved in the IAA.

The IAA did eventually establish itself on the Blood reserve. In fact, in February 1946 two locals were formed because of the enormous size of the reserve: one at Standoff and one at the Old Agency. Those who attended the organizational meeting included individuals previously involved with Blackmore, and Gladstone became an informal leader of the IAA supporters.[33]

The Peigan had some contact with Jim White Bull and John Blackmore and their activities to improve life on the Blood reserve; however, by the spring of 1945 the Peigan leaders had organized their own IAA local. In this community the Reverend B.S. Green, principal of the St. Cyprian Indian Residential School, assisted the IAA. Green wrote as follows to IAA secretary Laurie in March of that year: "The Indians of the Peigan reserve have been talking to me about the Association and I gave them permission to have their meetings in our school. They had a meeting yesterday and being very interested, I became a member."[34] Following a visit to the Peigan in April of that year, Secretary Laurie informed President Callihoo that "I had a very nice time at Brocket. The Peigan Executive are real fine chaps."[35] By the annual convention of 1945, the Peigan delegates presented resolutions calling for social security and opposing the alienation of reserve lands.[36] Members of the Peigan local eventually became some of the most dedicated supporters of the IAA. Bob Crow Eagle and his wife assumed leading roles in the organization shortly after it was established on their reserve. The Peigan community was not as well off as was the Blood community and, therefore, was interested in an organization that might improve their lot. In addition, it seems that suspicions of the IAA did not run as high on the Peigan reserve as it did on the Blood reserve.

Like the Blood, the Blackfoot reserve fared better economically than did most reserves in the province; consequently, the Blackfoot were less interested in joining an organization supported by poverty-stricken communities. As a result of the huge sale of their reserve lands at the turn of the century, the Blackfoot established a large trust fund that they used to supply band members with food, clothing, houses, and farming assistance. Money from this fund also served to establish a reserve hospital. Indian Agent Gooderham, who assumed a post at the Blackfoot reserve in 1920, referred to the Blackfoot reserve as "an ideal welfare state – the first of its kind so far as I was aware."[37] In the 1920s the Blackfoot community had over 100 successful farmers on the reserve, all of whom benefited from the trust fund money.

Over time, however, low grain prices brought on by the Great Depression coupled with drought undermined these successful farming operations. Compounding the problem, non-Indian farmers who had purchased or leased Blackfoot reserve lands began defaulting on their payments to the council. Furthermore, in the 1940s power machinery and larger farms became a trend in agriculture; Indian farmers, with their limited land-base, could not participate. Through this combination of factors, Blackfoot farmers found themselves in a position in which they had more labour than capital.[38]

Initially, Blackfoot farmers continued their marginal farming because the trust funds provided them with regular rations and seed, something many non-Native farmers lacked during the Depression. Unfortunately, the combination of poor crops and low incomes gradually discouraged even Blackfoot farmers. By the 1940s the band council began to see a decline in its total trust funds as more families began relying on them for survival. When the trust funds became insufficient to meet the ever-increasing financial needs of the band, the reserve economy suffered a severe blow. Agent Gooderham claimed that, by 1946, "most small farms [on reserve] were consolidated and rented to white operators. Most of the stock, cattle and horses, had been sold"[39] and the Blackfoot found themselves subsisting on their trust funds and falling further behind in the postwar Alberta economy. By the 1940s the farm program, begun in 1911 with the money from land sales, had failed.[40]

The declining economic situation and local dissatisfaction with the actions of the chiefs and council on the Blackfoot reserve created some interest in the IAA.[41] Specifically, Ben Calf Robe, Henry Low-horn, and Teddy Yellowfly approached IAA provincial organizer Malcolm Norris about forming an IAA local on their reserve. Norris encouraged them. Calf Robe had been active on the Blackfoot reserve as a critic of the reserve council, and in the early 1940s he organized meetings in the community where he openly attacked its workings. In this same period he even travelled to Calgary with a handful of supporters to discuss, in the presence of a lawyer, his dissatisfaction with the reserve chiefs and Indian Agent Gooderham. Although he lacked extensive formal education – he had attended the Calgary Industrial School until Grade 4 – Calf Robe was clearly interested in what he considered to be his rights, and he studied the Indian Act in order to better challenge the established authorities on the reserve. His desire to improve conditions on the reserve also saw him encourage and lead others to challenge the Indian Agent and chiefs. During the Depression, many Indian men worked in a small but successful coal mine on the reserve. A miner himself, Calf Robe organized a strike for better wages.[42]

Overall, his actions did little to endear him to either the chiefs or the Indian Agent, and the latter was blunt in his assessment of him: "Ben Calf Robe is a red."[43]

In this case it is evident the IAA represented an opportunity for Calf Robe to circumvent leadership within a reserve community. Local conflict thus encouraged political action at a higher level. A successful IAA local was not established until 1951 (at the east end of the reserve), and, at that time, John Laurie noted local band council dissatisfaction with IAA activity.[44] The first president of this local was a Mr. Medicine Shield, who was assisted by secretary Steve Many Fires. For many years the Blackfoot community remained relatively disinterested in the IAA, until Clarence McHugh, from the reserve, held the IAA provincial presidency from 1954 to 1956.[45]

Another southern community whose members joined the IAA at a later date was the Sarcee (Tsuu Tina) community, located on the edge of Calgary. Again, as in the case of the Blood and Blackfoot reserves, this farming community fared better economically than did those located in central and northern Alberta. David Crowchild, a farmer and chief, brought the IAA to the reserve. Born on the Sarcee reserve in 1899 and raised in the local Anglican residential school, Crowchild started farming upon graduating from that institution at age eighteen. He became well known for his rodeo skills and horsemanship. Crowchild met John Laurie for the first time in 1945 at an IAA annual meeting in Seebe, where Crowchild was an observer. Laurie made an instant impression upon Crowchild: "He [Laurie] looked just like a farmer and seemed to have a real bitterness about the way that white people were treating the Indians."[46] Laurie and Crowchild quickly became close friends and were happy to find they shared common interests in horses, education, and a commitment to the Anglican Church. They also shared a strong political will. Crowchild adopted Laurie as his "brother" and, with his help, he organized the first IAA local on the Sarcee reserve in 1945. Both Crowchild and his wife, Daisy, were active and important IAA supporters throughout the 1940s and 1950s.

Ultimately, local problems and conflicts were the primary force driving reserve communities to join the IAA. Initially, in the southern reserve communities, local band councils were extremely suspicious of the IAA; however, over the course of the 1940s southern reserves eventually created their own IAA locals. The northern reserves in the Edmonton area provided a great deal of impetus for the spread of the IAA across the province, but it was not until the late 1940s and early 1950s that the far northern communities beyond Lesser Slave Lake became involved with it.

After 1944 the IAA gradually settled into a routine of regular executive council meetings and annual conventions. Through these regular meetings the association increased its influence, and, gradually, a feeling of collective identity emerged among the IAA membership. Harold Cardinal, son of early IAA member Frank Cardinal, notes that his father saw the IAA as an opportunity, with the help of other chiefs and tribes, to change the dire circumstances facing so many reserve communities.[47] Frank Cardinal was among those who believed that collective action was the answer to the problems facing Indian peoples, and it was this sense of collective action that gave the IAA membership a lasting feeling of purpose and unity.

IAA Meetings

After the Hobbema convention of 1944, the IAA held regular annual conventions during the summer months on reserves around the province. The right to host these annual meetings, which were social occasions as much as political meetings, became a highly sought after honour. Because of the high degree of community involvement, over the years the IAA contributed to a sense of collective identity among Alberta First Nations.

Host reserves made tremendous efforts to accommodate guests and to provide for their needs. Delegates attending a meeting were billeted at the host reserve, staying at the homes of family and friends. Secretary Laurie prepared information bulletins in advance of the annual meetings, and it was common for him to urge delegates to "bring your blankets or you are likely to sleep cold!"[48] as, sometimes, tents were the only available accommodation. Attendance at these large meetings was sometimes problematic because people had difficulty travelling long distances and/or lacked the money to leave their home reserves. As a result, the IAA tried to provide transportation (buses or cars) for delegates travelling from Calgary or Edmonton to the host reserve. In most cases, the delegates paid their own expenses. Gordon Crowchild recalls "people just got together in an old car and drove to meetings ... everyone helped each other."[49] Arriving at the host reserve, delegates received a warm welcome as guests of the IAA local.

One of the highlights of an annual convention was always the feast held by the host reserve. In some cases, women of the host reserve community spent up to a year preparing for the event.[50] Because of the expense involved in feeding the large number of delegates, band funds were occasionally allocated for convention-related activities.[51] Those who attended remember fondly the food at the meetings: "They had beautiful lunches!"[52] People not involved in the IAA also assisted with the preparations for a meeting: for example, even women whose husbands were not politically inclined helped cook meals for the visitors.

At the annual meetings, which usually lasted two or three days, proceedings began early in the morning and continued well into the night. Community halls on reserve were common meeting places, though sometimes local residential schools were used. At times committees or subcommittees holding separate or concurrent meetings were relegated to the out-of-doors.[53]

Meetings opened with a prayer, and, beginning in 1945, a representative from Indian Affairs often welcomed the delegates to their own meeting. Over the course of the convention, after sharing, debating, and recording local resolutions, a final brief was drafted by the IAA secretary for presentation to Indian Affairs. According to Hugh Dempsey, who sometimes acted as unofficial secretary (after Laurie's time), this was the IAA's most valuable function: it brought people together from all over the province and allowed them to see and document their shared problems. Even though many locals were concerned with only their own specific issues, the meetings gave members a sense of group strength and reaffirmed the importance of fighting for common goals.[54]

At these meetings women, if not always prominent, played noteworthy roles. Although women were not commonly involved in the public politics of reserve communities during this era, several took an active and public role in the IAA. Women generally attended the IAA conventions, were significant as supporters, and, of course, were vital as hosts, preparing and cooking meals for the delegates. Women assumed new prominence in the organization beginning in 1952, when the executive encouraged the first official female delegates to attend the IAA annual meeting. The reticence of many women to become involved was not easily overcome, however, and Mrs. Dan Minde of Hobbema challenged this fear when she confronted the female delegates at the 1952 meeting:

> I wish to speak to the women and the younger women present. Here is our opportunity of speaking for ourselves in our own organisation ... We women should not be afraid to talk for ourselves. Even as I stand here now, I feel as if I were a mouse running across the floor but as women you must make every effort to help yourselves by becoming members of the IAA. We women must learn to speak on our difficulties and problems in our own organisation, the IAA.[55]

Clearly, there was a sense within the IAA that women had special interests in certain issues and that their views were valuable.[56] In its early decades of operation, the more prominent women in the organization included Daisy Crowchild of the Sarcee reserve, Mrs. Bob Crow Eagle of the Peigan community, and Victoria McHugh of the Blackfoot reserve. These individuals assumed active leadership roles in the IAA and took it upon themselves to focus upon issues related to education.

Daisy Crowchild, for example, became involved in the IAA through her husband, David Crowchild. Daisy Crowchild, of Manitoba Sioux ancestry, was educated at a Portage La Prairie Presbyterian boarding school, and she strongly believed that formal education would provide her people with a better way of life. She joined the IAA in 1947, initially using her boundless energy to head the catering committee, but she later turned her attention to education issues. Daisy Crowchild sent her own children to school in the City of Calgary, and, through the public school system, she became involved in the Home and School Association. She was so enthusiastic about the Home and School group that, in 1941, she set about forming the first Home and School Association in a reserve community (the Sarcee reserve).[57] She soon became a link between the Home and School Association and the IAA, and she reported regularly on problems in education. At the 1953 annual convention, for example, the meeting minutes indicate she reported "that more than one million dollars had been cut from the estimates for construction and maintenance of Indian day schools in Canada for the year 1953-54. This was a serious matter. In Alberta, education had barely begun on a satisfactory basis. So many day schools had been requested through the Association, even in the present year, that the need was still very great."[58] Day schools were scarce in Alberta after the Second World War and were in high demand in reserve communities across the province.

Other women involved in the IAA took similar leadership roles. Victoria McHugh became treasurer of the organization in 1953; Mrs. Crow Eagle, in turn, supported the improvement of education on all reserves and was very prominent on her reserve as an IAA member; others spoke up on issues of health care. Perhaps the most telling comment retained on the records of an IAA annual convention about the role of women came from a Mrs. English: "Mr. President, I am here for the first time and I am surprised and pleased to see so many women here as delegates."[59] Women may not have been present in the IAA records or public events in an obvious way, but, in the early years, their presence and influence at IAA meetings was significant and unmistakable.

The Indian Affairs Branch also had a presence at IAA meetings, starting in 1945. Initially, the local Indian Agent attended these meetings as an Indian Affairs representative, although his role was passive: he was generally not called upon to speak or act in any way. After the 1946 appointment of George Gooderham to the position of Regional Supervisor of Indian Agencies, this former Indian Agent of the Blackfoot reserve became the official Indian Affairs representative at IAA conventions. Gooderham was empowered by the the Branch to receive IAA resolutions and to make recommendations concerning each. In the eyes of the DIA: "By following this procedure it is hoped that this and other Indian Associations will be encouraged to deal with all matters through the office of the responsible Regional Supervisor."[60] Gooderham seemed to enjoy the meetings, attended as often as he could, and became good friends with IAA executive secretary John Laurie.

Not all Indian Affairs employees were equally supportive of the IAA and its aims, despite official Branch approval for the association in 1945. In contrast to Gooderham, Regional Supervisor R.F. Battle was not well disposed towards the IAA.[61] Battle saw IAA meetings as mere publicity opportunities, and he wondered whether his attendance was worthwhile. He questioned his supervisors as to whether the association was representative and argued that it was usurping the power of local band councils.[62] In a letter to the director of Indian Affairs, he complained: "I am still not sure if I accomplished anything by attending [the IAA annual convention at Driftpile in 1955]. Whenever questions arose which required explanations, I volunteered the information but I was not able to have any of the resolutions withdrawn. In other words, what is the point of my being there ... ? ... I know Dr. Falconer and Dr. Orford also consider it useless to attend these meetings."[63] Battle continued travelling to meetings, but he also went so far as to send his complaints about the IAA straight to the minister responsible for Indian Affairs.

Police surveillance of IAA meetings did occur, although it was carried out under the guise of monitoring possible infractions of the Indian Act, particularly the clause that forbade Indians to be in possession of liquor.[64] It is not clear that the federal government sought to interfere in the IAA meetings. For instance, in 1951 the RCMP were present at the IAA convention-closing celebrations held at Whitefish Lake Indian reserve. According to the RCMP report, "No difficulty of any kind was encountered and there was no suggestion of liquor being on the reserve whatever, very close attention was paid to anyone entering or leaving the reserve and very few white persons attended. The convention was very orderly and well conducted."[65] In fact, the chief of the reserve, also an IAA member and host to the convention, assisted the police in their monitoring activities.

Of all the meetings held by the IAA, the annual conventions were perhaps the most significant and influential. These meetings brought leaders from around the province together to discuss common concerns and to draw up resolutions that could be forwarded to Ottawa for consideration by Indian Affairs. Although expensive and sometimes difficult to attend, meetings affirmed a sense of collective identity among those participating. IAA members were generally not a majority in any reserve community, but the actions of members did generate a feeling of common purpose, and those who remember the meetings in the 1940s and 1950s have the following recollections: "people loved the meetings ... there was a sense of action"; "the IAA gave the people a sense of strength ... to fight the government for their rights"; "the IAA didn't *create* an identity but did give a *voice* to an Indian identity in Alberta."[66]

The influence of the "outside" world on the daily existence of members of reserve communities was tremendous during the interwar and postwar periods. In fact, it appears that, following the founding of the IAA, outside help became an influential factor in the activities of the association. As the IAA was founded because of outside influences – including the MAA, the farmers unions, and the Great Depression – it is not surprising that it continued to function with the assistance of outsiders. Though broader social trends cannot be dismissed, with regard to stimulating Indian political activity, it is clear that local and regional factors were extremely important. Only through oral history, and through investigating sources still held within the communities involved, can one achieve a deeper understanding of the IAA.

4
"Outside Help": John Laurie and Non-Indian Supporters of the Indian Association of Alberta

> White help is necessary because they are the people who can influence government.
>
> – John Laurie to Pat Lalonde, 1945[1]

> Unfortunately, these do-gooders get involved in spheres of activity ranging from simple, charitable church projects to the political arena, where self-appointed spokesmen for the Indians do incalculable harm. Their view of the Indian almost always, even if subconsciously, is that native people are incapable of handling their own affairs.
>
> – Harold Cardinal, *The Unjust Society* (1969)

In the year he first taught English and drama at Calgary's Crescent Heights High School, John Laurie was known among his students for asking, "Any questions?" This stern young teacher, slight in build, joined the school staff in 1927. He remained with the school well into the 1950s and always lived within walking distance of the building. Although little in his background or career seemed to guide John Laurie towards becoming involved with Alberta's Indian communities, Crescent Heights served as a foundation upon which he built his career as secretary of the Indian Association of Alberta in the 1940s and 1950s.

From its inception in 1939, the founders of the IAA recognized the importance of "outside help" to their cause of improving the position of treaty Indian people in Alberta. Malcolm Norris, IAA provincial organizer in the early years, insisted that the association reach beyond its treaty Indian membership to actively seek the support of non-Native liberal progressive groups. At the time Norris was all too conscious of the war in Europe, and he felt that the minority status of Indian peoples within Canada put them in special danger of falling prey to the evils of fascism. For this reason, he encouraged members of the IAA to merge their concerns with the members of other like-minded organizations in order to strengthen the IAA's position. It was through the urging of Norris that John Laurie and, subsequently, a whole range of citizens groups came to support the IAA.

Although it was Malcolm Norris who inspired the connection between the IAA and outside help, it was high school teacher John Laurie who encouraged and cultivated that connection. Laurie recruited politicians and housewives alike to assist the IAA. He personally directed special requests for help and functioned as a liaison between the IAA and potential supporters. Officially, his position as executive secretary of the IAA facilitated much of this networking activity as he handled all of the association's correspondence. As secretary he could easily draw up letters calling for help and speak on behalf of the IAA. Some of the connections Laurie drew to the side of the IAA actually stemmed from his personal involvements. For example, two of the most important groups Laurie enlisted to help the IAA were the Edmonton-based Friends of the Indians Society, and the Crescent Heights Home and School Association. These two service groups did a great deal to promote the causes of the IAA, and it was because of Laurie that they came to its assistance. Finally, Laurie also gained the assistance of influential individual MPs and members of Alberta's Legislative Assembly. Together, these individuals and groups gave the IAA important connections within government and the press, and increased its credibility in the eyes of the public.

Interestingly, the outside help drawn to the IAA through John Laurie acted as a conservative influence on the association. This outside help primarily supported improving Indian education and employment opportunities and applying new social legislation to Indian peoples. However, it never explicitly challenged the administration of Indian Affairs; rather, non-Indian supporters of the IAA encouraged it to seek reform through existing government channels. Indian peoples' unique treaty rights, a priority clearly spelled out in the IAA constitution, represented an important IAA concern that its outside help never actively promoted. What outside help offered the IAA was very much in keeping with contemporary Canadian concerns about the postwar social and economic reconstruction of Canada, with conservative views of treaty rights, and with liberal democratic notions of equal civil rights for all citizens.

The non-Indian help received by the IAA was conservative because that was the intellectual climate of the time. Between 1944 and the mid-1950s, popular thinking emphasized the idea that education and employment for all citizens would regenerate Canadian society after the war. It was also believed that the political equality of all citizens was a necessity in postwar Canada. In assisting the IAA, outside help sought exactly that for Indian peoples: their integration into the social, economic, and, to a lesser extent, political structure of Canadian society. Indian peoples were not seen as different from Canadian citizens: they were viewed simply as people who needed to catch up to the rest of society, especially socially and economically. In the immediate postwar years, social and economic integration took precedence over political integration.

In addition to involving non-members in the IAA, Laurie also directed its daily functioning. First and foremost a teacher, he believed strongly that the IAA could act as a modernizing force in Indian reserve communities by teaching individuals important skills. Laurie felt that the IAA could improve both morale and morality in reserve communities and that, with the assistance of other responsible citizens, the association could "advance" Indian people. He wrote extensively on Indian subjects for various popular magazines and newspapers, including the *Calgary Herald*, the *Albertan*, and the *Canadian Cattlemen*. He also spoke publicly on Indian issues, sometimes even exaggerating his examples for effect. Based on his writings and presentations, it appears that he was driven by the belief that the Canadian public and Indian peoples could be taught to appreciate each other. Laurie promoted the idea that Canadian society could learn about the plight of reserve communities and appreciate their traditions. He also felt that Indian peoples could be taught many of the advantages of modern life. This Calgary high school teacher's views closely reflected contemporary stereotypes about Indian peoples; that is, Indian communities shared in a glorious and romantic past, but this past, with its outdated traditions, hampered their ability to become industrious citizens.

Laurie's desire to assist Indian communities in Alberta, and his genuine concern with the special "rights" of Indian peoples, was reconcilable with his notion of integration. His attempts to integrate Indian peoples into Canadian society could and did co-exist with the IAA's emphasis on treaty rights. Laurie (and the IAA's outside help) saw integration as more important than treaty rights because, like many contemporaries, he believed that Indian communities lacked formal power. This view was evolutionist and was predicated upon the assumption that access to political and economic power would serve to free the reserve communities, which he saw as underdeveloped and stagnated, and would provide them with the tools of social change.[2]

In their work with the IAA, John Laurie and the outside help perceived Indian reserve communities as requiring "improvement" – something that could come about only if these communities gained access to political power. Whereas, before the existence of the IAA, Indian communities were seen as powerless, John Laurie and the outside help believed that, with the help of the IAA and its leaders, reserve communities would become empowered. Once empowered, Indian peoples would finally be able to extricate themselves from the limitations of their subsistence economies (and their technological inferiority) and become fully functional, economically contributing members of Canadian society. This way of thinking justified Laurie's focus on "training" IAA members in the fundamentals of democracy and having them interact with the Canadian state. Indian peoples needed to be politically integrated into Canada in order to ensure their own social and economic advancement. This goal took precedence over treaty rights, which simply reinforced and represented the unique status of Indian peoples outside the Canadian political system.

In existing histories dealing with Indian political organizations, the role of non-Indian "outsiders" in these organizations is noted, but their involvement is rarely investigated in detail.[3] More often, Euro-Canadian involvement in Indian political groups is discussed within the context of Canada's postwar concern with Indian issues. For example, historian J.R. Miller identifies how Canada generally became concerned with human rights as a result of the experience of the Second World War.[4] In general, these studies contain neither detailed analysis of the form of this outside assistance nor of the ideas motivating it; instead, the focus tends to be on *effects* of outsider involvement in Indian organizations.

In the case of the IAA, Euro-Canadians were not the instigators of political action, but they did have a strong hand in directing it. Furthermore, aid to Indian peoples in the postwar era was often motivated by more than just humanitarian concern. In fact, the history of the IAA suggests that the idea of "improving" or directing the lives of Indian peoples continued to motivate outsiders to help Indian communities, particularly during the first years after the war. Outsiders involved with the IAA were concerned less with the special rights of Indian peoples than they were with making sure that Indian peoples were included in general Canadian society, so that they could better contribute to the nation.

John Laurie Before the IAA

John Lee Laurie joined the IAA as executive secretary in 1944, after he was recommended for the position by IAA leaders Malcolm Norris and Albert Lightning.[5] During his years of involvement, Laurie came to play a critical role in the association. First, he attracted and recruited politicians and citizens to assist the IAA, sometimes through his work as a teacher and sometimes through his activities as IAA secretary, which placed him in contact with a variety of politicians and civil servants. Second, through the IAA John Laurie promoted his personal vision of what would benefit Indian peoples. He was most interested in advancing Indian education, achieving social equality, and attaining what he believed to be the moral improvement of Indian peoples. His influence on the IAA was neither consistent nor all-powerful; however, between 1944 and his death in 1959, it was persuasive.

John Laurie invented his own life story. Strangely, although he spent a great deal of time in the public eye following his 1944 appointment as secretary of the IAA – working with government officials and addressing audiences across Alberta – few knew many details of his early life. When he died in his Calgary home on 6 April 1959 following several years of illness, he left behind little but a few old suits of clothing, his buckskin outfits, a small suitcase of papers, and miscellaneous personal items.[6] He left Calgary as quietly as he came to it.

Laurie's life has a number of different versions. Those who knew him in his early teaching days at Crescent Heights believed he was an Englishman and a war veteran.[7] His official personnel file at the Calgary School Board states that he was born in London, England; and his Teacher's Permanent Record states that he received a great deal of his primary schooling in England.[8] In 1955, when he received an honourary doctorate from the University of Alberta for his teaching and for his work on behalf of Alberta's treaty Indians, it was claimed that he had been born in Scotland and educated in England.[9] Somehow, Laurie led others to believe that he had served overseas with the Royal Air Force during the First World War. His quiet nature was interpreted as being the result of permanent shock induced by wounds sustained during the war.[10]

Those who worked with Laurie and the IAA believed he was from Ontario and that he had Aboriginal ancestry. According to his good friend Ruth Gorman, when Laurie spoke of his childhood: "I never heard him talk about his family ... no one talked about their relatives ... I had heard him say 'I was raised by the Iroquois when I was little,' I'd heard him say that."[11] During the war years, he claimed to have Indian ancestry. In a letter appealing to the sympathies of MP Dorise Nielsen a few months before he assumed the position of IAA secretary, he wrote: "I am far from being wholly Indian – in fact I have only a little Indian blood but I am an adopted son of one of the Stoney chiefs ... I have been pretty well accepted as an Indian by them all and I think as one of them rather than as a white man and I speak as one."[12] John Laurie plainly wanted others to believe that he was directly connected to Indian peoples, perhaps in order to explain his interest in Indian issues or to bolster his credibility as an expert on Indian affairs.

For unknown reasons Laurie tried hard to obscure the real details of his own life. In a partial deathbed autobiography dictated to a former student, Laurie claimed that he was born in England, that he was raised in Ontario, and that, at a young age, he was taken by his grandmother to England to be educated by tutors and govenors.[13] He remembered having a great fondness for his father, with whom he enjoyed spending Sunday afternoons in the woods of Ontario watching birds and wildlife, and that his mother never approved of his Indian playmates.[14] In the same account, he also recalled that his favourite childhood pastimes were reading and hearing stories read aloud during the long winter months while on the farm with his parents. Perhaps it was his love of stories and literature that drove Laurie to fictionalize his own life. This "autobiography" is only a few pages in length and ends with Laurie's brief "memories" of his childhood in England.

Laurie's efforts to reinvent his childhood and life, making them exotic and exciting, hint at personal insecurities. It also reveals his tendency to exaggerate – a tendency that, in later years, he employed in his attempts to draw attention to the plight of Indian communities. In reality, he was born in 1899 on a farm in Blenheim Township, Oxford County, near what is now Cambridge, Ontario. His Canadian-born parents, Andrew and Isabella Laurie, lived on the family farm with John's maternal grandmother (who had emigrated from Scotland) and his much younger sister Marion. The Laurie family was staunchly Presbyterian, and it was always the wish of John's mother that her son become a minister. Since he did well at both primary and secondary school, he eventually chose to attend Trinity College at the University of Toronto, an undergraduate college affiliated with the Anglican Church. The strong English atmosphere and traditions at the college probably encouraged the rural Ontario farm boy to later invent an English background for himself. John's studies were only briefly interrupted when he enlisted as a cadet with the Royal Air Force in the summer of 1918.[15] The armistice of 11 November 1918, however, cut short his military career. Despite his own later attempts to create a different impression, he never served overseas. He returned to Trinity at Toronto in 1919, taking English, history, and modern languages.[16]

Following the war, Laurie was restless and was not content to remain in Ontario. A young man of twenty-one, he decided to leave his family and venture to the Canadian Prairies. He arrived first in Manitoba and, later, found employment as a teacher in the small towns of Evergreen and Hespero, near Eckville, Alberta.[17] By 1923 he had moved on to Calgary where he obtained a position as the Latin and English master at Western Canada College, a private boys school. He became quite attached to Calgary, and this job marked the beginning of his long teaching career in that city. In 1927 Laurie graduated from the Calgary Normal School with an Alberta teaching certificate, and, that same year, he joined the staff at Crescent Heights High School, where William Aberhart, the future premier of Alberta, was the principal.[18]

Students and colleagues at Crescent Heights found him to be well dressed, distinguished, and a romantic who loved literature.[19] Photos of Laurie from this time show him as a slim young man with a well trimmed mustache, looking rather stern. He supervised work on the yearbook, the Public Speaking and Debating Club, and even wrote plays for the students.[20] Fellow teacher Douglas Harkness recalled that Laurie was a "good conversationalist," and social studies teacher Aylmer Liesemer also formed a fast friendship with him. Both Liesemer and Harkness were politically active, with the former leaning to the left and the latter to the right. It was Liesemer who introduced Laurie to the left-wing Co-operative Commonwealth Federation (CCF) party founded in Calgary in 1932. Liesemer served as a city alderman in the mid-1930s and, from 1944 to 1952, he sat as a CCF member in Alberta's Legislative Assembly. It seems that Laurie's association with Liesemer, both at school and as a friend, encouraged his politicization, eventually leading him to come into contact with the IAA's Malcolm Norris. This meeting occurred during the early years of the war, when all these men were in Calgary for a CCF meeting.[21]

Despite all his extra-curricular commitments at Crescent Heights and his budding political interests, Laurie was alone – a bachelor rather far removed from his Ontario family. Although he forged many acquaintances in the Calgary area, these did not seem to satisfy his need for close social contact. Around this time, seeking companionship, young Laurie directed himself to the Stoney Indian reserve community west of Calgary. In later years Laurie, rather romantically, claimed he was first introduced to the Stoney reserve in 1926 while driving polo ponies to Rocky Mountain House. It is true that Laurie enjoyed horses and riding a great deal and that, by his own account, he stopped in at the agency blacksmith of the Morley reserve when his horse lost a shoe. Forced to spend the night on reserve, this event served as his introduction to the reserve community and to the poor state of the reserve lands at the foot of the Rockies. These lands were rocky, dry, and not good for farming.

Laurie came back to the reserve a few years later when he befriended the Reverend E.J. Staley, missionary and principal of the reserve residential school. The Calgary teacher frequently visited Staley on reserve, and the reverend introduced him to the reserve community and encouraged him to be involved in some of the United Church events on reserve. Laurie was particularly interested in the children and the schooling of the community, and, in 1939, he even went so far as to help one boy, Eddie Hunter, attend music lessons in Calgary. Through his involvement with Eddie Hunter, Laurie spent a great deal of time with the Hunter family. Their relationship was a close one, and Laurie finally gained a place in the community when, in 1940, the Hunter family adopted him as their son.[22]

Throughout the war years, Laurie continued travelling out to the Stoney reserve from Calgary, spending weekends as a guest at the residential school where there was always a variety of activities to enjoy, including music performances, outings, and plays.[23] A young teacher at the school remembered the bachelor as a somewhat cool and aloof gentleman who visited the school regularly, taking an interest in the students. Laurie, it seems, even attempted to forge a liaison with one of the older girls at the school. On a hot summer evening in 1944, when the school children were in bed, Laurie proposed to her from the residential school courtyard, to no avail.[24] From his association with the Hunter family, his connection with the residential school and Reverend Staley, and his search for companionship, it appears that Laurie wanted to belong in the reserve community.

In Calgary he missed the intimacy that a small community could provide. Spending so much time at Morley, Laurie was introduced to the poverty that existed in many reserve communities.

Laurie began to research government Indian policy at the local library and to discuss the topic with local non-Indians who were familiar with the condition of the Stoney and other reserve communities.[25] As he recalled: "Through Mr. Norman Luxton of Banff and others I found out about their [Stoney] efforts to readjust matters settled in 1877 to the new world of the late 1930s. Their efforts had not met with much success."[26] Luxton was a prominent entrepreneur in Banff; he sponsored the Banff Indian Days and, in the early 1930s, attempted to protect the Stoney economy. At this time hunting was vital to the Stoney, and Luxton wanted to ensure that this right was protected. As a result, he supported the legal battle that ensued in the Alberta courts on behalf of the Stoney. Although the *Wesley* case was originally defeated, the appeal judgment recognized the Stoney's treaty right to hunt for food on unoccupied Crown land: Luxton had scored a small but immediate victory for the Stoney.[27] His own research findings, his growing personal commitment to the Stoney community, and Luxton's example led Laurie to seek political and legal solutions to the reserve's problems.

In the early years of the war, Laurie made a concerted effort to publicize the poor state of the Stoney community. He thought a systematic approach to Stoney problems was needed. Later, the Calgary high school teacher even went so far as to suggest that he himself was responsible for the political organization of the Stoney.[28] It is not clear to what extent the Stoney leaders formed a cohesive group with Laurie's help. However, as early as 1941, with the assistance of Norman Luxton, various church groups, and the advice of his politically oriented co-workers at Crescent Heights, Laurie began a campaign to pressure the federal government to assist the Stoney community and to address the "Indian problem."[29] In this crusade on behalf of the Stoney, Laurie spoke on Indian issues to groups such as the University Women's Club in Calgary, provided newspapers with short articles on Indian issues, and became involved with the League of Nations of North American Indians.[30] By 1944 Laurie was trying to form a group he wanted to name the "Indian Rights Association" – an organization seeking to grant full rights of citizenship to Indian peoples and supported by influential Calgarians.[31] The ever-earnest teacher wholeheartedly engaged himself in solving the social inequities he saw on the reserve. As a lone activist Laurie felt that his goal was to "help," to improve life for Indian peoples, and the federal government became the target of his concerted reform campaign.

Even before he became IAA secretary, Laurie had approached elected officials to seek help for Indian peoples. MP for East Calgary, George Ross, was among the first to support Laurie's calls to have federal Indian policy adjusted for the benefit of Indian peoples. In a letter to Ross, Laurie set out his position:

> My contention is that a paternalistic policy such as we have had in Canada is out of date and certainly can achieve little except to create a "begging" attitude on the part of many Indians, here in the West particularly. A new policy which will throw more responsibility upon the Indian by giving him better social and economic conditions of life, and by giving him a greater voice in the conduct of his affairs, will certainly do more good than the present system.[32]

At this early date, Laurie was already seeking a greater voice for Indian people within the Canadian political system.

Ross took Laurie's ideas for greater Indian self-government and improved social and economic conditions and presented them before Parliament and the federal Committee on Reconstruction and Re-establishment (an influential government committee struck to consider the postwar reconstruction of Canadian society).[33] Ross mentioned Indian issues in Parliament as early as 1940, and, when he spoke as a member of the Committee on Reconstruction, he pressed Indian Affairs officials to explain the government's plans for rehabilitating the Stoney reserve economy. He questioned the assistance being given the community as well as the education available to the youth on reserve.[34] Ross boldly called for a new policy, indicating that the old policy had failed. Speaking directly to the secretary of the Indian Affairs Branch, T.R.L. McInnes, Ross said: "You have pointed out that the Indians are capable of doing great things ... But we have not got those great things from the Indians as yet ... we are in the horse and buggy days so far as the Indians are concerned. We need a new policy ... It is the policy of the government that it seem to me needs revising."[35] Undoubtedly, it was the information provided to him by John Laurie that enabled Ross to feel confident about questioning the workings of Indian Affairs.[36] Even before he joined the IAA, Laurie was directing debate on Indian issues.

In 1943, Laurie struck up a correspondence with MP Dorise Nielsen. Nielsen looked to Laurie for advice concerning the needs of Indian peoples. Already perceived as an "expert" on Indian issues, Laurie cultivated this perception by telling Nielsen that, even though he only had a little "Indian blood," he spoke as an Indian.[37] Laurie impressed upon her that education should be considered a priority in Indian affairs, and he even suggested that Indian self-government should proceed along the lines adopted under the Indian Reorganization Act in the United States.[38] The importance of Indian education was a theme Laurie pursued throughout his career with the IAA. Even before his appointment as secretary of the IAA, Laurie helped

Eddie Hunter from the Stoney reserve attend high school at Crescent Heights.[39]

In Laurie's view, the "Indian problem" could best be attacked by improving Indian education, gaining greater responsibility for band governments, and using the media and Opposition members in Parliament to embarrass the federal government into adjusting its Indian policy. He firmly believed that if Indian children were better educated, they could assume greater responsibility for their community and that, subsequently, reserve life would improve. He felt that Indian education should include provisions for higher education or technical training for Indian children, that mandatory school attendance should be extended to the age of eighteen years for Indian children, and that funding for Indian schools should be increased.[40] Furthermore, Laurie saw federal Indian policy as too restrictive and in desperate need of revision: Indian policy prevented Indian communities from taking initiatives to improve Indian lives. Fundamentally, John Laurie suspected the federal government and did not believe that it had the interests of its Indian wards at heart.[41] Despite these suspicions, Laurie never challenged the existing system of Indian administration; rather, he appears to have thought that the system could be revised to the benefit of its Indian patrons. He did not pursue issues relating to treaty rights.

Notwithstanding what appear to be honourable intentions and a deep personal commitment to the Stoney cause, Laurie did have a penchant for the dramatic and for generalization. At the same time as he was petitioning MPs, he was also writing in the *Calgary Herald*, describing the plight of the Stoney, their lack of education, health care, and old age security. And he was speaking at the University Women's Club, criticizing the administration of Indian Affairs and encouraging citizens to get the government to explain its Indian policy. As a result of his speaking and writing, Laurie spurred members of the University Women's Club, the Optimist Club, and MPs to take action.

Unfortunately, Laurie's claims were not completely sustainable, even though they did appeal to the sentiment of the public and the media. One of Laurie's central criticisms was that the Stoney were so poorly clothed that old clothing had to be collected for them. If Laurie had checked with the school and reserve community, he would have discovered that the Stoney had no use for this collected clothing. In addition, in his discussion of schools, Laurie falsely compared the Canadian system of school funding with the American system. Despite these errors, Laurie's petitions led several prominent citizens to challenge the government and to put the Indian Affairs Branch on the defensive.[42]

In the spring of 1944 John Laurie was finally brought a step closer to his dream of systematically fighting for his cause when he met IAA organizer Malcolm Norris, who was stationed in Calgary with the armed forces.

According to Norris, "I was first introduced to him by people who knew of his Indian activity and since then I have regarded him as a very good friend."[43] Norris and Laurie were both intellectuals and avid readers who were deeply concerned with social issues. They shared an interest in the CCF, and Norris frequently visited Laurie at home to discuss politics. Norris was so impressed with Laurie that, in February 1944, he wrote about him to his long-time friend Johnny Callihoo. In this letter Norris described Laurie as "a High School Teacher at Crescent Heights school in the city of Calgary. He has a trace of Indian blood in his veins through his father." He also described him as someone very sympathetic to Indian peoples.[44]

Norris's mention of Laurie was not trivial. Callihoo had struggled throughout the war to keep his fledgling IAA in operation, fighting unsuccessfully to extend its influence to other reserve communities in Alberta. Lacking confidence in his own ability to increase the power of the IAA and embarrassed by his rudimentary education, Callihoo relied heavily upon Norris for advice and direction. During the war Norris was prevented from being directly involved in the IAA because of his position as an officer in the armed forces; however, he did promise to help Callihoo and, in the spring of 1944, suggested that Laurie would also assist.[45] The result of Norris's connection with Laurie was that, in May 1944, at the Fifth Annual Meeting of the IAA held on the Hobbema reserve, Laurie was nominated for the position of secretary in absentia. A vote was held and Laurie was awarded the position by acclamation. His career with the IAA was launched.

Laurie's work as IAA secretary clearly and directly extended from his previous involvement in Indian matters. Not surprisingly, from the moment of his appointment in May 1944, Laurie zealously threw himself into his work. Based on the voluminous notes and correspondence Laurie produced over the course of his terms as IAA secretary, it is obvious that he invested a great deal of time and energy in the association. Gordon Crowchild, who stayed with Laurie while attending school in Calgary, recalls that the chain-smoking Laurie regularly worked deep into the night in his main floor suite, typing IAA correspondence.[46] Laurie lived near his school and, despite his full-time teaching career, did some of his IAA work at home during lunch hours. On weekends he travelled to reserve communities on behalf of the IAA and even took leaves from his work in order to pursue IAA business. In some cases, he became so tired he could not work as a teacher. In 1951 an exhausted Laurie wrote to his friend: "I did not go to work on Monday at all but went to bed when I got home and have missed most of the week. Today was the first day I really felt like myself again."[47] In 1956 a progressive heart condition eventually forced him to resign his position as IAA secretary but not before he had spent considerable money, time, and energy on the association.

Outside Help and the IAA

Numerous individuals and organizations, ranging from concerned citizens groups to politicians, came to offer help to the IAA through John Laurie. Officially, John Laurie's secretarial duties were limited to keeping accurate minutes of all association meetings and being in charge of the IAA's business correspondence.[48] In keeping with his official assignment, Laurie arduously typed, copied, and circulated minutes of the executive meetings and conventions to all member locals. He also received and processed agenda items for convention meetings, kept locals notified of important issues via informational bulletins that he personally drafted, and circulated IAA resolutions for local approval.[49] Officially, therefore, Laurie was a mere extension of the IAA membership, documenting its wishes and words.

In reality, however, John Laurie took his role in the IAA far beyond its official description. He broadly interpreted and exercised his duties as secretary and, unofficially, had a strong hand in directing the activities of the IAA. Laurie felt empowered by his involvement in the IAA, which gave him a sense of purpose. The IAA founders needed and admired Laurie's skills, and he zealously pursued his IAA duties.

No sooner had Laurie assumed his duties as secretary than he began to exercise his own vision of what the IAA should do and be for the Indian peoples of Alberta. In his view, the IAA would function most successfully as a lobby group, pressuring the government to change federal Indian policy by cultivating public support. One of the more significant of Laurie's moves was to encourage politicians and citizens groups to support the IAA. The extent of his connections and lobbying activities was revealed in a letter he wrote to IAA treasurer Sam Minde following the 1944 Annual General Meeting at Hobbema (in preparation for the presentation of the IAA's first memorial on Indian affairs to the Indian Affairs Branch): "I have written personally and at my own expense to the following members at Ottawa, Messrs. Edwards, Ross, Castleden, MacNicol, Blackmore, Mrs. Nielsen and Mr. Bracken, as eloquently as I could seeking their support of our protest ... I have called a meeting of two service clubs ... asking – and they will give it gladly – their support which will be duly forwarded to Ottawa to where it should do the most good."[50] Laurie was broadening the reach of the IAA.

Controlling the correspondence of the IAA was Laurie's key to recruiting outsiders to assist the association. It allowed him to establish personal contacts with Indian Affairs Branch administrators and Opposition MPs, and he took full advantage of these contacts when he travelled to Ottawa. For example, in September 1944, following the IAA's presentation of its first memorial on Indian affairs to the federal government, Laurie travelled to Ottawa at his own expense to visit all those individuals he hoped to convert to the IAA. During this very brief visit, which kept him away from Crescent Heights, he met with the director of the Indian Affairs Branch and former Calgarian Harold McGill as well as with other Branch staff. Outside Indian Affairs he met with reporters, hoping to ensure that the IAA received favourable press coverage when Indian issues were brought up in the House. He further extended his range of influence by contacting other citizens who showed concern with Indian affairs, including Canadian Pacific Rail executives and the Canadian Handicraft Association.[51]

Among the politicians drawn to the IAA through their contact with John Laurie were MPs Douglas Harkness and G.H. Castleden and Alberta MLA Aylmer Liesemer. Harkness and Liesemer were perhaps closest to Laurie because all three had worked together at Crescent Heights High School in the 1930s. Liesemer provided Laurie with strategic political advice and contacts at the provincial level when he sat in the Legislative Assembly as a CCF member. Harkness, a veteran of the Second World War who, in 1945, had left Crescent Heights for a political career with the Conservative party in Ottawa, provided Laurie with political contacts and personally voiced many of his issues in Parliament. Castleden, in turn, had supported Indian issues as a member of the 1944 Committee for Reconstruction and Re-establishment, and Laurie had petitioned him for assistance with Indian matters soon after becoming IAA secretary. Harkness and Castleden were particularly important to the IAA because they gave it significant exposure in the House of Commons, and their criticisms of Indian administration were brought directly to bear on the minister of Indian Affairs.

Harkness began advancing Indian issues in the House as early as 1945. In his first year as an MP, he raised the question of extending social legislation to Indian peoples in a debate concerning old age pensions. Pensions had been available to Canadian seniors since the Old Age Pensions Act, 1927; however, Indian peoples were not eligible because the Liberal administration viewed the application of pensions to elderly Indians as both bureaucratically complex and unnecessary (apparently because Indians already received rations).[52] Thanks to John Laurie, Harkness had first-hand experience with the problems of the aged and elderly registered Indian population. In the fall of that same year, Laurie spurred Harkness to visit the Stoney reserve to witness first-hand the poor economic conditions prevailing in that community, especially among the elderly. With the high school teacher's help, Harkness took the opportunity to graphically report his findings in Parliament:

> At the first home we visited we found an old woman whom two other people had to help up off the floor where she was sitting. The old woman we found was a charge upon the son. This man had a family of three children, whom he had considerable difficulty in supporting. In fact, shortly before our arrival his only food stock, which was potatoes, had been frozen. Upon making inquiries we found that this old woman did not draw the old

> age pension and further that the Indians alone amongst all our citizens are the only ones who do not come within the provisions of the Old Age Pensions Act.[53]

Harkness acknowledged John Laurie in the House as a valuable source of information on the subject, and he described the poverty of the reserve. He argued passionately against the injustice of excluding Indians from receiving social benefits simply because these were administered by the provinces while Indian peoples were wards of the federal government. In his view, to allow Indian peoples to fall victim to federal-provincial jurisdictional disputes was unfair: to grant social benefits to elderly Indians was a matter of "simple justice."[54]

Support for the idea of treating Indian peoples on an "equal" basis with other Canadians was voiced by other parliamentarians, although not many. Some MPs suggested that Indians should gain the pension because "they are human beings, the same as you and I," or as a reward for their enlisting during the war.[55] These arguments would seem to support the idea that parliamentarians endorsed the notion of political equality for Indian peoples. In fact, however, this argument was not extended to other Indian issues. Parliamentarians focused more upon the poor state of Canada's reserve economies than they did upon the right, in principle, of Indian peoples to equal social benefits. If social welfare could relieve poverty, then social welfare was deemed necessary for Indian peoples. The rationale for helping them was economic rather than ethical and was rooted in the ideal of political equality. Harkness's motion to extend pensions to Indian peoples received a great deal of support, despite its rejection by Minister of Indian Affairs J.A. Glen.

Indian pensions was but one of several issues Harkness promoted in Parliament, and it reflected how the political agenda and needs of Indian peoples intersected with the postwar desire to reshape Canadian society through education, employment, and social welfare programs. Harkness continued to be helpful to the IAA when he was appointed to the 1946 Special Joint Committee investigating the Indian Act. He supported the discussion of Indian issues in Parliament throughout the 1940s and 1950s. And, numerous times, he went on record in the House to criticize the Liberal government's handling of Indian Affairs, focusing upon such issues as the improvement of Indian education, Indian health services, and agriculture.

Laurie also cultivated the support of Saskatchewan CCF MP G.H. Castleden. In a 1945 letter asking him for help, Laurie emphasized the need for better Indian education and social services for Indian communities.[56] An elegant orator, Castleden frequently spoke on Indian issues in the House, and, of all those who supported the reform of Indian Affairs, he was perhaps the most liberal in his approach.

Taking Harkness's argument for "simple justice" for Indian peoples further, Castleden called for Indian Affairs reform on the grounds that the basic rights of citizenship should not be denied Canada's Indian citizens. Speaking in the House in 1945, Castleden remarked, "the time has come when we should look upon the Indian population as humans, with rights to citizenship. They need not be treated entirely as wards."[57] Castleden was among the first to consistently argue that Indian peoples be granted the same "human rights" to a decent standard of living and education as were enjoyed by other Canadians, along with the right to manage their own affairs. He believed that this was the surest way to improve their standard of living.[58] He repeatedly criticized the government for treating Indian peoples in an undemocratic manner by denying them a voice in government and, on more than one occasion, he brought Canada's neglect of its Indian treaties to the attention of the House.[59]

On the one hand, Castleden was exceptional in emphasizing treaty and human rights as the basis for granting Indian communities additional benefits and for reforming Indian Affairs. Most MPs who spoke in favour of Indian Affairs reform emphasized economic questions. They focused upon the poor state of reserve communities rather than upon theoretical questions of rights. Castleden did adopt the popular idea that education was the foundation upon which to improve Indian communities, stating, in 1947, that "education is a fundamental and basic thing upon which we must build these people if we are to make anything at all of them."[60] Castleden was clearly more liberal in his interpretation of Indian peoples' fundamental rights than were many other MPs. On the other hand, he believed that the education and employment of Indian peoples should be a central government goal. Castleden believed in the redeeming function of work and education, arguing that, through work, "[Indian people] could make a contribution to our country. Early in life we should discover what capacities they have and then train them along those lines."[61] Through Castleden, the IAA agenda to improve Indian education, to ensure employment opportunities, and to protect treaty rights was given some exposure.

Besides Ottawa politicians, Laurie also recruited local citizens groups to aid the IAA. Two of these were: (1) the Crescent Heights Home and School Association of Calgary and (2) the Edmonton-based Friends of the Indians Society. These citizens groups gave the IAA valuable public exposure and emphasized the importance of education, employment, and social assistance with regard to helping Indian peoples "improve" their position in Canadian society .

It was no secret in John Laurie's classroom at Crescent Heights that the condition of Indian peoples in Canada concerned and upset him.[62] Students were well aware of his sentiments. Not surprisingly, his interest in Indian education filtered through to the Crescent Heights Home and

School Association. At a meeting in December 1944, members of the Home and School Association discussed the lack of educational and vocational opportunities for young Indian students. That night a resolution was passed calling for Indian children to be given the same educational opportunities as non-Indian children. The issue did not rest here, and, hungry for more information on the deplorable state of Indian communities, the members invited Laurie to make presentations to them concerning Indian issues. Laurie attended their spring meeting, and, in response to his information, the Rosedale parents resolved that,

> as Indians have no vote, no representation in Parliament and no voice in their own affairs, nor any rights of citizenship and yet the men of the tribes are conscripted for service in the armed forces, that these peoples should no longer be regarded as a subject race but should be given the same educational opportunities as other Canadians, as *education is the only hope for rehabilitation* of the Indian [emphasis added].[63]

Clearly, the Home and School group was interested in educating Indian children for the purpose of reforming and improving them. The resolutions emerging from the above meeting reflected an underlying concern with social change, calling for improved school facilities, better teachers, a federal investigation into Indian educational services, and, most significantly, access to welfare training officers.[64] Education and social change were solidly linked in the minds of these middle-class parents. The 1944 and 1945 meetings were among the first Indian-related encounters between Laurie and the Home and School Association, and, over the years, the latter became a solid supporter of the IAA, particularly with regard to Indian education.

Much of the Home and School Association's interest in improved Indian education came from its president, Anne Downe. Downe, an immigrant from England, was a poet and member of the Canadian Authors' Association, and her young daughter and son attended Crescent Heights. Downe loved English literature, which made her sympathetic to a literary person like Laurie, to whose charm and influence she quickly succumbed. Through her efforts, the issue of Indian education was carried all the way to the national Home and School Association. By 1945 the Home and School Association's membership endorsed the IAA in its petitions to Parliament, and Downe personally immersed herself in helping Laurie with his IAA-related administrative and secretarial duties.[65] Her involvement with the IAA soon deepened, and, beginning in 1945, she began regularly attending IAA meetings as an honourary association member.

Education remained Downe's primary concern when it came to pressing for the reform of Indian Affairs. According to her daughter, she travelled to reserve communities with Laurie and was particularly moved by the separation of children from their families when the former were forced to attend residential school.[66] Downe saw education as offering "salvation" to Indian peoples, and she took it upon herself to organize adult education classes for IAA members in Calgary. Held at the Anglican Cathedral Hall in the 1940s, these focused upon conducting meetings, job interviews, and writing business letters.[67]

Downe's efforts also extended to garnering support for the IAA from other citizens groups. She used her connections with the University Women's Club to promote the plight of Indian peoples and the work of the IAA; and, in 1946, the Canadian Authors' Association submitted a brief to the Special Joint Parliamentary Committee appointed to investigate the Indian Act.[68]

A second citizens group that became involved with the IAA immediately after the war was the influential, Edmonton-based Committee of Friends of the Indian, known as of 1951 as the Friends of the Indians Society. Unlike the Home and School Association, the Friends of the Indians Society existed specifically to support the IAA and emphasized a slightly broader range of reforms to Indian administration. The Friends of the Indians Society pushed for greater employment opportunities for Indian peoples and the revision of the Indian Act; furthermore, its members immersed themselves in legal matters pertaining to Alberta's Indian population. Like the Home and School Association, the Friends of the Indians Society sought improvements in Indian education.

The Committee of Friends of the Indian was founded in December 1944 by Reta Rowan, wife of University of Alberta zoology professor Dr. William Rowan. Reta Rowan actively participated in various groups concerned with minority rights at both the civic and provincial levels. In this instance, the Committee of Friends of the Indian derived from the Council for Canadian Unity, of which she was a member. Rowan was known to move in social circles that favoured Fabian socialism, and she was a strong believer in community development. According to Harold Cardinal, son of founding IAA member Frank Cardinal and later president of the IAA, "She always struck me as a kind, gentle soul whose only interest was to help."[69] In the Depression years Dr. Rowan assisted Indian Affairs with Manitoba fur rehabilitation projects aimed at helping Indian trappers, and Reta was also interested in assisting Indian communities in Alberta.

The decision to organize the Committee of Friends of the Indians resulted from a council session entitled "Indians as Canadians," where members of the council had suggested that a special committee be set up to study the conditions in Indian reserve communities. Five influential members decided to form the original Committee of Friends: C.F. Baker, Reta Rowan, Edith Nave, Morgan Pitcher, and the Edmonton lawyer H.A.

Mackie. With the exception of Pitcher and Mackie, who had previously involved themselves in Indian issues (Mackie had been recruited by the League of Indians of Western Canada to answer legal questions),[70] in Rowan's view, "this small group knew but little about the Indians and their many problems, or how they tried to meet them with their Native activities curtailed."[71] In 1944 the members of the Committee of Friends set out to educate themselves on Indian matters by studying, among other things, the Indian Act, the annual reports of the Indian Affairs Branch, briefs by non-Indian welfare societies in Canada and the United States, and the U.S. Indian Reorganization Act, 1934, which was brought forward by John Collier, the reform-minded Bureau of Indian Affairs commissioner. In addition, the committee studied the first memorial on Indian affairs submitted to Ottawa by the newly restructured IAA. Although membership in the group was initially small, by 1949 several affluent and influential people in Edmonton society were members, including university professors, provincial government administrators, lawyers, missionaries, and Indian people from the Edmonton area.[72] Even IAA members Malcolm Norris, Johnny Callihoo, and Albert Lightning eventually joined the Committee of Friends.

At an early date, through its constitution, the committee pledged itself to several goals: to promote a better understanding between Indians and the Canadian public, to improve the living conditions on reserves, to raise the educational level of Indian communities, to work in harmony with the IAA for better health and opportunities for Indian peoples, and to press for changes in the Indian Act. Nor were treaty rights ignored, as the Committee of Friends affirmed "the need for consideration of the terms of Treaty, and consultation with representative Indian bodies, before any changes be made affecting treaty rights."[73] Treaty rights, however, never became one of the committee's prominent issues. Clearly, the Committee of Friends had a close relationship with the IAA, and it sought to assist Alberta's Indian population in matters of employment and education as well as in changing Indian Affairs policy. The committee took a conservative approach to reform, emphasizing the need to work with government and other organizations to improve conditions for Indian people. Part of this conservative approach included minimizing treaty issues and focusing upon the Indian Act.

Within the first year of its existence, the Committee of Friends consistently lobbied the government to reform Indian Affairs, and it attempted to educate the public on Indian issues. In 1945 alone, the committee canvassed northern Alberta communities for support, wrote editorials for newspapers, and sent letters to Premier Manning and various MPs advocating the institution of a Royal Commission on Indian Affairs. In addition, the committee held an Indian art exhibition in Edmonton and sponsored public discussions of Indian issues. Reta Rowan herself attended IAA meetings, and much of the information she gathered there (with the help of John Laurie and people like Johnny Callihoo) became the basis for the committee's lobbying activities. At all times, despite the wide range of its activities, the committee stressed the need to reform Indian education in Canada.

Perhaps one of the most direct actions the committee undertook for the benefit of Alberta's Indians, particularly for members of the IAA, was the launching of an adult education program. As early as February 1947, the Committee of Friends arranged a week-long adult education program at the Bissell Memorial Institute in Edmonton for interested Indian students. Much like the classes sponsored by the Home and School Association in Calgary, these classes aimed to improve the language skills of Indian students and offered instruction in parliamentary procedure, leadership, first aid, and other practical skills. Where the Home and School Association led by Anne Downe served the Indian population of southern Alberta, the Committee of Friends served the Indian population of northern Alberta.

The first session of the education program appeared to be relatively successful and ten students attended the classes. Unfortunately, the following spring the second adult school saw fewer attendees and, by 1949, the program was dropped. In 1951 and 1952, the education program was briefly resurrected in the form of "Parliamentary Projects," with students attending lectures given by Alberta government administrators in the Legislative Building on subjects related to provincial matters, including health, education, forestry, agriculture, and fish and furs.[74] These classes, too, were not well attended and were discontinued after 1952.

Despite their short lifespans, the adult school and the Parliamentary Projects, both of which were aimed at "improving" Indian peoples, were hailed by the Indian Affairs Branch as important. In a letter written by the Branch director R.A. Hoey, John Laurie was heartily congratulated for the initiative taken by the Friends of the Indians group:

> the information sent forward by you with respect to the organization of Indian groups for the study of worthwhile subjects is the most encouraging bit of news I have heard since I entered the department almost eleven years ago ... The organization of such groups, coupled with the organization of homemaker's associations, will do more than anything else I can think of at the moment for the advancement of the Indian population.[75]

In the immediate postwar era, the education of Indian people was an issue prominent in the minds of many Canadians, particularly those who wanted to "help" Indian communities. It was thought that, through education, Indian people would learn the duties of citizenship in a democracy and could then assume their rightful position as productive citizens within postwar society. In other words, outside help was consistent with federal attitudes about what was important for Indian peoples. Interestingly, some IAA members who attended the adult education programs valued them because they showed that non-Indians were concerned about Indian issues. In a Friends of the Indians Society meeting in 1951, Albert Lightning said "that the people back on the Reserve were beginning to understand the efforts being made by those outside the Reserves for improving the conditions in which our Treaty Indians live."[76]

IAA executive members appreciated the efforts made by the Friends on behalf of their cause, and they worked to inform it of issues concerning Indian people. IAA president Johnny Callihoo, himself a member of the Friends, publicly acknowledged his appreciation for the group: "Many thanks for your good work ... As Indians we are very weak in making any kind of protest as we are a conquered race so we must depend on all the christen [sic] people of this Dominion of ours for help. I know you people in Edmonton have done your very best."[77] Other IAA members, including Malcolm Norris and Albert Lightning, also frequently attended the monthly meetings held by the society, eagerly providing it with their perspective on issues facing Indian peoples in Alberta and sometimes challenging the information the society received from other sources. At a June 1946 meeting on Indian education, for example, Archdeacon H.S. Middleton of St. Paul's Anglican Indian Residential School of Cardston, Alberta, told of the great successes of his school and the high standards of living on the Blood reserve (where the school was located). During the discussion, Callihoo and Lightning leapt up and directly contradicted Middleton, stressing the "incompetence and inability of northern Indians to become self-reliant and self-supporting," despite their access to some degree of education.[78] Norris attended Friends meetings regularly in the late 1940s and often gave presentations on current issues facing Indian communities. Through their involvement in the Friends of the Indians Society, IAA members helped the concerned non-Indian middle class appreciate Indian perspectives on pressing issues.

It is important to note that, despite its efforts to assist and support Indian peoples in Alberta, the Friends of the Indians Society bypassed opportunities for discussions on treaty rights. In contrast, time and time again, IAA members from reserve communities who attended the society's meetings brought up the issue of treaty rights. Johnny Callihoo was a tireless promoter of treaty rights and raised the issue of their neglect at every possible opportunity.[79] Even though IAA members clearly stated that treaty rights had been diminished and that their erosion lay at the heart of many of the problems facing Indian communities, the society never pursued this issue to any great length.[80]

That outside help, like that represented by the Friends of the Indians Society, did not focus upon treaty rights is not surprising. Rather than taking treaty rights as the basis for its activities, the society chose to justify its assistance of Indian communities by arguing that "the Indian people need help in their relations with the Indian Affairs Branch, and the governments, both Provincial and Dominion."[81] The aim of the society was to address the socio-economic inequity in Indian reserve communities and to integrate Indian peoples into Canadian postwar social and economic policies. It was thought that political integration would follow. In the words of Reta Rowan, "the Friends of the Indians Society has been able to act as 'liaison.'... a go-between, to help both sides towards a better understanding of each other. Their basic needs are: – better health care, including training in sanitation and preventive habits; general education and training in livelihood skills, especially the latter, to develop earning capacity; and knowledge of the citizenship process to enable them to participate in local and national affairs."[82] The society acknowledged that Canadian society had finally realized "the fact that it is no use to plan unless planning is shared by the Indian people themselves."[83] The purpose of the Friends of the Indians Society, then, was to include Indian communities in Canadian society rather than to address their unique rights.

Last, Laurie forged a close relationship with George Gooderham, a devoted civil servant in Indian Affairs who, in 1946, was promoted to the position of Regional Supervisor of Indian Agencies in Alberta. Gooderham entered the Indian Affairs service in 1920, when he replaced his father as Indian Agent for the Blackfoot reserve. Gooderham, a rather gruff and efficient individual, was knowledgeable about farming, and his goal for the Blackfoot reserve was to create a community of self-sufficient agriculturalists. He believed that Indians should be made "industrious in the white sense," and, to this end, he attempted to teach Indian farmers and workers to save their income and harbour their resources.[84] At the same time as he promoted this Protestant work ethic, Gooderham also encouraged Blackfoot traditions: he attended Sundances and spoke in support of traditional religious practices. In his work as Indian Agent, Gooderham appears to have been respected by the local leaders and by the band in general.

Once the IAA established itself as a credible organization in the eyes of the Indian Affairs Branch, Regional Supervisor Gooderham became the central contact between the Branch and the IAA. As a result, after 1946, when IAA resolutions were to be discussed with the Branch, or when the IAA had any other special concerns, Gooderham became its first government contact. Secretary Laurie met with Gooderham on many occasions, sometimes with IAA executive members and sometimes on his own.[85] Over the years the two men developed a close friendship,[86] and, by the late 1950s, their views on Indian issues converged.

The conservative nature of the IAA's outside help was reflected in its focus on Indian education and the state of income/employment in reserve communities. Anne Downe, the Home and School Associations, the Friends of the Indians Society, and parliamentarians supporting the IAA all directed their energies towards solving problems related to these particular areas of concern. This preoccupation with Indian social welfare, education, and employment was far from radical. Indeed, towards the end of the Second World War, Canadian opinion in general was highly sensitive to the memories of the interwar Depression and the political and social strains that accompanied heavy and prolonged unemployment.[87] Throughout the war years, the federal government concentrated a great deal of time and energy planning to reformulate Canadian society so as to avoid the unstable and frightening social conditions of the 1930s. Canada's aim was to reconstruct its economy and society so that unemployment and poverty would never again reach the levels experienced during the Great Depression. Social welfare programs, education, and employment were hailed as three of the most solid and promising building blocks for postwar reconstruction.

Throughout the war years, the importance of social welfare programs, education, and full employment were reflected in discussions of postwar economic policies that took place in intellectual and government circles. In a series of lectures delivered at the University of Toronto in the fall of 1942, for example, the participating faculty emphasized the need for full employment after the war and considered the need for government intervention in smoothing the transition from a wartime to a peacetime economy.[88] Unemployment was definitively linked to human destitution and misery:

> The obvious fundamental need ... is full employment: a job at decent wages for everyone able to work ... It is the idleness of the heretofore industrious workman which is the insidiously destructive factor: the fruitless search for work, the repeated rejections, the long-continued humiliation of being at home, underfoot in a crowded and tense family situation, but denied the opportunity to work for its support; these are the factors which steadily undermine morale ... the right to work is more than an idle phrase.[89]

Unemployment was viewed as a grave threat to national progress and had to be addressed before it undermined the morale of the population.

According to the popular thinking of the day, postwar attempts at full employment required broad government intervention, including protection for those unable to work (e.g., old age pensioners) and continued education for those not yet established in the workforce. Social programs (e.g., social insurance, public assistance, health care, family allowances, and pensions) were all viewed as important ways for the government to protect its citizens. During the war years, human welfare was hailed as a new government responsibility as it was felt that the "spiritual aim" of a true democracy was "the fullest development of human personality."[90] In addition, human welfare had to be actively promoted through "employment for all seeking it, security from want, and adequate services for the health, education, and cultural development of all the people."[91] The intelligentsia of the day saw the improvement of society through work and welfare as the goal of a new age. A nation's human resources were its "true" national wealth, and the wasteful management of those resources could not continue. There was a great hope during the war that, upon the arrival of peace, Canadian society could be reshaped and remoulded through social programs, thus yielding a stronger nation: "Our reconstructed vision of Canada must add to the beauty of our landscapes the beauty of healthy childhood, of vigorous manhood, and of gracious age. To achieve these, a national dynamic for human welfare is essential; the social services will be its medium of expression."[92] Social and economic ideas thus melded to form an approach to reconstruction that emphasized improving society through work and welfare.[93]

Social and economic improvement as a medium for the moral and social improvement of Canada was also linked to the political ideal of democracy and equality for all citizens. In 1945 high levels of stable employment and income, and higher standards of living, were proclaimed as a major aim of government policy, "transcending in importance all sectional and group interests."[94] All Canadians were, theoretically, to receive equal attention; as a result of this, it was thought, Canada would become a more democratic nation. In 1946 G.H. Castleden beautifully illustrated the connection between democracy and the struggle to address the "Indian problem": "The fight of the Indian today is a fight against ignorance, poverty, against fear; and it will be a fight for democracy."[95] Ignorance could be fought with education, poverty could be alleviated through work, and all of this would lead to the betterment of Canadian democracy and the stability of the nation. According to this line of thinking, political ideals flowed directly from social and economic change.

In keeping with this view, Indian peoples were not ignored in government postwar reconstruction discussions. In 1944 creating work and welfare for Indian peoples was discussed at some length by the House of Commons Special Committee for Reconstruction and Re-establishment, and this discussion was continued in Parliament by men like Castleden and Harkness. The welfare of Indian peoples gained public support primarily because of an overall national concern with human resources, which many believed had been squandered during the Depression and the Second World War. National stability and security were deemed to rest on the more equal distribution of wealth, and the government was to be responsible for that democratizing action. John Laurie supported this notion through his work with the IAA, and, in turn, citizens groups were drawn to the IAA because they were similarly democratically inclined. In essence, the IAA's outside help was conservative in its striving for social security and its belief that work, education, and welfare would lead to political stability and civil equality.

Despite the significance of the postwar focus upon the reconstruction of Canada and upon achieving democracy and equity, the question remains: In a postwar world where the state of Indian communities was seen as deplorable, and where Indian peoples themselves called for a reassertion of treaty rights, why did the IAA's outside help not pursue this issue? The explanation seems to be that treaty rights were seen as unrelated to government postwar reconstruction policies as well as to notions of democracy and equity, and that they were perceived as vague and difficult to realize. John Laurie himself believed that treaty rights were too esoteric and that asserting them could lead to their degradation. Popular sentiment at the time supported the idea that treaties were not law and that, therefore, they could be ignored.[96]

The whole notion that treaty rights were difficult to assert and protect had, at the time, been asserted in the Ontario case of *Rex* v. *Commanda,* a hunting rights case heard in the Supreme Court of Ontario in 1939. The judge ruled that "it does not matter whether the Indians have any rights flowing from the reservation in the Robinson treaty or not. Such rights (if any) may be taken away by the Ontario Legislature without any compensation."[97] The case was further significant because the Crown had also argued that, as Indian peoples were never treated as an independent power, treaties between them and the Crown were simply agreements, or contracts, rather than treaties in the strict sense of the word. Under this argument, upholding treaty promises was a question of the Crown's honour rather than of Indian Peoples' rights. The federal government never appealed this case, which set a precedent that undermined the sanctity of Indian treaty rights in Canada.[98] Plainly, the idea that these rights could and should be protected was not popular at the time, nor was it supported by either the courts or the government. As a result, solving the practical social and economic issues of Indian peoples was deemed a priority, and the actions of outside help significantly contributed to this way of approaching Indian issues.

Laurie and the IAA

Though John Laurie enlisted the assistance of numerous non-Indian organizations and individuals in his efforts to champion the causes of the IAA, he also had a strong hand in directing its activities. In fact, Laurie represented a source of both "outside help" and "inside help." From his privileged post as provincial secretary, John Laurie worked tirelessly to infuse the IAA with his personal vision of what was important for the advancement of Indian peoples. Primarily, he saw the IAA as representing an opportunity for Indian peoples to learn the principles of democracy, to educate themselves, and to improve their moral fibre. He also saw it as a vehicle with which to educate the Canadian public on issues confronting Indian communities. He did not openly voice this idea in his early years with the IAA, but by the late 1950s he openly acknowledged the importance of integrating Indian peoples into Canadian society. In his view, the IAA was an instrument that would contribute to the attainment of that goal.

Since Laurie had a direct hand in planning IAA meeting agendas and political strategies, he was easily able to promote his own ideas. Initially, Laurie and Malcolm Norris worked together to devise IAA strategies. Norris and Laurie often discussed politics before the latter joined the IAA, and they continued to do so in the first year after he became secretary. In 1945 they set the tone for the IAA general meeting by helping Johhny Callihoo with his presidential message. Laurie wrote to Callihoo: "Dear Brother Johnny, Malcolm and I are sitting here pounding out a little medicine for you and sharpening a few arrows which we hope you will shoot because you are the best marksman of us all. What we really mean is that we have a few ideas which we would like you to put into your President's message."[99] Later, Laurie worked on his own, advising the IAA leadership on various issues. For example, in a 1953 letter to IAA president Gladstone, Laurie made several suggestions as to how the IAA should proceed with its activities: "I should like to send out a questionaire [sic]," "what do you think of appointing a committee from several parts of the province ... to collect and ... put together all suggestions about the [Indian] Act?"; "I just thought tonight of trying to get on CFCN with a talk"; "I feel strong protests should be made about the medical services being cut down and about the cut in estimates for schools and education generally."[100] Obviously, Laurie had many ideas about what types of actions the IAA could or should take, and he was never hesitant to share them with the IAA executive.

John Laurie saw the IAA as a modernizing force in Indian reserve communities, as a provider of educational opportunities, and as a training ground for democracy. In his view, the IAA was a force that would improve Indian peoples and win them respect. To this end, he insisted that the IAA be run "properly." Laurie created "instructions to locals," which he distributed to newly organized locals in the hope that this would ensure that all members of the IAA would use parliamentary procedures.[101] In a letter to Rod Callihoo of the Villeneuve local, he explained: "I like very much to receive well-ordered reports for two reasons – first, they make it so much easier for me to keep up the records, second – they show how quickly our members follow the rules of Parliamentary procedure, increase the respect outsiders have for us and our Association."[102] Laurie emphasized the importance of following proper form, and he even pressed this point home to President Johnny Callihoo, stating: "Unless there is a proper organization with responsible elected officers the department will pay absolutely no attention. The first questions they ask are 'whom do you represent,' and 'how many paid up members have you.'"[103] A democratically run organization based on parliamentary procedure was the only hope Laurie saw for the advancement of Indian peoples. Unless Indian peoples organized themselves "properly," they would make no progress.

Laurie also saw the IAA as an opportunity to modernize Indian communities. He believed that the organization could provide its members with educational opportunities that would help them distance themselves from their "ancient animosities" and assist them to gradually move away from a position of isolation.[104] As a result, he encouraged these adult education classes more than he did those organized by the Home and School Association and the Friends of the Indians Society. In 1948, for example, he organized an Adult Education Week, which was to be held for IAA members in the hall of the Anglican Cathedral in Calgary. These classes were to instruct Indian members in legal issues and practical matters. He composed an advertisement for these classes, and it contained the following phrases: "Adult Education School ... Good Teachers ... Interesting Subjects ... Useful things to know ... Show the Government that the Indian people really want education ... Let us stop talking, Let us do things ... Success or Failure is up to you ... Be on time."[105] Classes offered instruction in hygiene, cattle management, English, spelling, first aid, the Indian Act, the Game Act, parliamentary procedure, "civics," and special courses for women. Even IAA president Callihoo attended, and local newspaper coverage featured a photo of "students" enthusiastically bandaging each other. The text read: "An Indian chief and five Indian braves are back at school this week learning things which were neglected in their own education and which they will pass on to their own tribesmen in adult education classes."[106] Laurie firmly believed these classes would educate Indian peoples about legal issues and would also improve their personal moral and intellectual development. According to him, education was "to preserve pride of race and culture and to rescue the rapidly disappearing self-respect of the Indian is important ... To create a feeling of unity among the Indians and to assist to break down the ancient inter-tribal prejudices, to assist Indians towards greater responsibilities through education, practice self-reliance."[107]

Classes were not the only means Laurie used to increase IAA members' self-reliance and to improve their morals. At times he devised inspirational readings that were to be included with the bulletins he sent to locals. For example:

> This looks like the season when feed will be scarce. Crops are not threshed yet. What about your stock? What about your family? Do you need food or do you need a trip or a new car? You cannot eat a car. It will not feed your children. Many people want to run their own business. They have asked for this privilege. A smart man provides for the winter and for spring work. How smart are you? ... Pay your bills first. Then put away enough for a winter grubstake. Then think about seed grain for next spring. Think about hay you may have to buy. Let us show that members of the IAA are smart enough to take care of themselves. The government is watching every step our members take. Let us show them, Brothers, that we are MEN who can provide for ourselves.[108]

Laurie spread this same message, emphasizing improvement through education and moral restraint, in IAA speeches. In a speech he prepared for President Gladstone, Laurie included a call to IAA members to educate themselves:

> Please remember that many of you came here in cars and trucks; you did not come on horseback and bring your equipment with travois; you are living in the atomic age and please don't forget it ... We must learn to live in the modern world; we have to earn the respect of other people outside the reserves. They will not give us this respect for nothing. We have to earn it by behaving and living properly.[109]

Education, democracy, and moral improvement were key goals that the IAA could set for Indian peoples in an attempt to ensure their success in the twentieth century. Laurie's drive to assist Indian peoples was unmistakably moralistic and paternalistic.

For Laurie the IAA was not simply another Indian lobby group. In his view, the association would save Indian peoples and their cultures. He believed that Indian peoples would and could become fully integrated members of Canadian society once they had been educated and had been given the chance to improve themselves. In a 1956 speech delivered to Rotarians and Lions Club members, Laurie stated: "Integration is a noble ideal to which we should direct all our efforts; the brotherhood of man is the essence of civilization and the hallmark of humanity." He believed that educating Indian peoples was the key to helping them to overcome their dependence on treaties, reserves, and special status. In the same speech, he went on to say:

> Our Indians face difficult times. Generally they are socially rejected; in most cases their lack of training makes them industrially unacceptable, routine is psychologically difficult and routine seems so vital in our world.

> The reserves are a security to them which they find nowhere else. They have not been trained for responsibility and educated for the white man's way.[110]

Laurie was convinced that, with time and proper education, Indian peoples could overcome their difficulties and become contributing members of Canadian society. It should be noted that, although he did not openly advocate treaty rights, he never openly disputed their validity or significance either. In many ways, the vagueness of his message regarding the future of Indian peoples within Canadian society made it all the more appealing to the Canadian middle-class public whom he canvassed for support. Laurie never challenged the stereotypes many middle-class Canadian citizens held regarding Indian peoples, and he appealed to them on the basis of their postwar interest and support for democracy and equality.

Laurie's views very closely echoed those of the Indian Affairs Branch. In a 1958 internal government memo, former regional superintendent George Gooderham, reaffirmed the importance of the IAA with regard to the integration of Indian peoples:

> The job of integrating the Indian into white society is a full-time one and I believe the Indian Affairs Department is now fully aware of that and is formulating policies to deal with it ... the Indian Association of Alberta, in which Dr. John Laurie and other responsible whites have worked with Indians, have made many constructive suggestions. They are working very closely together to solve problems ... Integration is bound to be slow. The Indian must be prepared to study hard, and adopt the white man's way of life before he will be freely accepted. Few good families will adopt an Indian family that is uncouth and uneducated, but the colour barrier will dissolve when the two races "speak the same language."[111]

Indian peoples would be successful if they adopted the ways of Whites. This idea was something both Laurie and the government promoted.

Finally, Laurie attempted to use his position as IAA secretary to educate the Canadian public about Indian issues and culture. His IAA executive position enabled him to be viewed as an expert on Indian issues. Between 1950 and 1958, Laurie published numerous articles and opinion pieces on Indian history and Indian issues in the *Canadian Cattlemen*. This magazine featured articles on current and historical themes, and it represented one of the few venues available for publishing local history pieces. The aim of the magazine was to emphasize the romance of the west, and Laurie's Indian articles fit well with this goal.[112] His fictional pieces included romanticized renditions of traditional stories and descriptions of the communities he visited. His writings on contemporary issues, which were meant to explain the complexities of Indian issues in a simplified manner, were mainly critiques of federal Indian policy and revealed his deep distrust of government power.[113] No doubt a magazine with a western agricultural and conservative focus welcomed critiques of federal policies. In addition to producing magazine articles, Laurie documented biographies of various Indian leaders, collected and reworked traditional stories, and attempted to make a complete study of Stoney history and culture. Finally, he wrote many speeches, some for himself, some for other IAA executive members. His writings were critical and highly readable, though not remarkable for either their style or rigour. It was primarily through his writings that Laurie succeeded in popularizing Indian issues.

Despite their often contradictory messages and arguments, Laurie's writings did emphasize one important idea: Indian peoples required assistance in integrating into Canadian society. He believed that the government had not pursued this goal in a democratic manner and that it had pushed Indian peoples into a world they were ill-prepared to handle. In one of his many speeches aimed at enlightening non-Indians about the Indian problem, he asserted: "Integration cannot be established merely by passing laws. It is a matter of changing beliefs, hearts and minds. This is a slow process as world history illustrates ... only a very gradual adjustment can be truly beneficial ... If our policy-makers at Ottawa could only admit ... that a long range policy for the next fifty or seventy-five years should be instituted!"[114] Laurie believed that slow change was positive because it allowed Indian peoples gradually to realize the superiority of modern society: "By demonstrating that our pattern is the best the human mind has ever conceived, we are on the right road ... we have taken the right steps towards acculturation."[115] Laurie was plainly an integrationist who assumed the superiority of his own culture; his firm belief that he was bringing the benefits of his world to Indian communities motivated him to become involved with Indian peoples.

The form and content of outside assistance changed little between the 1940s and the 1950s. If anything, its influence over the IAA increased. For example, in 1945 attendance at Friends of the Indians Society meetings ranged from between five and ten individuals; by the 1950s the society was holding large group dinners and membership burgeoned. As membership grew, so did involvement in IAA activities. By 1957, the Friends of the Indians Society founded a new branch in Calgary and sponsored the creation of a special advisory board to the IAA (consisting of a group of concerned citizens from the Friends of the Indians Society, the Farm Women's Union, Quaker groups, and others who wanted to provide the IAA with advice on various matters). Harold Cardinal suggests that, over time, "there is some indication [these outside groups] assumed too much control" and that, by the late 1950s and into the 1960s, this might have alienated IAA support at the reserve level.[116]

John Laurie and his outside help assisted the IAA, but it also infused it with an ideational paradox. On the one hand, IAA members sought the fulfillment of their treaty rights; on the other hand, Laurie and his outside help sought equality for Indian peoples within Canadian society. These two sets of ideas were popular with two different audiences – the first with the Indian population of Alberta, the second with the Canadian public. At no time during Laurie's involvement with the IAA was there an attempt to resolve this incongruity, for it provided the IAA with a convenient short-term popularity on all its fronts and allowed it to press for change in Indian Affairs in a variety of venues.

5
The Indian Association of Alberta and Its Relations with the Indian Affairs Branch, 1939-46

> Unless there is a proper organization with responsible elected officers the department will pay absolutely no attention.
>
> – John Laurie to Johnny Callihoo, 1945[1]

> All the efforts of the Indian Association of Alberta have been towards developing a better understanding among various groups of people, and seeking and GETTING SUPPORT of the various progressive groups ... we are also opposed to the fundamental causes of war – one of which is petty nationalism.
>
> – Malcolm Norris to John Tootoosis, 1944[2]

During the war years, the Indian Association of Alberta organized itself into a viable provincial-level Indian political union, and, by 1945, it had established itself as a legitimate voice of Alberta's treaty Indian population. A close look at the interaction between the IAA and the Indian Affairs Branch during this period reveals issues that the association pursued with the federal government and how it gained recognition in Ottawa. Although in 1939 the Branch discouraged Indian political activity, by 1944 the IAA managed to induce a change in this attitude, and it used this momentum to push for the reform of Indian Affairs policies.

The IAA succeeded in gaining respect for its activities by frequently interacting with the government and politicians and by linking its agenda to contemporary concerns. First and foremost, the IAA worked hard to focus attention on Indian peoples' social and economic problems in Alberta; and, in seeking a resolution to these problems, it appealed to liberal ideals of democracy and equality. The IAA also sought to spawn private links within government circles. Its first non-Native secretary, John Laurie, forged personal connections with Indian Affairs staff and parliamentarians, and IAA representatives worked hard to create support for their cause among concerned citizens groups. Furthermore, the IAA succeeded in gaining credibility, as well as government support and attention, because its demands for change to Indian policy were essentially conservative. Unlike some Indian groups in eastern Canada, whose demands were rooted in claims of nationhood, the IAA worked within the administrative system of the Indian

Affairs and never challenged the status of Indian peoples within that system. In fact, in its first petitions to the government, it put minimal emphasis on treaty rights. Finally, the IAA actively pressured the government at a time when existing Indian policies were thought to be in need of revision.

The climate of change brought on by the Depression and the Second World War worked to enhance the government's receptivity to suggestions for policy reform from outside its civil service. At the end of the Depression there emerged a sense that the government needed to take a fresh approach to the growing "Indian problem." It was thought that it needed to revise its policies in order to address the poverty of reserve life, to educate Indian children, and to improve the lives of Indian peoples across Canada. The emergence of this reformist attitude within government circles and among civic activists was revealed at a two-week meeting of Canadian and American Indian Affairs bureaucrats, missionaries, academics, and concerned citizens in September 1939. The Toronto-based conference, entitled "The North American Indian Today," was jointly organized by the University of Toronto and Yale University in order to address issues of Indian welfare. The content of the presentations and discussions revealed many of the prevailing attitudes concerning Indian policy in Canada. It was precisely these attitudes that the IAA sought to reform and influence by involving itself directly with government.

Contrary to the opinion of some that, "in the period 1933-1945, little attention was paid to Indian matters," and that government and civil servants of the Indian Affairs Branch did not appear to have any policy,[3] the presentations at the Toronto conference reveal that distinct policies in the areas of Indian education, land use, and economic development were indeed in place. The 1939 Toronto conference indicates that the policy of the day emphasized segregating Indian education and improving Indian health (so as to enable them to exploit reserve-based natural resources). Within a few years, the IAA would directly question much of the thinking aired at the conference and, in the form of carefully prepared briefs to politicians/civil servants and direct lobbying of government representatives in Indian Affairs, offer its own solutions.

The IAA's submission of two memorials to Ottawa, in 1944 and 1945, respectively, initiated the relationship between Indian Affairs and the IAA. These memorials, or "Bluebooks," as Secretary Laurie called them, were formulated in direct response to existing Indian policy and reserve conditions. Although relations between the IAA and Ottawa were initially tenuous, the IAA gradually formed a bond with Indian Affairs director Robert A. Hoey. Once this friendship was established discussions between the IAA and the government increased in scope and depth. The first memorial was significant simply for initiating and setting the tone of dialogue between the IAA and the Indian Affairs Branch by introducing the issues that Alberta's Indian communities considered to be most important. This memorial addressed questions of Indian health, education, and reserve lands within the context of 1939 Indian Affairs policy. The second memorial spoke to similar issues within the context of the changes brought about by the war and gave the IAA a chance to reiterate its suggestions to Indian Affairs. Both memorials were forward-looking, anticipating the end of the war and the reform of federal social and economic policies.

During this period the IAA attempted to work within the bounds of Indian Affairs administration and legislation. The IAA memorials eventually encouraged a close relationship between the Branch and the IAA, as well as inspiring what proved to be a significant invitation to IAA members to make presentations to the 1946 Special Joint Committee investigating the Indian Act and the Indian Affairs Branch.

The 1939 Toronto Conference and Canadian Indian policy

When employees of Canada's Indian Affairs Branch and the American Bureau of Indian Affairs joined approximately eighty academics, church representatives, and Indian participants at the Royal Ontario Museum in Toronto on 4 September 1939, their goal was to spend twelve days discussing the social and political problems of North America's Indian population. This was the first scholarly conference to discuss North American Indian welfare and the first to invite Indian delegates.[4] Two Alberta treaty Indians, Blackfoot band members Earl Calf Child and Teddy Yellowfly, were among the dozen Aboriginal participants. The conference was also noteworthy because it represented one of the rare occasions when Canadian Indian Affairs policy was openly discussed and publicly considered. Organizer and anthropology professor T.F. McIlwraith later explained, "the members felt their responsibility to deal with social problems in the democratic way, by discussion, and trusted that they would have the opportunity of profiting from the knowledge gained."[5] The management of Canada's Indian peoples was seen as a pressing social issue, one requiring expert consideration. This had not always been the case. Earlier, in 1932, Canada's pioneering anthropologist (and a delegate at the conference) Diamond Jenness predicted, in his *Indians of Canada*: "Doubtless all the tribes will disappear. Some will endure only a few years longer, others, like the Eskimo, may last several centuries."[6] It was commonly believed that Canada's First Nations would eventually "disappear" as distinct peoples, thus mitigating any need for future consideration of their unique status or needs. At the conference, however, it was mentioned that the status Indian population in Canada had stopped its decline and was increasing at the rate of 1 percent annually.[7] Bureaucrats, missionaries, and academics now confronted the realization that the Indian population in Canada was no longer declining and set themselves the task of tackling the implications of this fact.

While historians have written a great deal about Canadian Indian policy, little attention has been paid to the nature of that policy between the late 1930s and the end of the Second World War. Historian John Tobias, in his important overview of Canadian Indian policy, claims that, during this period, the government made only ad hoc decisions regarding Indian peoples. In his view, the policy direction of the time was in a state of flux or, more dramatically, lacking completely.[8] Tobias argues that, prior to 1945, Canadian Indian policy focused upon "civilizing" Indian peoples in Western Canada as rapidly as possible. Originally, he contends, Ottawa aimed to educate and train Indian peoples in settled economic pursuits, such as farming or manual labour, within the sheltered confines of the reserve, the aim being to eventually integrate them into Canada's non-Indian society. Then, according to Tobias, the federal government changed its outlook: it began to see reserves as a major stumbling block in the assimilation of Indian peoples into Canadian society because they acted as a check on the economic development of the areas in which they were located. Reserves gained reputations as stagnant backwaters, hampering Indian peoples' integration. As a result, in an effort to reduce the distinction between Indian and non-Indian communities, in the 1920s and 1930s, the government took measures to gradually break down reserve boundaries through land sales, leases, and the application of provincial laws to reserve members. By the 1930s, Tobias claims, government policy focused upon the gradual demise of the reserve for the purpose of promoting the rapid assimilation of Indian people.[9]

Other historians of Indian Affairs policy, including E. Brian Titley and F.L. Barron, offer similar views. According to Titley, up to the 1920s and 1930s, Canada's Indian policy emphasized the "amalgamation" of Indian peoples with the rest of the Canadian populace, the idea being that Indians would eventually disappear as separate peoples. Titley claims that the reserve system functioned as a temporary component of a transitional phase during which Indian communities were guided by Church and State into mainstream Canadian society, the goal being to abandon the reserve system.[10] Similarly, Barron argues that the overall aim of Canada's Indian policy was "assimilation through integration."[11] In Barron's view, after the 1890s the government adopted the idea that Indian peoples should gradually abandon the reserves in order to join the non-Indian community. These authors suggest that, from the late nineteenth century through to the late twentieth century, the goal of Indian Affairs was to slowly move Indians off reserves.

Interestingly, an analysis of the 1939 Toronto conference suggests that, in the 1930s, Canadian Indian policy was being modified. Without denying that the IAB strove to include Indian peoples in Canadian society, bureaucrats and social engineers of the day believed reserves were key to the socio-economic progress of Indian peoples. In the late 1930s, policy makers saw reserves as vital components in a policy aimed at making Indian people economically self-sufficient; Indian peoples would become contributing members of Canadian society from a reserve base. In fact, judging by the conference presentations made by members of the Indian Affairs Branch, reserves were seen as the "proper" place for Indian communities, a place where Indian people could assume their station in life as manual labourers and farmers. Consequently, the Canadian Indian Affairs bureaucrats who outlined the essence of Canada's Indian policy emphasized four main elements: reserve land use, reserve education, health, and economic problems.[12] Conference speakers related all of these elements to life on reserves. Not surprisingly, the views espoused by bureaucrats were precisely those that the IAA questioned and challenged in the years to follow.

One of the first speakers at the gathering was Dr. Harold W. McGill, the director of the Indian Affairs Branch. McGill had entered into the Indian Affairs administration through a patronage appointment made by Prime Minister R.B. Bennett in 1932. Before this appointment, McGill's experience serving Indian communities consisted of his having been a medical officer to the Sarcee (Tsuu T'ina) peoples near Calgary prior to the First World War. McGill enlisted during the early months of the war and served until its end, during which time he was promoted to the rank of major. With his military background and experience with Indian peoples, McGill was quickly promoted to director of the Indian Affairs Branch, a position he administered in a rigid and conservative manner until his retirement in 1945.[13]

As one of the opening speakers at the conference, McGill presented the barest outline of Canada's Indian Affairs policy: "It is simply this: so to treat our Native races that they may become self-supporting and enjoy thereby some degree of economic security and increase their welfare and happiness besides being a source of strength to the nation."[14] McGill's statement cleanly summarized the federal government's prevailing attitude towards its Indian charges – to prepare Indian peoples for gainful employment so that they would be able to contribute to the economy of the nation. T.R.L. MacInnes, secretary of the Indian Affairs Branch, echoed McGill's words a few days later: "The economic adjustment of the Indians to modern life is a large problem engaging close attention of the Department ... the policy of the Department and the efforts of the staff are directed towards making the Indians self-supporting" so that they might eventually lead the "normal life of the ordinary Canadian citizen."[15] Both MacInnes and McGill had touched on the most basic goal of Indian administration in Canada: creating Indian reserve communities that were economically self-sufficient. Junior civil servants with the Branch gave more detailed descriptions of the policy.

D.J. Allan, a bureaucrat from within the Branch, discussed Indian reserve lands and their use, thereby building on the foundation laid by his superior, McGill. In Allan's view, Canada had been more than generous in its allocation of land reserves to Indian peoples. For the most part these land resources constituted "good land from the standpoint of agriculture, and the greater part of the balance is economically useful to the Indians and suited to their traditional requirements for hunting, trapping, fishing."[16] He believed that, by means of the various historical treaty processes, Canada had granted Indian peoples land that could serve as an ample resource base if properly managed. Allan believed that the contemporary challenge was "to yield the maximum in the cultural, economic, and social development of the Indian, to preserve him as a useful, competent, and picturesque entity in our national life."[17] The idea that management of reserve lands was the key to success breathed new life into the role of Indian Affairs vis-à-vis reserve communities. At a conference devoted to the networking of bureaucrats it was logical that such thinking would prevail.

Whether Allan's assessment of the reserve lands as "good" was fair or not, Indian Affairs clearly viewed reserve lands as key to sustaining Indian communities. This view of reserve lands encouraged two types of economies: agricultural, and hunting and fishing. Reserve lands were to support subsistence economies. Allan himself stated that such economies were preferable because they were perceived to be compatible with the Indian "tradition and temperament."[18] In his conference presentation, he emphasized that much work still had to be done because only a small start had been made towards the "full" utilization of Indian land in the Indian interest.[19] His statements reveal the underlying attitude in the Indian Affairs Branch at this time: Indian peoples were to be useful to the Canadian economy, but their economic advancement was to be in keeping with their traditional modes of existence. Thus, Indian peoples would be working the land.

The notion that reserve lands should function as a base for Indian economies was also reflected in Indian Affairs practice. Not only had the DIA been actively encouraging such activities as gardening, community farming, and individual farming for decades prior to the 1930s, but, in 1938, it also created a revolving loan fund to encourage Indian farmers to use either their own or borrowed funds to develop their farms.[20] By advocating the use of band funds and loans for agricultural expansion on reserves, the Branch felt that it was giving Indian peoples distinct "advantages that ma[d]e for contentment and happiness."[21] Happiness and contentment were linked to lives spent working reserve lands.

In regions of Canada where farming was impossible, the Branch promoted hunting, trapping, and, occasionally, harvesting of natural resources such as timber. In 1934 it began new projects aimed at increasing beaver and muskrat populations near northern reserves on leased provincial lands. By 1939, Branch administrators anticipated that these fur management operations would yield large annual cash fur crops for their Indian participants. Again according to D.J. Allan, despite their cost, the fur development projects represented a new way of using lands to develop local economies and to teach the Indian participant "that by his own wisely directed effort he can again achieve the self-sustaining independent status that was his."[22]

Indian education was another area in which Branch officials felt they could direct Indian peoples to self-sufficiency and, thereby, encourage their participation in national development. Not surprisingly, as they did with economic development, they placed Indian education within the context of reserve life. Indian education was not meant to encourage students for life off reserve or for a life beyond a reserve-based subsistence economy. At his presentation at the Royal Ontario Museum in 1939, Reverend J.F. Woodsworth, principal of the United Church's Edmonton Indian Residential School, echoed sentiments commonly held both by members of the Indian Affairs Branch and educators. Woodsworth, like many during this interwar period, believed that Indian education should aim at instructing Indian pupils in "Christian citizenship" and should provide them with "an adequate and substantial economic foundation for Indian life."[23] The implied connection between citizenship and economic activity was both unmistakable and telling. Education would create students who worked to contribute to the common life in Canada. At the same time, however, "Indian life" was seen as remaining separate from the lives of other Canadians, mostly because, in 1939, Indian peoples were expected to remain within the economy of their reserve communities. Indian education, therefore, was viewed as rightfully focused upon vocational training as it prepared "the vast majority of our Indian youth for the life which he must live still for many years *upon his reserve* [emphasis added]."[24] Woodsworth's presentation was in keeping with this view. Understood within the context of the conference, his remarks reveal how Indian students were expected to become functional within their own separate world: "I am of the opinion that the surest way of ultimately incorporating the Indian in our national life is by the gentle method of cultivating the ground of his own nature and letting him find employment in his own environment."[25] Only if a distinct social and economic niche were created for Indian peoples would their potential be realized. This niche would be located on reserve lands.

Indian health represented yet another element of Indian Affairs policy discussed at the Toronto conference, this time by the superintendent of medical services of the medical division of Indian Affairs, Dr. E.L. Stone. Until the onset of the Great Depression, Indian Affairs had gradually expanded its health care facilities and staff in the Prairie provinces. In the west, it sought to reduce tuberculosis, which was perceived to be the primary threat to both the Indian and non-Indian population in the region. When in 1938 new funds became available for Indian health, they were applied to controlling and eradicating the disease in both residential schools and reserve communities located near larger urban centres.[26] In the 1930s a small number of departmental hospitals existed in the Prairie west; however, the aim of the Branch, as identified by Dr. Stone, was not to duplicate public hospitals with Indian Affairs facilities. In Stone's words, "this Department has never undertaken to compete with other public authorities doing the same work, or adopted policies towards the segregation of Indians on any account."[27]

The Branch's stance of offering a minimum number of health care facilities to Indian peoples very much reflected its reticence to become wholeheartedly involved in an area of Indian administration generally not considered a treaty right or covered by the Indian Act. As a result, health care initiatives involving Indian peoples remained conservative. In 1939 the Branch's focus was on prevention: on inoculation programs to curb infectious diseases such as diphtheria, measles, whooping cough, and typhoid fever. In addition, it acquired or built facilities to function as isolation hospitals and sanatoria in southern areas.[28] In regions where Indian people could attend provincial facilities, the Branch subsidized the treatment of Indian patients in provincial hospitals.

Indian health care was discussed at the Toronto conference because those attending it were motivated by humanitarian concern for Indian peoples. However, another reason for discussing the state of Indian health was related to the fact that continued poor health on Indian reserves clearly hindered the economic advancement of those communities. In the Edmonton Agency of Alberta, for example, tuberculosis caused economic hardship for many families, who subsequently turned to Indian Affairs for financial assistance.[29] The subtext at the conference was that a healthy Indian community would be a more productive, self-reliant community.

Finally, at the Toronto conference R.A. Hoey, superintendent of the Welfare and Training Service of the Indian Affairs Branch, presented a paper entitled the "Economic Problems of the Canadian Indian." Hoey received a patronage appointment to the civil service in 1936, following a short career as a Conservative MP.[30] Born in Ireland and educated in Manitoba, he spent several years working in the farmers movement, organizing the western wheat pools, and eventually serving in Manitoba premier Bracken's government as minister of health and welfare, and minister of education.[31] This experience gave Hoey the credibility to address the welfare problems of Indian peoples.

Much like Director Harold W. McGill, Hoey emphasized the Branch's "very clearly defined objectives – the establishment of the Indian population of this country on a self-supporting basis" and the idea that Indian peoples should strive to become "progressive, resourceful, and self-reliant."[32] Hoey's presentation is noteworthy because it indicates just how depressed the industries and economies sustaining Indian peoples were in this time of national economic crisis. Just as Indian farmers had been hard hit by the Great Depression, so the economy of the hunting and trapping Indian populations declined after suffering the dual blow of a drop in fur values and increased competition from non-Indian trappers in the north. Hoey's view, like that of Allan, was that the agricultural potential of reserve lands in Canada was still under-utilized. Hoey specifically pointed out that these reserve lands were fully capable, "if cultivated ... of sustaining an Indian population far in excess of the population now living on these lands."[33] Similarly, he expressed the belief that, with the help of new Indian Affairs-managed fur projects in the middle-north, Indian trappers and hunters could again become productive.[34] The Branch identified the underdevelopment of reserve economies as the central economic problem facing Indian communities, and it saw a clear rationale for increased management of Indian reserve resources.

The statements and presentations of the various Indian Affairs Branch employees at the 1939 Toronto conference reveal their concerns about Indian reserve lands, Indian education, and Indian health. Branch bureaucrats emphasized having Indian peoples make efficient use of their respective reserve lands, educating Indian children for their future lives in reserve communities, and improving the condition of Indian health within those reserve communities. As Director Harold McGill indicated, the Branch was primarily interested in creating viable and sustainable economies on reserves, using Indian peoples' own natural and human resources. This policy was clearly informed by a notion of race and class that placed Indian peoples in a separate sphere from the rest of the Canadian population. Reserve communities were encouraged to have separate economies, Indian education was held apart from non-Indian education, and even health care was largely segregated. Despite this separation, the Branch expected Indian communities to contribute to the development of the country as a whole and, ultimately, to be absorbed into the Canadian body politic.[35]

The views expressed by the participants at the Toronto conference on the eve of the Second World War were far from radical. In fact, they represented a continuation of the basic ideals and policies advanced by Indian Affairs throughout the 1920s. For example, when Deputy Superintendent General of Indian Affairs Duncan Campbell Scott described his views on Indian policy in 1931, he emphasized the importance of Indian self-sufficiency: "The policy of the department and the efforts of the staff are directed towards making the Indians self-supporting," either through agriculture or, "for Indians in the outlying districts where other sufficient employment is not available," hunting and trapping.[36] It is obvious that Scott's policies on Indian health and education continued to influence policy makers in 1939. Scott believed that Indian health and education could help make Indian people self-supporting and, therefore, required more administrative attention than other areas. Indian education focused upon training Indian children in agriculture and the domestic arts, vocational training being viewed as the most important aspect of residential school instruction. Vocational training was meant to prepare Indian students for work deemed appropriate for their race and class. Furthermore, an improvement in Indian health could transfer "Native energy to the channels of modern life."[37] Scott viewed the reserve as an important haven for Indian peoples, "designed primarily to provide them with a refuge where they could live, move and have their being without danger of exploitation or molestation."[38] In 1939 this legacy of protection and of building on the potential economic reserve base still exerted a powerful influence on federal Indian policy.

The conservative nature of Canadian reserve land policy in 1939 is underscored when one compares the statements made by Canada's Indian Affairs bureaucrats with those made by American Indian Affairs administrators. In the United States, a reform movement in Indian policy had been initiated through the Indian Reorganization Act, 1934. Unlike Canada's Indian Affairs Branch administrators, the Americans consciously sought to reverse their long-standing integrationist policies. Before the reformist move, ownership of reserve lands was gradually individualized, and tribal control over these lands was diminished. From the passage of the Dawes Act, 1887, to the 1930s, the bureau worked to individualize the reservations and to undermine the integrity of Indian communities. With the passage of the Reorganization Act, 1934, however, the United States Indian Bureau reversed this process. That year it sought to return to tribes all their inherent powers, including the right to determine their own membership, the right to self-government, and the right to tribal property. Unlike their Canadian counterparts, American Indian bureau workers sought to return to reservation communities their self-determination. As John Collier, commissioner of the Bureau of Indian Affairs in Washington, said in his conference paper: "The way is open for an Indian tribe to assume a political and economic control over its internal affairs as complete as that exercised by an incorporated municipality."[39]

American support for Indian self-determination stood in stark contrast to Canada's paternalistic and authoritarian Indian policies. Canadian officials were obviously enthusiastic about increasing their management role in, and authority over, reserve communities. This approach did little to impress the Americans, who viewed the entire intellectual atmosphere of the conference as outdated and even backwards. J.C. McCaskill, an assistant to Collier, later reported his impressions of the Toronto conference back to Washington:

> The Canadian missionaries as well as the Canadian officials were almost entirely historical in all of their efforts to deal with problems. Their accounts usually brought the subject up to about 1914 and then ended. A more tight-lipped, defensive group I have never encountered. They had no problems, knew all the answers, and the Indians were doing beautifully.[40]

McCaskill hoped that the presence of American opinion at the conference "served to awaken the Canadian group from their lethargy ... after hours one after another of the Canadian group came up to some of our own people and began to confide that they too faced some of the same problems we were facing."[41]

Like the American visitors, Alberta Indian delegate Teddy Yellowfly was singularly unimpressed by the conference and the Canadian government pronouncements. He later recalled: "It was just a seminar, no problems really solved ... policy is just the customary British native policy – regimentation, which is a short view with only temporary goals achieved."[42] Yellowfly was sceptical that the conference would lead to any lasting change.

Although, until the Second World War, the Canadian government and its allies continued to view reserves as safe havens, or training grounds, for Indian people, the ultimate goal of gradually encouraging Indian peoples to leave the reserves and join Canadian society through the process of enfranchisement was never completely subverted. Duncan Campbell Scott's policies of the 1920s and 1930s directly reflected the goal of enfranchisement. Shortly before his retirement in 1931, Scott predicted that "the Government will in time reach the end of its responsibility as the Indians progress into civilization."[43] However, it must be emphasized that, in 1939, the desire to enfranchise registered Indian peoples ranked second to the drive to make Indian communities self-supporting. The distinction between the two programs was subtle but clear and significant.

Even the administrative structure of the Indian Affairs Branch in the late 1930s reflected this heightened concern with reserve lands and the maintenance of segregated, yet self-sufficient, Indian communities. From 1880 to 1936, Indian Affairs operated as a distinct department under the direction of the minister of the interior: it consisted of a headquarters in Ottawa and an outside service composed of two Indian commissioners and an army of department inspectors, Indian agents, medical officers, and other field staff employed to manage daily life in reserve communities within the bounds set by the Indian Act. In 1936, however, the Liberal government restructured Indian Affairs to emphasize the importance of Indian lands and, in so doing, placed it under the control of the Department of Mines and Resources.[44] Following this move, Indian Affairs consisted of four services: field administration, medical welfare and training, reserves and trusts, and records.[45] The redistribution of powers and responsibilities within the Branch indicated the new emphasis placed by the federal government on Indian reserve lands, education, health, and economic development on the eve of the Second World War. The downsized Indian Affairs Branch promoted increased reserve self-sufficiency in order to reduce federal expenditures during the continuing economic crisis. The specific goals and emphases of this policy remained in effect until the Second World War, when outside influences forced the federal government to re-evaluate its priorities in Indian administration.

Failure of Pre-War Indian Policy: Alberta

Despite the hopes and aspirations of Indian Affairs policy makers, on the eve of the Second World War much remained to be done to make reserve communities economically independent and self-sufficient. When the IAA was formed in 1939, what it sought redress for was precisely the failure of Indian Affairs' reserve-oriented Indian policy of the 1930s. This clarifies why concerns about land, education, and health became the basis of the IAA memorials sent to Ottawa in 1944 and 1945. The failure of Indian policy in the areas of reserve development, Indian health, and education can perhaps best be illustrated by the experience of the Stoney reserve community in Morleyville, Alberta, now known as Morley. Although the poor conditions on this reserve appear to have been more pronounced than those on other reserves in Alberta,[46] the shortfalls of Ottawa policies in this community are clear, and the IAA did not hesitate to cite the Stoney reserve in its petitions.

The Stoney reserve, located sixty-four kilometres (forty miles) west of Calgary along the Canadian Pacific Railway, was surveyed in 1879 for the three Stoney bands cited in Treaty 7. From the start, it was clear that the rugged and dry Stoney reserve lands at Morleyville in the foothills of the Rocky Mountains were unsuited to farming.[47] Despite an enlargement of the reserve in 1914, climatic conditions and topography hindered the successful establishment of agriculture. Gradually, at the turn of the century, the pressure on the reserve's limited resources led members of the Wesley band to leave the area for the Kootenay Plains – a traditionally favoured hunting area northwest of their reserve. Members of the Bearspaw band moved to the Highwood Pass region south of their reserve, where hunting opportunities were also deemed better.[48] Those who remained at Morleyville, mainly members of the Chiniki band, lived by ranching, harvesting timber from the wooded portions of the reserve, and, to a lesser degree, wage labour and tourism.[49]

The onset of the Great Depression further aggravated economic conditions on the Stoney reserve. Those who had worked off reserve for local ranchers soon found themselves unemployed. Furthermore, the advance of non-Indian settlement in the region, along with the creation of Banff National Park, had reduced territories where Stoney hunters harvested country foods. As usual, since the 1880s, crops regularly failed on the reserve. Consequently, the reserve population relied increasingly on rations provided by Indian Affairs.[50]

The poor state of the Stoney reserve was noticed by the government. In the interwar years Indian Affairs tried to expand the reserve economy and to make it "self-sufficient" through education and resource development. In the early 1930s, Ottawa made plans to establish a fur-ranching facility on the reserve, and students at the Morley Indian Residential School began receiving training in carpentry, blacksmithing, and handicrafts. According to a contemporary newspaper report: "A rising generation of Stoney Indians may, in the near future, forsake the trap line for the fur farm ... They will be encouraged to take up this work as part of the scheme now being developed in the department of Indian Affairs to make the Indian more self-sustaining." The unidentified reporter continued: "Only such material as they would likely have on the reserve is utilized."[51]

The development of natural resources on the Stoney reserve presented another opportunity for Indian Affairs to stimulate the Stoney economy. As a result of oil discoveries in Turner Valley, Alberta, in 1929 attention turned to Indian reserves seemingly located within the range of the oil-bearing formations. This led directly to leases being granted to oil companies on the Stoney reserve, with Indian Affairs holding lease profits in trust for the community. Interestingly, when trust fund moneys were eventually paid to the Stoney people, the federal government payments were made partly in cash and partly in agricultural implements.[52] From a federal perspective, natural resource development on reserve was meant to contribute to further agricultural development as well. The determination of Indian Affairs to stimulate a land-based economy on reserve never wavered.

Despite the efforts of Indian Affairs to increase Stoney economic activity on reserve throughout the 1930s, by the end of that decade none of the initiatives in agriculture, fur farming, oil development, or education had significantly altered the poor state of the community. The oil-lease moneys accruing in the Stoney trust accounts proved insufficient to fund adequate rations for band members, and many continued to go hungry.[53] In fact, conditions on the reserve were so dire that, in the summer of 1935, the Stoney petitioned Indian Affairs for increased assistance. They requested more reserve pasturage and range lands, and a return to their Treaty 7 ration system.[54] Though Director McGill did visit the reserve in response to the petitions, assistance was slow in arriving. A news reporter investigating the state of the Morley reserve in 1936 noted the continued lack of band resources. Following interviews with band members, he later wrote: "I talked with some of the old men when they rode down for their weekly rations. They do not complain for themselves though their allowance of meat, flour, tea and sugar, has recently been reduced 20 per cent, the longer to eke out the meagre band funds."[55]

The poor state of the Stoney reserve received a great deal of publicity in newspapers and through local ranchers and businesspeople, despite its situation being relatively common for reserves in Alberta. In fact, the founding of the IAA, whose purpose was to improve the social and economic position of treaty Indian people in the north-central part of the province, confirms the idea that other reserve communities were similarly underdeveloped. Among those who wanted to help the Stoney was the Calgary schoolteacher John Laurie. To both Laurie and other IAA members, it was clear from the conditions on the Stoney reserve and elsewhere that Indian Affairs policy of the 1930s disregarded the true needs of Alberta's Indian communities. In their view, federal policy on education, reserve land development, and Indian health needed to be refined and revised so as to give Indian peoples more control. Their critical view of Indian Affairs policy led the IAA to formulate and send to Ottawa the two unprecedented memorials (in 1944 and 1945, respectively) suggesting policy changes.

First IAA Memorial, 1944

The IAA made its first extensive representations to the Indian Affairs Branch in 1944 as a result of resolutions passed at its fifth annual general meeting, which was held at Hobbema in central Alberta. Prior to 1944 the IAA sent short petitions to Ottawa through Indian Agents; however, these received very little attention.[56] The Hobbema meeting was the first substantive meeting held by the IAA since its founding in 1939, and it involved delegates from Hobbema, Morley, and Gleichen as well as from reserves in the Edmonton agency and as far north as Cold Lake.

The meeting was well attended, and delegates brought with them resolutions emanating from their own locals, which they hoped to have endorsed for presentation to the Indian Affairs Branch. Not surprisingly, delegates representing the poverty-stricken Stoney reserve in Morley brought forward resolutions demanding improved social benefits and education for Indian peoples. The central and northern delegates, in turn, sought changes in provincial trapping regulations and recognition of the primacy of the Indian treaties. Northern and southern locals voted unanimously in support of each other's resolutions. All of these issues were then quickly distilled and transcribed directly into a memorial to be presented to the Indian Affairs Branch. Secretary John Laurie drafted and typed the final document at his home in Calgary and ensured its wide distribution to citizens groups, church organizations, Opposition MPs, and other Indian political organizations.

IAA secretary Laurie sent the first "Memorial on Indian Affairs, 1944," directly to Dr. Harold W. McGill, director of the Indian Affairs Branch.[57] Another copy was forwarded to the minister of mines and resources, T.A. Crerar, this time accompanied by the signatures of concerned citizens.[58] The memorial arrived at the Branch at the height of the 1944 parliamentary session, and its credibility was bolstered when, shortly afterwards, letters in support of it flooded in from many individuals and organizations, including the Society for the Furtherance of BC Indian Arts and Crafts, the Okanagan Society for the Revival of Indian Arts and Crafts, the Optimist Club of Calgary, the University Women's Club of Calgary, the Canadian Authors' Association, the Calgary Council of Home and School Associations, and influential individuals from the Calgary area. The Okanagan Society for the Revival of Indian Arts and Crafts even went so far as to send a letter to Prime Minister Mackenzie King, emphasizing the importance of the memorial.[59] Finally, John Laurie sent the memorial to Opposition MPs known to be sympathetic to the IAA, including Messrs. Edwards, Ross, Castleden, MacNicol, Blackmore, and Mrs. Dorise Neilsen.[60]

In its introduction, the memorial boldly emphasized the right of Indian peoples to make their views known in a democratic manner. It alluded to a connection between the Second World War, the oppression of minority groups, and the condition of Indian peoples:

> The delegates express their confidence that the authorities cannot but look favourably upon the extension of democratic rights and privileges to the Indian People. They are certain that the authorities recognize the principles at stake in the present global conflict and are, as members of a governing body, eager to assure to the French, the Poles or other oppressed peoples of Europe, an extension of democratic privileges, of free speech, right of assembly, and intellectual freedom. They feel that, not only as the Aboriginal inhabitants of this Dominion, but as "Wards" of the administration not only British subjects, but as men and women with human rights and privileges, they will NOT be overlooked.[61]

The IAA made its appeals on the grounds that, if the federal government respected minority rights in Europe, then it was morally bound to grant its Indian "Wards" the same attentions. Since the Indian Act had, to date, limited the ability of Indian peoples to form associations for the purpose of petitioning their rights, the IAA, by making obvious connections between the principles behind the conflicts that led to the Second World War and Indian peoples' limited freedoms, astutely, effectively, and legitimately pressed its case.

The memorial focused upon five main issues: (1) the extension of social legislation to Indian peoples, (2) Indian education, (3) band membership, (4) matters of general policy, and (5) gaining official DIA recognition for the IAA. Obviously, the IAA's concern with education and social security derived directly from the practical effects of Indian policy on reserve communities in Alberta.

The IAA resolutions on education stressed the need to revise the existing system in order to allow Indian children to benefit from higher education to the same extent as did non-Indian children; to increase funds available to residential schools; and, most important, to increase the number of day schools available to Indian children in Alberta. At this time there was only one day school in Alberta (in the Edmonton Agency), and the IAA made a point of linking this substandard educational system to the poor social conditions on Alberta reserves: "The inadequacy of the system hitherto followed is evident in the social conditions on many reserves."[62]

The IAA also emphasized its wish to have the country's relatively new social legislation extended to Indian peoples across the nation. Appealing to the federal government's sense of democracy and equality, the memorial stated:

> Whereas members of other races in Canada are eligible for the benefits of Old Age Pensions, Widows' and Mothers' Allowances, Indigent Relief and other social benefits, and Whereas needy Indians receive only rations under a system which is unsatisfactory ... Be it resolved that the Federal Government extend to Indians ... all other social legislation as may be provided from time to time by legislation, and on the same basis as white citizens.[63]

The IAA also openly criticized the Indian Affairs Branch for its policy of trying to create self-supporting reserve economies. It pointed out that many reserves lacked sufficient resources to support their populations. Moreover, through the memorial, the IAA emphasized that Indian peoples should be provided the same opportunities to support themselves as were non-Indians: "The Association feels that Indians should receive the same as white citizens receive, since so much is being expected of them in these days. Home gardens, herds of goats, etc. are far from being a solution to the pressing needs of many bands whose geographical location is such that both are rendered impractical or whose reserve is so economically inadequate neither gardens nor goats survive the infertile soil and the rigours of the climate."[64]

These resolutions pertaining to education and social legislation appealed directly to the political ideals being promoted by the Liberal federal government of 1944. During the early years of the war, the Liberal government and its leader, Prime Minister Mackenzie King, felt increasing pressure from a massive shift to the left in public opinion. The rise of the leftist CCF party in the early 1940s – a party that challenged the government with new and dynamic socialist ideals that were palatable to a large number of Canadians – stimulated the Liberals to devise an interventionist program for postwar reconstruction as early as 1943. By 1944 it became the duty of the highly trained civil service to devise a practical program to implement such restructuring.[65] The Liberal policy that emerged emphasized that "the assurance of opportunity of employment for all who are willing to and able to work is the cornerstone of the government's program to achieve prosperity and social security."[66] Through this new plan, the Liberals promised improved social security and health care measures. In a timely manner, the IAA asked that these ideas apply equally to Indian citizens and non-Indian citizens. Goats and gardens were not viewed by the IAA membership as viable options for Indian peoples when the rest of Canada was anticipating new industrial jobs and unprecedented social security benefits.

One of the memorial's prominent resolutions protested the Branch's revision of the membership lists for two bands in central Alberta. Band membership questions frightened Indian communities. This fear was revealed by John Laurie's comments to MP Manley Edward just after the memorial was submitted: "I am informed from reliable sources at the Coast that many groups of Indians are in sheer terror that they will be enfranchised against their will. There have been too many utterances by officials of the Department ... to make any subsequent official denials ring true."[67] At the IAA's Hobbema meeting, the resolution was discussed at great length by delegates from all parts of the province, which indicates that concern over this issue was widespread.

In the memorial, the IAA protested Branch interference with band membership, arguing that the two individuals concerned, James Ward and Fred Hodgson, had been accepted into treaty without proper investigation. It asserted that "the onus should rest upon the Department and not be put upon these men by means of a legal device such as Section 18, of the Indian Act. Can a man be convicted of a crime for which he has once been acquitted?"[68] The IAA further questioned the accuracy of Branch research into the ancestry of the men and, indeed, promptly began its own investigations into their family history.[69] The memorial described the cases as exemplary of the Branch's arbitrary Indian Act enforcement and its "dictatorial" behaviour, pointing out that the act was applied only to individuals whom were reported to Indian Affairs.[70]

The remaining resolutions of the 1944 memorial dealt with matters of general Indian Affairs policy. They requested the exemption of Indian peoples from military service under the terms of the Natural Resources Mobilization Act, the abolishment of Indian Affairs' long-standing permit system, and the recognition of the IAA as a bona fide association representing the collective wishes of its large Alberta membership. A surprisingly short resolution tucked away at the end of the document demanded that the Indian Act be amended to better conform with the rights granted the Indians of Canada through the treaties.

Interestingly, the concept of national, or Aboriginal, rights was not raised by the IAA, and treaty rights were only mentioned in the final resolution within the context of education, where the federal government clearly had a treaty obligation. Promoting the social and economic advancement of Indian peoples was the priority of the memorial. "Indian nationalism" was certainly not viewed positively by administrators within the DIA at this time, and the IAA avoided any hint of it.

Federal government reaction to the IAA memorial was ambiguous. Indian Affairs accepted the memorial; however, it did nothing to encourage the IAA or other First Nations political groups. At the time the IAA presented its memorial to Indian Affairs, the minister of mines and resources had recently refused to meet individuals who claimed to represent "the Indians of Canada." These individuals included Jules Sioui, a Huron leader from Loretteville near Quebec City.[71] Yet at the same time Indian Affairs had acknowledged the Native Brotherhood of British Columbia to the extent that Branch officials attended and spoke at a brotherhood convention in 1944.[72] In the case of the IAA, Indian Affairs accepted the memorial for consideration, and Director McGill promptly requested information regarding the association's membership and organization.[73]

Officially, Ottawa discouraged the formation of political associations or any other kind of pressure groups by Indian peoples, although, as historian Richard Leuger notes, this policy was nowhere explicitly stated in legislation, annual reports, policy statements, or articles produced by Indian Affairs administrators. From an early date the federal government simply and paternalistically believed it had the right and moral duty to protect and direct Indian peoples as they adjusted to Canadian society and that Indian Affairs administration should not be subject to partisan or pressure politics. The general attitude was that Indian peoples could not be trusted with the details or uncertainties inherent in the management of their affairs; therefore, information was not shared with them. According to Leuger, Ottawa looked upon Indian associations as interfering with the efficient administration of Indian Affairs, as inspired by "trouble-making Whites," and as too demanding of special considerations to which they had no rights.[74] However, this attitude began to change in the 1940s.

The IAA was among the few organizations stimulating and encouraging this shift in government sentiment. It became one of the first and few associations to be received in Ottawa as well as one of the first whose representations were acknowledged and dealt with to any great extent. When Fred Loft attempted to organize Indian peoples in western Canada in the early 1920s, for example, Indian Affairs worked actively to discourage him personally as well as his organization. Loft's League of Indians of Western Canada failed to create a dialogue between reserve communities and the federal government because Indian Affairs actively closed off the association's avenues of communication.[75] Not until the mid-1940s was Indian Affairs again confronted with a Prairie western Indian organization: the IAA. This time the mood within the Branch had changed, and it considered this new group's petitions.

Upon receiving the first memorial, administrators carefully analyzed the document as it circulated within the Branch for several weeks. Written assessments of its demands, which subsequently emerged, were generally negative. For example, Dr. P.E. Moore, superintendent of medical services, opposed officially recognizing the IAA. He curtly recommended that correspondence pertaining to Indian peoples welfare be conducted through departmental channels "rather than through such an organization." On the other hand, Moore did fully support the memorial's call to have social legislation extended to Indian peoples.[76]

Superintendent of Training and Welfare R.A. Hoey offered a much more detailed and scathing assessment of the memorial than did Moore. Hoey's response reads like that of a senior civil servant whose administrative expertise has been called into question: "A casual perusal of this document is sufficient to convince one that it was prepared by an individual or individuals wholly unfamiliar with departmental policy and administration and equally unfamiliar with conditions on our reserves and Indian characteristics." Considering the origins of the memorial, and Hoey's distance from western Canada, it is distressing to consider how he arrived at this conclusion. But Hoey's criticism went beyond questioning the credibility of the memorial. He continued: "The resolution relating to old age pensions, mothers' allowances, etc. is based on the common assumption that by the mere distribution of money the social and economic status of the Indian can be improved ... These so-called social services might well be held out, in my judgement, as an inducement to the more progressive Indians to leave the reserves, seek enfranchisement and assume the full duties and responsibilities of democratic citizenship."[77]

Hoey's statements neatly summarized Branch policy: Indian peoples should be encouraged and assisted only insofar as this contributes to their assumption of productive citizenship. He dismissed any suggestion that additional assistance might make Indian peoples more productive. The concept that such assistance might be in keeping with the original treaties was left unaddressed. Not surprisingly, Hoey believed that, because it circumvented Branch administration, recognition of the IAA would only cause trouble. In his view, only senior administrators should hold the right to recommend changes to the Branch. Accepting any Indian association petitions only undermined the authority of the department. In his words, "I can see nothing but disaster ahead of us unless we can enhance the reputation and standing of our inspectors and field officers." In his opinion, the Indian Affairs Branch had the ability and expertise to control and improve the lives of Indian peoples. The single concession the superintendent of training and welfare made was to agree that a review of the Indian Act was desperately needed.

Although Indian Affairs officials appeared to disagree with the 1944 IAA memorial, the document did facilitate and stimulate further dialogue between the Branch and the Indian peoples in Alberta. Director McGill's official response to the memorial was cautious and unyielding. Within three months of having received the document, the Indian Affairs informed IAA secretary Laurie that it was doubtful the points raised by the memorial could be cleared up by correspondence. The Branch suggested that Indian Affairs officers be allowed to attend future IAA conferences and that, in the meantime, the inspector of Alberta Indian agencies be the conduit for IAA concerns.[78] The Branch obviously had little intention of accommodating the IAA's demand for official recognition, although it did invite the IAA to continue communicating with the government. Indian policy was not adjusted to accommodate the IAA, but an acceptance of Indian political activity was implied. The IAA saw this as an incentive to continue its work. IAA organizer Malcolm Norris decisively claimed the memorial as a victory for the IAA when he wrote to the Blackfoot local: "I am pleased to report that the Memorial submitted by the Association to the Dept. of Indian Affairs has been favourably received."[79]

This initial IAA memorial has great significance. It first indicates that the IAA functioned successfully both as a protest and as an innovative movement. The association acted as a venue through which Indian members could object to Branch policy, yet it also provided an opportunity for members of reserve communities to suggest new directions in Indian policy. Through its resolutions seeking official recognition of the IAA and its motions pertaining to band membership, the IAA openly protested Indian Affairs policy. At the same time, in recommending the equal application of social legislation to Indian and non-Indian Canadians, the IAA proposed that Indian policy be brought in line with broader social trends in Canada.

During the war years, the Canadian public became increasingly concerned with plans for "reconstructing" Canada after the war. In Ottawa, bureaucrats busily devised schemes for the rehabilitation of Canadian society. The IAA's efforts sought to ensure Indian peoples a place in these discussions on a national level, and, indeed, it did succeed in having Indian Affairs implement some of its ideas. For example, the IAA's call for the development of social legislation for Indian peoples preceded Ottawa's passage of the Family Allowance Act and its subsequent application to registered Indian peoples.

The memorial submitted to Ottawa in 1944 reveals much more than the IAA's early success as an innovative movement, making clear its strong grassroots focus. Local issues affecting members and their communities formed the basis of IAA actions. Through the 1944 memorial the association sought to improve living conditions on Alberta reserves, to protect the members of those communities, and to provide a better future for new generations through improved education. Despite Hoey's belief that the memorial was written by someone unfamiliar with reserve life, the document truly reflected the concerns of reserve communities.

Within five years of its founding, the IAA, as evinced by the memorial, had begun to evolve beyond its initial mandate of protecting treaty rights. Increasingly, it concerned itself with issues pertaining to the Indian Act and provincial legislation. The memorial did include a resolution to have the Indian Act brought in line with treaty rights; however, its focus was clearly on issues related directly to the Indian Act (such as band membership and the administration of Indian education). Malcolm Norris had originally envisioned the IAA as a treaty protective association, and he openly remarked that one of its primary purpose was to "seek the betterment of their [Indians'] social and economic conditions as promised under Proclamation and Treaties made with them by representatives of his Majesty's government."[80] The 1944 memorial still acknowledged those treaty rights, but it placed decidedly more emphasis upon the Indian Act.

A grassroots focus, an emphasis on the Indian Act over treaty rights, and an appeal for greater self-determination for Indian communities – these three points characterize IAA policy as presented in its 1944 memorial. With regard to self-determination, for example, the resolution on band membership relating to the cases of Hodgson and Ward emphasized that their expulsions were contrary to the expressed desire of the bands involved. Similarly, the call for official recognition of the IAA stressed the importance of the association as a vehicle through which Indian peoples could assume greater responsibilities for their own affairs: "such an Association is a step towards fuller responsibilities of citizenship and is in accordance with the principles of democratic life."[81] In both cases, the IAA sought to have Indian communities gain increased input into issues directly affecting them.

Ultimately, the first memorial represented an initial attempt by Alberta reserve communities to work for change within the established Indian Affairs system of governance. Through the memorial the IAA was brought into closer contact with Opposition MPs and John Laurie. In subsequent years, alliances forged between the IAA and MPs became increasingly important to the IAA and contributed to its maintaining a relatively conservative approach to reform.

The Branch's consideration of the first IAA memorial encouraged the association to continue its conventionalist tactics. Far from being discouraged by the cool response of the Branch to their demands, IAA executive members began working immediately on additional government briefs. Their efforts over the next twelve months culminated in the IAA's second memorial on Indian affairs, which John Laurie delivered to the government in the summer of 1945. The second memorial proved critical in establishing the association as a credible and relatively powerful lobby force on behalf of Alberta's treaty Indian population.

Second IAA Memorial, 1945

The second memorial represented the crystallization of Alberta First Nations demands and concerns during a time of accelerating change. Between the issuing of the first memorial in 1944 and the second memorial a year later, life in Alberta reserve communities underwent noteworthy changes (which, for the most part, were directly attributable to the impact of the Second World War). Towards the end of the war, reserve economies experienced the effects of increasing wage labour opportunities for Indian people off reserve. Furthermore, the IAA had expanded its membership on new reserves in the interim and spread its influence. Finally, as a result of the war, health and education services on reserves were directly compromised.

Perhaps the most important effect of the Second World War on Alberta was to increase the demand for wage labour in various fields across the province. Before 1940 Indian policy emphasized that Indian peoples were to become self-supporting within the confines of the reserve; however, the loss of personpower throughout the war years resulted in new off-reserve work opportunities opening up to Indian labour. The increase in employment opportunities was felt as early as 1942-43, and Indian Affairs quickly sanctioned Indian involvement in the various divisions of war-related work.[82] In Alberta, Indian peoples increasingly laboured for wages as ranch hands, in the sugar beet fields in the southern parts of the province, in logging camps and lumber mills in the north, and on the construction of the Alaska Highway.[83] Even young boys and girls of school age found work so easily that, much to the dismay of the Indian Affairs Branch, they stayed away from school. The demand for Indian women as domestics and as war industries workers in the larger urban centres apparently exceeded the supply.[84] In Alberta specifically, the British Commonwealth Air Training Program brought a large military presence to the province and created opportunities in both service and construction industries.[85]

Initially, the Indian Affairs Branch viewed the increase in wage work for Indian workers positively. Much to the delight of Indian Affairs administrators, increased incomes reduced the reliance on Branch welfare payments in the southern regions.[86] In general, the war helped reserve communities to become more self-supporting and to somewhat diversify their economies. Only in northern communities did the Branch view expanding reliance on welfare negatively. In 1943-44 the Indian Affairs annual report identified this problem and placed the blame upon the Indian population of the northern communities:

> Prevailing economic conditions have enabled the Indians to enjoy a measure of prosperity throughout the year. There are still, however, a few districts where relief costs remain practically as high as similar costs during the worst years of the depression. These districts consist in the main of northern agencies such as ... Athabaska and Lesser Slave Lake. It would appear that the Indians of these agencies have neither the skill, training nor temperament to take full advantage of employment conditions in agricultural areas or in War industries.[87]

The Branch saw fur rehabilitation programs as one of the few ways these northern communities could become self-supporting.

Just as the war changed reserve economies, especially in the south, so it affected the staffing of Indian agencies as Indian Affairs teaching and health personnel joined the military. The difficulty of retaining teaching staff directly hampered the growth of day schools across the nation and compromised vocational training programs.[88] Indian health services were also understaffed, preventing the expansion of medical services. The Indian Affairs Branch annual report for 1944-45 revealed the problem: "Staff difficulties continued to increase during the year ... Owing to the shortage of help in departmental field work and on hospital staffs, many more nurses could be employed if they were available."[89] The issues of day school shortages and inadequate health care remained issues of central concern to the IAA.

Wartime shortages of petroleum further affected several Alberta reserve communities. New demand for petroleum products created a national interest in Alberta's energy supplies, and, as a result, mineral exploration on reserve lands increased during the war and the Branch approved more leases to oil companies.[90] Though no oil had yet been discovered on reserve lands, the leases themselves resulted in increased revenues for some Alberta bands.

Over the course of 1944 and 1945 Indian Affairs began to pay more attention to the IAA, partly as a result of the first IAA memorial. Following the presentation of the 1944 memorial, Secretary Laurie made a pilgrimage to Ottawa at his own expense for the purpose of championing the IAA cause and to ensure the Branch's goodwill towards it. To these ends, he was relatively successful. As Laurie recalled: "The reason behind it all was this: that a personal visit would clear the air for all of us. After a consultation with Calgary MP Mr. George H. Ross and Mr. Manley Edwards, now Judge Edwards, who supplied introductions to the director of the Indian Affairs Branch, Dr. McGill, and to Dr. Moore of the Indian Health Services, I found myself in Ottawa as representative of the Alberta Indians." Upon his arrival at Indian Affairs headquarters in Ottawa, Laurie initially received a rather cool reception. He remembered how nonchalantly McGill welcomed him into his office, leaning back in his chair with his boots on the edge of an antique table, not bothering to rise as he entered. After a perfunctory greeting, McGill confidently informed Laurie that the table formerly belonged to Prime Minister John A. Macdonald. As Laurie later recalled in his memoirs, R. A. Hoey of the education division then rushed into the office and accused Laurie and the IAA of over-working him![91]

Despite this inauspicious beginning, relations between the IAA and the Branch warmed in subsequent days and months. Laurie acknowledged that, when Hoey assumed the position of director upon McGill's retirement in 1944-45, "the Indian people of Alberta always were certain of a fair hearing; there was no further nonsense during his time, about not bringing problems to the attention of his particular office."[92] By 1945 the Branch had taken to actually inviting representatives of the IAA to visit Ottawa in order to discuss matters of Indian administration.[93] By the winter of 1944-45, in a small undated memo the IAA had the courage to call directly on the Branch for a revision of the Indian Act.[94] The initial personal visit of the genteel and charming Laurie did much to gain credibility for the IAA in government circles, and his emphasis on the IAA's willingness to work within the government system must have pacified some lingering opposition to the association.

The resolutions incorporated into the second memorial were formulated at the sixth annual general meeting of the IAA, held in June 1945 near the Stoney reserve in Morley. This meeting was noteworthy because it marked the first time other southern reserves participated. Until 1945 the IAA was an organization with a northern and central Alberta focus. With this meeting, reserve communities from the south joined the association, giving the IAA a truly provincial mandate. Specifically, delegates from the Peigan reserve came for the first time, and members of the Blood and Sarcee reserves attended as observers. In addition, "fraternal delegates," that is, non-member non-Indian supporters from the Friends of the Indians Society, the Home and School Association, the Association of Indians of Saskatchewan, and the United Farmers of Alberta attended. J.N.R. Iredale, Agent of the Stoney reserve, delivered the opening welcome message. In fact, in May 1945 the Branch officially sanctioned staff attendance of IAA meetings under the condition that "agents should only attend upon formal invitation from the Association."[95] Clearly, the IAA had successfully cultivated widespread support for its cause.

The second IAA memorial emerged out of these circumstances of changed reserve economies and a closer relationship between the IAA and Indian Affairs. This second memorial reflected the increasing confidence of the IAA and John Laurie's knowledge of the inner workings of Indian Affairs. Yet, in essence, the key resolutions in the second memorial remained very similar to those of the first. As in 1944, the 1945 memorial called for changes to the Indian Act (particularly Section 18, which dealt with band memberships), demanded the extension of social benefits to Indian peoples, and challenged the conscription of registered Indians. It sought to reaffirm treaty rights as well as changes to hunting and trapping regulations, and it contained extensive resolutions concerning Indian education, Indian health, and reserve lands.

Unlike the 1944 memorial, however, this second document contained numerous resolutions pertaining to reserve lands. Not surprisingly, these resolutions directly related to Alberta Indian communities' concern that their reserve lands might be alienated to benefit non-Indian war veterans returning from overseas.[96] Across the Prairie provinces, in 1941 the Department of Mines and Resources had been busy surveying Indian lands for the Soldier Settlement Board in order to determine which lands might be available for war veterans. This survey activity made many reserve communities uneasy. Indian reserve lands were also often leased out to neighbouring non-Indian farmers prior to and during the war. According to the memorial: "There is considerable fear that, under that pretext that Indians are not putting the land to use, outside groups may attempt to acquire further leases or to purchase Indian lands ... As leases now expire, the lands should be returned to the Band for its own use."[97] In the same vein, bands opposed the further surveying of their reserve lands for fear this might ultimately lead to their subdivision. In the memorial, reserve lands were seen as vital to the postwar "rehabilitation" of Indian peoples. The language of the memorial purposefully played into the single political priority of the day.

Health services also received more attention in the second memorial than they did in the first. Resolutions on this front demanded that local shortages in health care be addressed at the end of the war. In calling for a new hospital on the Hobbema reserve, the memorial stated: "Undoubtedly military needs have lessened the number of doctors and nurses available for the past six years. With the prospect of the end of the Japanese War, an opportunity will arise to make available the services of many experienced doctors and nurses."[98] During the war years, many reserves had to make do with doctors who served simultaneously on more than one reserve. The Stoney reserve, for example, had been serviced by the medical officer of the Sarcee reserve, which made medical emergencies difficult to attend to.

Again, the IAA presented forward-looking resolutions, anticipating a postwar improvement in reserve life.

The Indian education system suffered compromise during the war because teaching staff joined the military and because building materials for new schools were unavailable. With the war's end, the second memorial pressed for more day schools, which were still notoriously lacking in Alberta. The IAA called for day schools that could contribute to postwar Canada's national development. In the IAA's view, Indian children could benefit from higher education within a day-school setting – a setting that "might contribute much of value to the life of Canada as a whole."[99] Day schools and integrated education in municipal schools were viewed as the best ways to provide Indian children with proper training: "The day school can concentrate upon its proper function, academic or trades training ... there is a greater need of academic education unless Indians are to be intentionally maintained as an inferior race, capable of only manual and casual labour."[100] The IAA emphasized that Indian children must prepare for a future very different from that of their parents – one that included off-reserve employment.

Finally, the second memorial publicly called for the revision of the Indian Act consequent upon a Royal Commission investigation into the needs of Indian peoples. While both the government and the IAA had raised this issue previously, the second memorial brought it to general attention. In its call for a Royal Commission the IAA also suggested that Indian peoples should be directly consulted as to the nature of their needs: "This Royal Commission should have among its members, Indians; and should be empowered to visit All Indian reserves, and all bands of non-Treaty Indians ... Particularly, Indians themselves should be encouraged to testify freely and without fear of reprisal."[101] As early as March 1945, the Indian Affairs Branch still hesitated to begin a formal inquiry into the act. T.A. Crerar, minister of mines and resources, insinuated that finding a neutral commission would be virtually impossible: "Indian administration in Canada has been since its inception closely associated with the missionary effort. In this appointment of a Commission, it would be, in my judgement, exceedingly difficult to secure the services of men who would be acceptable to the Government on the one hand and to the religious denominations and the Indian population on the other."[102]

Like its predecessor, the second memorial had great significance. As the relationship that developed between Indian Affairs and the IAA encouraged further dialogue, the second memorial made its demands more explicit. The 1945 memorial indicates that the IAA astutely associated its calls for reform with the national drive to reconstruct and rehabilitate Canadian society. The IAA was not fixated on protesting old Indian policy; rather, it actively suggested changes to that policy in response to changes in reserve economies over the course of the Second World War. The IAA successfully pressured a reluctant government to take action. The association was not alone in its lobbying effort, but it did exert a powerful influence because it now had the confidence of MPs and of some senior administrators in Indian Affairs. Over the course of the fall of 1945, the IAA gained publicity for this cause through the press, at political rallies, and even in Parliament.[103] When, in October 1945, the matter was brought up in the House by IAA supporter MP Castleden, the IAA's influence was unmistakable:

> Mr. Castleden: What steps have been taken by the government to set up a Royal Commission to inquire into the conditions of the Indians across Canada prior to the amendment of the Indian Act? Have any organizations in Canada petitioned or requested the government for a commission? If so, what organizations?
>
> Mr. Glen: Consideration has been given to the desirability of appointing a royal commission to inquire into the needs of the Indian population. No decision, however, with respect to the matter has been reached. A number of organizations have recently petitioned the government for the creation of such a commission. Committee of Friends of the Indians, the Alberta council on child and family welfare, Okanagan society for the revival of Indian arts and crafts, Indian Association of Alberta, North American Indian Brotherhood.[104]

In this case, the petitioning organizations Glen named were almost all directly linked to the IAA. Only the North American Indian Brotherhood (NAIB) was fully independent of the IAA. The remainder had a direct and personal link to the association through John Laurie and relied upon it for direction in fighting for the social and economic betterment of Indian peoples in Canada. Laurie himself acknowledged the personal relations he cultivated with MPs when he reported as follows to the IAA membership: "Our friends, who are Members of Parliament, especially Col. D.S. Harkness and A.L. Smith took great care of your secretary. I ... met with many important Members interested in the IAA ... These men are strong for us and every day they think of us and try to help us."[105] Laurie enjoyed his important role. Inside and outside the House of Commons, the Calgary high school teacher had become an important link between the federal government and the status Indians of Alberta.

The Indian Affairs Branch's response to the 1945 memorial was noticeably warmer than was its response to the 1944 memorial. R.A. Hoey now seemed to take an interest in the findings and views of the IAA and its secretary John Laurie. Following the submission of the second memorial,

Hoey invited Laurie to meet with him in Ottawa to further discuss the issues it raised: "There are so many matters to discuss with respect to the administration of Indian Affairs at the moment and Indian Rights Associations, which appear to be multiplying rapidly throughout the Dominion, and I would appreciate very much indeed an opportunity to discuss a number of matters with you."[106] The new Branch director also intimated that he was striking a parliamentary committee to revise the Indian Act. Thus, before the public announcement, he entrusted the IAA with information on important developments within the government.

Hoey appeared to prefer having informal policy discussions with the IAA through Laurie. As he wrote to him on 20 October 1945, "a great deal of preliminary work has got to be done and some very important decisions reached before such matters can become the subjects of public discussion."[107] Secretary Laurie met Hoey's request, obtaining another leave from his school. When he returned from his trip, he said to IAA members: "Mr. Hoey told me that the IAA was very welcome at the Department. The IAA is the best Indian organization in Canada. Its Council does business in the right way ... They have made two good Memorials of their needs. The Department has studied their Memorials carefully ... The officials prefer to do business with the IAA."[108] Evidently, the "right" way for the IAA to succeed was to work through established government channels, to lobby behind the scenes, and to not challenge the supremacy of the DIA. Laurie's willingness to travel to Ottawa, and his ability to obtain leaves from school, worked to the IAA's advantage vis-à-vis its relationship with the government.

By the spring of 1946 Laurie managed to extract a statement of official support from J.A. Glen, minister of mines and resources. In a letter to Glen, Laurie politely requested to know the exact status of the IAA within the Branch: "The Indian Association of Alberta has no wish to take upon itself undue matters nor bring matters to the attention of the IAB or you, Sir, if these matters can be settled within the powers of the Agent."[109] Glen, in turn, quickly replied that, although he personally supported the IAA, he was unaware of an official policy on Indian political groups: "I have taken the position on more than one occasion that the members of Indian associations working under capable and trustworthy leaders should, with their intimate knowledge of conditions on the average Indian reserve, be able to assist the officials of this department in a very real and substantial sense."[110] Glen hoped that, with the revision of the Indian Act, the role of Indian associations would be more clearly defined. The work of the IAA had evidently not been in vain.

The IAA operated at a time when Canadian society was undergoing great change. At the end of the Second World War, the government struggled to devise new policies to promote Canada's reconstruction and rehabilitation.

The IAA, through its memorials, sought to place Indian peoples within this discussion. Whereas before the war Ottawa had actively discouraged Indian political organizations, by 1945 it was favourable towards the IAA. The IAA was kept informed of government activities through regular correspondence between its executive and the Indian Affairs Branch, and the latter's civil servants were directed to attend the former's meetings. The success of the IAA in gaining government support is most clearly revealed by that fact that it was invited to make representations before the 1946 Special Joint Committee, which was created in order to revise the Indian Act.

The IAA members, 1947. Albert Lightning, John Samson, and Howard Beebe all served as IAA presidents at one time. Back: Peter Burnstick, Samson, and Beebe; front: David Crowchild, Lightning, and Ed Hunter.

IAA meeting at Saddle Lake, 1948. This photograph shows John Laurie addressing group members.

David and Daisy Crowchild and family on the Tsuu T'ina reserve, c. 1950. John Laurie was a close friend of David Crowchild and took this photograph of his family.

John Callihoo at the Blackfoot Indian reserve, 1952. Callihoo travelled extensively by car during his tenure as IAA president. His wife Sophie accompanied him on this trip.

John Laurie in regalia at his home in Calgary, 21 July 1952. Laurie was very proud of his connection to First Nations in Alberta.

John Laurie, 1953. A very personal photograph of the longtime IAA secretary.

IAA meeting, 1955. Albert Lightning is at the microphone. IAA meetings often went on late into the night.

Anne Downe (second from left) and her husband, H.E. Downe (far right), c. 1957. They were avid supporters of the IAA through the Home and School Association, and Anne Downe was friendly with IAA secretary John Laurie.

IAA women delegates at the IAA general meeting of 1957. Left to right: Daisy Crowchild, Reta Rowan, and Mrs. Sam Currie. Reta Rowan was a member of the Friends of the Indians Society. Daisy Crowchild was one of the few women on the IAA executive.

IAA meeting tent on reserve, 1957. IAA general meetings were held in a variety of locations, sometimes outdoors, and often on reserves.

John Laurie's cabin in Canmore, c. 1957.

IAA banquet at the Ermineskin Indian Residential School, Hobbema, 1958. Food was a significant part of all IAA general meetings. Left to right: Unknown, Peter Burnstick, Unknown, James Gladstone, Howard Beebe.

Minister of Indian Affairs Jean Chrétien addressing Aboriginal leaders at the presentation of the Red Paper to Cabinet, 1970.

Harold Cardinal at the presentation of the Red Paper to the Trudeau Cabinet, 1970.

6

Reconciling Citizenship and Treaty Rights: The IAA and the Special Joint Committee of the Senate and House of Commons, 1946-48[1]

> We believe as an association that the revised Indian Act must be based upon broad principles of human justice. It must, we know, provide for the development of the Indian people of Canada.
>
> – Johnny Callihoo, Special Joint Committee Hearing, 1947

In the spring of 1946, J. Allison Glen announced a public inquiry into Canada's federal administration of Indian Affairs and the Indian Act. In Parliament on 13 May 1946, this minister of mines and resources, who was responsible for Indian Affairs, moved "that a joint committee of the senate and house of commons be appointed to examine and consider the Indian Act ... with authority to investigate and report upon Indian administration in general[,]" including treaty rights, band membership, enfranchisement of Indians, Indian schools, and "any other matter or thing pertaining to the social and economic status of Indians and their advancement."[2] This much-awaited announcement led numerous MPs to rise to their feet to congratulate the minister on his motion. Following lengthy discussions both sides of the House enthusiastically endorsed the proposal. For once, Canada's concern for Indian peoples seemed deep and widespread.

The Special Committee appointment, workings, and final report are significant for several reasons. The appointment of a special committee reflected the Liberal government response to pressure to "improve," or address, the condition of Indian peoples in Canada. As the committee worked through its mandate, its vision of the role of Indian peoples as workers and citizens in postwar society emerged. The investigation process represented an important opportunity for Indian groups across the country to publicly air their views on their place within Canada.

The hearings of the Special Committee are particularly interesting because they reveal Indian and government views on the relationship between Canadian citizenship and treaty rights. The Indian Association of Alberta's presentations argued that treaty rights could be reconciled with citizenship, that the treaties between Indian peoples and the Crown were the source of citizenship rights for Indian peoples. In the brief it submitted to the Special Committee, the IAA outlined that the treaties promised certain rights to Indian peoples, including the full right to education and social security, so that Indian peoples might take their place as citizens within Canada.

Similarly, the committee was also concerned with Indian peoples' assumption of full citizenship rights. Unlike the IAA, however, committee members believed that only by being educated in their civic duties and gaining a place within the Canadian economy could Indian peoples assume full citizenship. In short, the committee denied that Indian peoples could become Canadian citizens simply through the treaties. Instead, they believed that Indians remained wards of the Crown under the Indian Act until they had "risen" to the standards of British citizenship.

Although the parties had different perspectives on citizenship and its meaning, both believed that Indian peoples had to gain social rights before they could gain political rights. Consensus on these ideas formed the basis for a common dialogue between Indian leaders and the federal government – a dialogue that, in the subsequent decade, led to full-scale changes in Indian administration.

The move to consider testimony from Indian representatives at the committee hearings was not particularly innovative on the part of the government, but the degree of Indian involvement was. The Branch had been receiving petitions from various Indian sources for decades, and demands that it deal with petitions had increased since the 1920s. The government did not ignore these calls. As early as 1920, for example, it responded by inviting thirty-five Indian spokespersons to attend a House of Commons committee hearing on Bill 14, which dealt with the compulsory enfranchisement of educated Indians.[3] By the 1940s the IAA was pressuring the government to create a committee to investigate Indian affairs. The Alberta association was one of the few Indian organizations to lobby consistently for a review of Indian administration and Indian needs, and it was among the first to throw itself into the fray of the committee's workings.

Between 1946 and 1948, the Special Committee issued a series of reports on its findings. Its final non-binding recommendations became public in 1948. In the end, its work represented a conservative critique of Indian administration in Canada and marked the beginning of a co-optation process whereby Indian groups selected by Indian Affairs were brought into the Canadian governmental process. The IAA's participation in this process was critical. Since 1944 the IAA pressured the government into addressing the needs of Indian communities, and its involvement with the Special Committee was an extension of that strategy. By participating in the investigations, the IAA realized John Laurie's goals of establishing cooperation between the government and Indian groups, and legitimizing

Indian political activity. At the same time, participation also served to co-opt the IAA, bringing it into the federal government's agenda.

Ian V.B. Johnson has written a short, general overview of the origins and workings of the Special Committee.[4] Other general descriptions of its activities can be found in the *Historical Development of the Indian Act* (1978), which discusses the evolution of Indian legislation in Canada, and in Leslie's *A Historical Survey of Indian-Government Relations, 1940-1970* (1993).[5] In addition to these works there are a handful of references to specific aspects of the committee's actions;[6] however, in-depth investigations into specific Indian groups testifying before the committee, and the context of their concerns, are lacking. This discussion aims to highlight the interests of one Indian political group that came before the committee. The IAA made important contributions to the committee: it sent submissions to it, and its executive travelled to Ottawa in 1947 to make presentations before the government body on behalf of the IAA membership. The central IAA message was the need to protect treaty rights, for treaty rights represented Indian peoples' link to full citizenship.

Creating the Special Joint Committee

The constitution of a special joint committee to investigate the Indian Act and Indian administration-related questions responded directly to concerns within government circles over the role of Indian peoples in postwar Canadian society. It was also the result of outside pressure on Ottawa to reform Indian Affairs. Within the government, discussions pertaining to the role of Indian peoples in reconstruction programs began before the end of the Second World War. As early as 1944, for example, the Special Committee on Reconstruction and Re-establishment heard witnesses speak on plans for including Indian peoples in Canada's postwar economy. At this time the prevailing sentiment was that Indian peoples could best be kept self-sufficient on their reserves or in their communities. It was believed that Indian workers would best be recruited into schemes related to their traditional pursuits so that returning Indian war veterans would not compete with non-Indians in more "preferred employment." In addition, the committee noted that Indian workers would most likely be the first to lose their jobs when the war ended and non-Indian veterans returned to the domestic workforce. Failure in urban areas would probably lead them to want to return to their communities.[7] In the words of one of the witnesses before the committee, "That is what we have to guard against in the immediate post-war years."[8]

Thus, anticipating changes in Canada's economy and Indian unemployment, the government planned to initiate programs encouraging Indian peoples to work in their own communities and to concentrate on fur trapping, handicrafts, and housing projects. Cooperative fur conservation and production programs were promoted for northern parts of the Prairie provinces, including Alberta, and handicraft industries were encouraged across the country. Housing projects, in turn, "would take care of the returned soldiers among the Indians pretty well, and it would do a remarkable job in clearing up the deplorable conditions which exist in many Indian communities as to housing."[9] Government concern was squarely focused upon encouraging unskilled and seasonal work in Indian communities rather than on training Indian workers for skilled off-reserve positions.[10] This attitude towards Indian labour was a carry-over from before the war, and it remained unchallenged until late 1945, when sectors of Canadian society – and the IAA – began to demand changes to the policy.

Public demand for the reform of Indian Affairs came from several sources. Historian J.R. Miller notes how Canadian society became more "human rights conscious" following the war and that this contributed to a public perception that Canada's paternalistic Indian policy was unacceptable.[11] Historian John Tobias similarly indicates that "the public was generally concerned with what was regarded as the treatment of the Indian as a second-class person and with the fact that the Indian did not have the same status as other Canadians."[12] Indian participation in the war effort was often touted as the basis for their rights to full citizenship and, thus, the need for reform. In 1946 the popular publication *Newsweek* reported: "More than 2600 Indian men and women served in the armed forces. Thousands took various war jobs. Many Canadians believe Indians should possess full rights of citizenship."[13] Canadian newspapers followed with similar reasoning, stating, "the war effort made by these original Canadians should have earned them a right to a hearing."[14] At least one opinion poll heralded that 85 percent of Canadians surveyed believed that Canadian Indians had come into their own and that they should have rights equal to those of their non-Indian fellow citizens.[15]

Canadians concerned themselves with Indian issues immediately after the war not only because they desired equal rights for all Canadian citizens, but also, and primarily, because they wanted to see Indian workers take their full place in the workforce (and, therefore, for Indian communities to be able to improve their condition). The *Edmonton Bulletin,* for example, asked the federal government "to educate the Indian along lines of self-help to assist them in holding their own in industry" because it was feared this group of people might otherwise "fall into a state of decadence or complete obliteration."[16] The widely read Canadian magazine *Saturday Night* claimed that the reason for the poor state of Indian peoples had to do with their isolation from the rest of Canadian society. It insisted "that the talents and resources of these people [were] admirably suited to fill a crying need in the economy of this country."[17] Rather than see Indian peoples become or remain state-dependent, citizens wanted the government to press for the "improvement" of Indian peoples by giving them work, preferably in industry.

Human rights, a full economic role for Indians in the workforce, and a desire to improve Indian community life: Indian reformers were motivated by all these factors. It was recognized that Canadian government and society had a responsibility to better the state of Indian communities as "the shameful conditions under which many of these people live[d] ... [was] ultimately the responsibility of all Canadians."[18] At public meetings average citizens and professionals alike deplored the social dependency of Indian communities and called for measures to alleviate the situation. Clearly, citizens across the nation believed that, unless Indian peoples were recruited into the workforce, their advancement would be thwarted and their communities would remain backward and, thus, would be a drain on the country's resources. Indian peoples were to be encouraged to use their own resources to help themselves. In short, after the Second World War conventional wisdom began to change: now it was clear that Indian peoples should not be expected to remain on reserves because that would only hamper their ability to contribute to the Canadian economy.

Thus, economic considerations were a significant factor leading to the creation of the Special Committee. Government policy with regard to the economics of reserve life was inadequate, and, at this time, the public demanded that Indian peoples no longer be kept apart and "dependent." In addition, the mood of the federal government and policy makers was changing due to years of petitions from Indian communities through organizations similar to the IAA in British Columbia, Saskatchewan and Ontario.

In May 1946 the Liberal government sponsored the formation of the Special Committee, which was composed of twenty-two MPs and twelve senators. The Liberals chose a parliamentary committee over a royal commission because, according to the Constitution, Indians were a federal responsibility; therefore, an analysis of Indian affairs should not involve other divisions of government.[19] Since Confederation, the federal government had invoked special committees for examining and processing legislation without placing increased demands on the House of Commons. Special committees also gave the government some opportunity to research policy issues in greater depth as the committee process allowed for the hearing of witnesses on certain questions and provided civil servants the chance to contribute to government policy formation. Committees also allowed the government to complete work within a less partisan atmosphere than existed in the House.[20]

Despite these advantages of the committee system, C.E.S. Franks has pointed out how, until the late 1950s, "committees were generally not active nor were they an important part of parliament."[21] Until the reform of the committee process in the 1960s, other problems also prevailed. Committees, for example, were prevented from acting in any independent fashion because they were tightly controlled by government and generally composed of individuals sympathetic to existing government practice and policy.[22] Furthermore, committee members were notorious for their low attendance records, and members were frequently inadequately briefed on the matters they were appointed to consider.[23] All of these problems were standard during the immediate postwar period, and the Special Committee on Indian affairs suffered from them.

As expected, the Special Committee on Indian Affairs suffered its limitations from the moment of it first convened. To begin with, the Liberal government strategically appointed Liberal member D.F. Brown as co-chair, with Liberal senator J. Fred Johnston. Together, these individuals controlled a rather large committee composed of twenty-two Liberals, eight Progressive Conservatives, two CCFers, one Social Crediter, and one Independent. Obviously, the committee was far from balanced, and this served to limit its capacity for critical policy and legislative analysis. Committee members were poorly informed on matters of Indian policy, history, and contemporary issues. As the hearings of the committee progressed, members struggled to understand the history of Canada's treaty signings, the contents of the Indian Act, and the nature of Indian communities across the country. As the committee engaged in its business, members who revealed themselves most interested in reforming existing government practices were the CCF representatives, W. Bryce and G.H. Castleden.

The Special Committee began its investigations in May 1946 with the questioning of Indian Affairs civil servants. Next, it held consultations with those whom the government recognized as outside experts on Indian issues. Finally, Indian representatives were called to speak before the committee, starting in June 1946 with the North American Indian Brotherhood's veteran leader Andrew Paull from Vancouver.[24] The IAA leaders followed in May 1947.

Witnesses from Indian communities were the last to be consulted because committees made a habit of first consulting with those who implemented policy and legislation – the administrators.[25] The committee's policy was that it "should not call witnesses from outside points until after it ha[d] completed the hearing and examination of officials of the Indian Affairs Branch and other government agencies"[26] because it wanted "to know what the picture [was] generally from the departmental point of view."[27] Indian representations to the committee were eventually solicited as the committee recognized its obligation to receive submissions from outside interests. This commitment to hearing the Indian perspective was not popular with all members, however, and, in July 1946, committee member Case decided that "watching briefs" of Indians or other representatives should be disallowed.[28] The involvement of Indian representatives in the committee investigations was contentious from the start. Perhaps the clearest expression of the contradictory attitude towards Indian participation involved the committee's rejection of CCF member Castleden's motion to have Indian members sit on the committee.[29]

Throughout the committee's sitting, members expressed an over-riding concern with the nature of Indian citizenship in Canada. Time and time again they questioned witnesses on Indian education, the state of their economies, and band governments. Not surprisingly, all of these issues related directly to a reformist liberal concept of citizenship that emphasized the importance of a minimum living standard for all, government responsibility for protecting its citizens from outside exploitation, and the redistribution of wealth within society. In postwar Canada it was believed that the government had a positive socio-economic role to play with regard to improving the lives of its citizens. In addition, the rights of citizens included the right to benefit from government protection and the right to exercise political rights. Notions of citizenship rights, therefore, encompassed both social and political rights. According to sociologist T.H. Marshall, the idea of expanding citizenship beyond its purely political function was partially a result of postwar prosperity. In his view, the diminution of economic inequality strengthened the demand for its abolition. The incorporation of social rights into citizenship rights was viewed as one way to reduce economic inequality.[30]

The Special Committee was quick to recognize that Indian peoples existed in a state of fundamental inequality. Committee members viewed the granting of citizenship rights, including both social and political rights, as the answer to Indian peoples' problems. Politicians believed it imperative that Indian communities gain their social rights through having access to a stable economic base and that Indians use their own local governments in a self-determining manner. Full citizenship was seen as something that would enable Indian peoples to become truly "free" and fully functioning members of the Canadian community. At the same time, the committee also believed that Indian peoples would not be able to assert citizenship rights until they had been suitably and sufficiently educated. This position was revealed by the committee's long discussions on the poor state of Indian education. In the eyes of the government, only formal education would properly prepare these peoples for their civic duties. When special committee member Case stated, "I can understand why Indians might not administer their own affairs"[31] during the hearings, he was confirming his view that they were not prepared for such duties.

Indian Representations to the Special Committee

Indian peoples began getting involved in the investigation process in 1946. In order to canvas input from Indian communities across the country, the committee empowered its counsel, Norman E. Lickers of the Six Nations on the Grand River and Ontario's first status Indian lawyer, to act as its liaison officer.[32] In early June 1946, Lickers sent a circular letter to Indian bands across Canada requesting their views on the eight separate issues within the committee's mandate. Over the ensuing months, Lickers received many replies, all filed for later consideration. Most submissions were relatively short, answering directly and in a few sentences the questions posed by the committee. Apparently, translation of Lickers's circular letter was a problem in some communities. Hugh Dempsey remembers that the chiefs of the Blood reserve in Alberta struggled to have the questions made clear to them. Only with the help of the local Indian Agent and IAA member James Gladstone, who was fluent in English and Blood, were they able to successfully answer the questions.[33] No attempt was made by the committee to ensure that Indian communities understood what was being asked of them, and it solicited little direct contact with Indian communities. All communications between the committee and Indian peoples was directed to Liaison Officer Lickers. Jim McMurtry suggests that Indian submissions to the committee were questionable because, "largely due to the substandard English writing skills and lack of political sophistication of the greater number of Indian leaders,"[34] they were most likely written by missionaries, lawyers, and others. This statement does not apply to the Canadian west. In Alberta, Indian leaders may have received assistance from "outsiders"; however, they lacked neither political sophistication nor an understanding of their position.

The IAA stood poised to address the Special Committee at an early date. Since 1945 it had petitioned for an investigation of the Indian Act and Indian administration, presenting Indian Affairs members of government with its second memorial that year. Over the winter of 1945-46, the leaders of the IAA continued to formulate material on the Indian Act and the needs of reserve communities. With the sitting of the Special Committee, the Alberta group finally saw an opportunity to present some of its concerns directly to the government. Unlike some other Indian groups in Canada, the IAA had been considering its brief to the committee for months prior to receiving requests for input.

The IAA executive leadership did not prepare its submissions in isolation, however. In fact, the submission of the Union of Saskatchewan Indians (USI) and of the IAA were written together. In mid-winter, incessant traveller and IAA strategist John Laurie participated in the organizational meeting of the USI in Regina. The newly elected Saskatchewan CCF premier Tommy Douglas worked together with Indian leaders from across the province in the hope of establishing a provincial-level Indian union that could help status Indians assert their rights before the federal government.[35] Douglas hoped to model the USI on the IAA, and, at this meeting, Laurie provided him and USI organizers with a copy of the IAA constitution.[36] Laurie's attendance at the meeting was critical. As a result of it, he re-established contact with one of his former high school students who now worked as a lawyer for Premier Douglas: Morris Schumiatcher. Undoubtedly, Laurie and Schumiatcher discussed the function of Indian associations, and, as a result of this meeting, Schumiatcher subsequently became involved in writing the IAA brief to the Special Committee. Not surprisingly, MP Castleden was also present at the Regina meeting and played an important role in encouraging Indian politicization. Thus two important Indian political groups became intimately connected on the eve of the Special Committee hearings. Links were built between Indian communities as well as with politicians and sympathizers such as Laurie and Schumiatcher. In 1946 the world of political activism in the Prairie provinces was small.

Although the record is not complete, USI lawyer Schumiatcher had apparently been preparing the IAA brief in the summer of 1946. At the IAA annual general meeting on the Peigan reserve that same summer, President Callihoo emphasized the importance of the committee to the future of Alberta's Indian population. In his opening address to attending delegates he pleaded with them to consider carefully their statements to the committee: "I beg you to think clearly and to speak wisely in these matters. You must keep in your mind that you are going to be blamed or praised by your great grand children for what you have done this year ... I say think carefully and speak wisely." In addition, he announced that the IAA was preparing an official brief for the committee, stating: "A very clever lawyer has been hired to work at a Brief for presentation to the Parliamentary Committee in Ottawa. He is one of the cleverest young lawyers in Canada and is in full sympathy with the aims of the Indian Association of Alberta. This Brief will be presented at the proper time."[37] The young lawyer was Schumiatcher.

The technical process involved in the creation of the IAA's brief reveals the important but limited input of IAA locals. Although Schumiatcher had already been engaged to write the IAA brief in July 1946, IAA locals around the province did not begin to consider the committee's request for information until Lickers circulated his letter that same month. The IAA executive had a stronger hand in creating the brief than did the locals. In order to assist the communities in preparing responses for Lickers, Secretary Laurie and President Johnny Callihoo spent the summer touring the northern part of the province and visiting bands. Laurie and Callihoo travelled many kilometres trying to convince the various communities to let the IAA speak for them before the committee, but they were not completely successful.

Both men were exhausted by the trip, and Laurie wrote to Blood president Gladstone: "In all I made about 1500 miles [2,400 kilometres] ... our president who was with me was finding it very tiring on a man of his age. As perhaps you know, Mr. Callihoo is suffering from high blood pressure and the constant travelling and strain of daily meetings wore him out completely."[38] Laurie, as a result of the heart condition that would force him to take sick leave a few months later, was not in top form either. Both men tirelessly persevered, however, and, as a result of their tour, managed to convince reserves in the Driftpile and Edmonton Agencies that the IAA should handle Lickers's letter. Meanwhile, reserve communities in the Hobbema, Blackfoot, and Blood Agencies remained unconvinced of the IAA's good intentions.[39] Laurie's goal to have the IAA speak for band councils did not appeal to all chiefs. In the end, the Blackfoot and Blood reserves submitted their own briefs to the committee. It is not at all clear that the submissions of the IAA-friendly communities were ever incorporated into the final brief devised by Schumiatcher for the federal committee. According to Murray Dobbin, writing of the brief apparently continued into the fall of 1946, with the assistance of Malcolm Norris.[40] John Laurie, in very poor health at the time, does not appear to have participated in the writing of the final product.

The IAA submission to the Special Committee was one of the most extensive and in-depth of all those made by Indian groups across the country. In addition to the official brief, IAA locals also contributed supplementary briefs, including a survey of education, housing, health, and agriculture in Alberta's reserve communities. The IAA also submitted to the committee yet another copy of its 1945 memorial on Indian affairs.

With its surveys the IAA locals made their most direct contribution to the Special Committee investigations. Previously, the IAA executive circulated to its various locals a questionnaire on agriculture and housing, and the returns were collated into a comprehensive survey of contemporary conditions in those communities. A short discussion of reserve health care needs was later added to the survey findings. Thus IAA locals and members across the province were able to submit short statements outlining their views on housing and agricultural problems. On the Blood reserve, for example, testimonials from individuals added personal insights to the otherwise dry list of facts produced by the survey, thereby increasing its impact and credibility. Mike Healy from the Blood reserve, for instance, gave evidence as to the poor state of housing and agriculture on his reserve:

> I do not own the house I am living in. I am living with my mother and she owns the house a frame house about 30′ × 20′, with two rooms kitchen and living room which we also live in. I have my wife and three children living in the house also my mother and her grandchild, 3 other children are at the residential school. I have no farm at present. I would farm if I had the implements to work with ... if I had a start in cattle I would take good care of them.[41]

Similar statements came from Bob Tail Chief and Frank Scout, father and son who lived and worked together:

> We live in the same house, a log house with 2 rooms and a kitchen lean to. These two rooms are approximately 16′ × 18′ and the kitchen is 10′ × 10′ made of lumber ... One part of the house is occupied by myself and wife and nephew. The other part by adopted son Frank Scout, and his wife and 3 children. This house was built in 1906 ... Although we've tried to keep farming we couldn't continue on account of not having any implements.[42]

Despite their brevity, these statements were probably the most direct evidence the committee received from a grassroots level, and they revealed first-hand many practical issues confronting reserve communities. The IAA chose agriculture and housing as issues of discussion not only because it was practical do so, but also because these two areas were of primary concern to the Indian Affairs Branch. In other words, because the surveys appealed to issues that the Branch already considered to be important, the IAA's presentations gained further credibility.

Unlike the surveys, the IAA's official brief focused upon three main issues: the concept of treaty rights, gaining social benefits for Indian peoples, and the shortcomings of the Indian Act. In many ways, the content of the brief stood in stark contrast to the survey material; the survey results represented the daily concerns of the communities while the legalistic brief represented the theoretical recognition sought by Indian communities, their leaders, and their supporters. The brief asserted that the government was obligated, through the treaties, to include Indian peoples in Canadian society and to give them increased self-determination.

The focus of the brief was treaty rights. Specifically, this document emphasized that treaty rights were the foundation upon which the relations between the government and Indian communities rested. It pointed out that treaty rights were originally intended to give Indian peoples equality: "As early as 1873 in Canada the Crown applied the concept of Brotherhood of Man to the Indians living among the whites. The Indian was to be elevated from the status of a serf and was to be educated so that he might be able to compete on equal terms with the white man."[43] The treaties were less important for their recognition of Indian nationhood and special, or distinct, rights than for their recognition of Indian people as full and loyal citizens. As stated in the brief: "It was then clearly the objective of the Treaties to promote progress among the Indians and make them self-sustaining, loyal citizens of the Crown."[44] The inclusion of the crucial words "self-sustaining" acknowledged the importance of the treaties with regard to sustaining the economies of Indian communities. Economic success and citizenship were related through the treaties. Finally, the brief employed the treaty right to education as the basis for arguing that only education and technical training would assist Indian peoples to become full citizens, as "only by fitting themselves to discharge the responsibilities of modern civilization [could] they hope to take their place in society today."[45]

These interpretations of the treaties formed the critical basis of the brief's thesis: that Indian peoples had the right to be treated as Canadian citizens with a full array of political and social rights. At the same time, the brief directly addressed the public outcry over Indian exclusion from Canadian society. In postwar Canadian society, the public and the politicians alike were concerned that Indian peoples did not enjoy adequate living standards. As previously mentioned, freedom from poverty and ignorance were deemed necessary for Indian peoples if they were to participate fully in the nation's affairs. In Canada the welfare state, which was instituted during and after the Second World War, was an expression of the state taking responsibility for its citizens in return for the latter actively participating in national life; however, this principal was denied status Indians because they were not viewed as full citizens. Here the brief simply argued that Indian peoples should be accepted as part of Canada's citizenry because this is precisely what the treaties had both promised and intended.

The focus upon treaties is not surprising since this was the primary concern of the IAA's founders. Although John Laurie consistently avoided addressing treaty rights in any meaningful way, Tommy Douglas, and specifically Morris Schumiatcher, were willing to venture into this uncharted territory. Schumiatcher's ability to highlight these unique rights could very well have been related to his own understanding of the treaties. A decade following the submission of the IAA brief, Schumiatcher himself published an article dealing with the treaties and citizenship in the popular magazine *The Beaver*. In Schumiatcher's view, the treaties were compatible with citizenship:

> He [the Indian] is prepared to be a citizen. Unfortunately, at the present time, becoming a citizen means that he must renounce the rights which

> his ancestors secured from the Queen almost a century ago. The Indian is given the hard choice of either remaining treaty bound – without status as a citizen – or of becoming a Canadian citizen by forsaking the rights guaranteed him by treaty. To me, there appears nothing inconsistent or contradictory in the concept of Indian Canadians sharing in the rights of citizenship and at the same time enjoying the special benefits that treaties grant them.[46]

Schumiatcher's approach to treaty rights appears little changed between 1946 and 1959. In him the IAA membership found a supporter of treaty rights at a time when most non-Indians were reticent to touch the issue.

Discussions pertaining to social legislation and the Indian Act further supported the brief's fundamental thesis. Extension of social legislation to Indian peoples was necessary as part of the state's duty to its own citizens. The Indian Act, in turn, needed to be reformed if it were to recognize the abilities of Indian communities and individuals to be self-determining. Recommendations emphasized the importance of self-government through band councils and the need to remove or change restrictive clauses within the Indian Act. The act was viewed as a piece of legislation that interfered with the treaties and their promise of progress, advancement, self-reliance, and equality for Indian peoples.

The document as a whole offered a complex argument against dependency. This was an issue upon which the public, politicians, and Indian peoples could all agree. Both parties – the government and the IAA – appeared to agree that employment, education, and self-determination were fundamental to improving the condition of Indian peoples in Canada. The IAA based its reasoning on the treaties; the government based its reasoning on a liberal democratic view of citizenship. The reform liberalism of the Mackenzie King government held that state intervention was necessary to ensure the sharing of wealth within the national community and a minimal standard of living for all. Through its brief the IAA reconciled the desire of Indian leaders for recognition of treaty rights and self-determination with the liberal political ideals that were then in vogue.

This interpretation of the treaties was reinforced when IAA representatives testified before the Special Joint Committee. In April 1947 a delegation of IAA members boarded the train in Calgary and headed for Ottawa. The government agreed to pay the expenses of three representatives from Alberta to testify – two representing the IAA and one unaffiliated representative – while others could attend as observers if the IAA financed their trip.[47] Those who boarded the train in April included IAA president Johnny Callihoo; IAA secretary John Laurie; Bob Crow Eagle from the Peigan reserve; Frank Cardinal from Sucker Creek; Albert Lightning from Hobbema; Mark Steinhauer from Saddle Lake; David Crowchild from the

Sarcee reserve; Ed Hunter from the Stoney reserve; and, finally, James Gladstone, Joe Bull Shield, and Cecil Tallow from the Blood reserve. The IAA selected Teddy Yellowfly of the Blackfoot reserve to represent the unaffiliated Indian peoples of Alberta; Callihoo and Crow Eagle were chosen as the official IAA delegates, one for northern Alberta, one for southern Alberta. As the men boarded the train, their mood was optimistic. Mark Steinhauer said to a waiting reporter, "You see, we hope to get our rights this time – full implementation of the treaties."[48] In Ottawa the IAA delegates were warmly welcomed by their parliamentarian connections, including Doug Harkness and Senators Dan Riley and W.A. Buchanan, who took time to host the representatives. Although their stay was brief, the Alberta men were also able to tour Ottawa.[49]

On their first day before the Special Joint Committee, Callihoo and Crow Eagle presented prepared speeches that summarized the most important parts of the IAA brief. Callihoo emphasized the significance of education and called for improvements in the educational system for Indian children so as to permit them to gain an education equal to that of non-Indian children. He also stressed the need for reserve communities to be able to govern themselves more freely, both through their band councils and by a loosening of restrictive Indian Act regulations (e.g., the agricultural permit system). Crow Eagle, in turn, pressed the point that improvements in housing and agriculture were critical to the reserve communities: "A successful farming community is the real strength of a country. This is also true if the Indian is to make the progress that our members wish for themselves."[50] Neither Callihoo nor Crow Eagle added any information to his presentation that was not contained in the brief. The committee did not press the IAA delegates for any additional information following the presentations, and Crow Eagle and Callihoo were invited to return the following day for a question period. Both Callihoo and Crow Eagle's presentations appealed to the committee's concern with citizenship. Both emphasized Indian education for future duties as well as economic advancement through social legislation and economic planning that would allow Indian communities eventually to take their full place in the Canadian political system.

On 22 April the question period, although it was intended to focus upon the testimonies of the IAA representatives, quickly turned into a free discussion involving all the Alberta delegates in the room, official and unofficial alike. Questioning became unsystematic and covered issues ranging from band membership, trust funds, and education to the powers of band councils. It was clear from the questions posed by the various committee members that their focus was, again, on matters pertaining to Indian status and the right to vote (the franchise and enfranchisement), and the ability of Indian bands to govern themselves in the present and future.

Both of these issues were related to the concept of citizenship. The concerns remained: Did Indian peoples want to gain the rights of full citizenship? And, if they did, would they be able to govern themselves in a responsible manner?

Upon completing their presentations, the IAA members quickly returned home. According to John Laurie, President Callihoo was not impressed with the proceedings, saying: "these people will not be allowed to make any serious and lasting change. I can see that the Federal Government is just going through the motions of satisfying the public."[51] The impact of the IAA on the Special Joint Committee investigations was not directly noticeable, and IAA members were initially disappointed. Upon their return to Alberta, the delegation disbanded and IAA business continued where it had left off. That summer, IAA concerns lay with organizing the southern reserves, including the Peigan and Blackfoot reserves, and holding the annual general meeting.

Similarly, some members of government remained sceptical of the Special Joint Committee, particularly representations made by such groups as the IAA. In his memoirs, Hugh Keenleyside, deputy minister of mines and resources at the time of the committee hearings, portrayed some of the Indian leaders who petitioned the government as self-interested: "In departmental dealings with the native organizations that were beginning to emerge, the irresponsibility, not unmixed with venality, of some of the more vigorous native leaders was a persistent factor. The active exploitation of their weaker brethren was not then ... confined exclusively to the white men."[52] Civil servants of the day were not always sympathetic to the pleadings of Indian leaders, despite their mandate to deal with their concerns. This lack of sympathy certainly would have had a negative influence on any attempts to later implement committee recommendations.

Perhaps the most dramatic outcome of the trip was that it appeared to tire John Laurie so much that he resigned his position as IAA secretary. Laurie had been suffering from heart troubles for some time, and the strain of holding down his teaching job at Crescent Heights High School and working for the IAA was more than he could bear. He had not been in the forefront of IAA action for some months, and he chose to rest in Banff and Windermere, British Columbia. In the summer of 1947, following the trip to Ottawa, he informed his friend James Gladstone, then an IAA director, that he was taking a temporary break:

> I have given up my place for a year because of bad health. I thought this over a long time, and was in hopes that a certain matter would come up this year in my private affairs that would set me free of teaching and so give full time to the IAA. But I did not get the thing I was after. I had no

> choice really but to ask the General Meeting to give me a rest. However, I am going to make an effort to get my secretaryship back at the next General Meeting.[53]

Laurie had dedicated a great deal of his personal resources and energy to the IAA, but his position on its executive was not necessarily secure. The announcement of his retirement immediately led to the nomination of Catholic Reverend Father Schmidt and Laurie's Stoney friend Ed Hunter for the position of secretary. The idea that others might be doing "his" work upset Laurie somewhat. In a letter to Gladstone, Laurie confidentially complained of possible troubles with the new secretary and emphatically stated, "I shall certainly be in the running at the next General Meeting."[54] Although, because of his poor health, he did not play a strong hand in the affairs pertaining to the Special Committee, Laurie was certainly not ready to relinquish control over IAA strategy and activities. In fact, despite his resignation, in the summer of 1947 Laurie continued to meet with Indian Affairs officials, whose confidence he felt he possessed, on behalf of the IAA.

Final Recommendations of the Committee

Despite their frustration with the process, IAA members did see some of their ideas advanced in the closing report of the Special Joint Committee. When the committee made its final report to Parliament in February 1948, after 128 meetings and after considering over 400 briefs, it concluded that the Indian Act should be completely overhauled and recommended that a new special committee be struck to formulate a draft bill amending the act. Most significantly, the report emphasized: "All proposed revisions are designed to make possible the gradual transition of Indians from wardship to citizenship." Despite the committee's broad mandate, citizenship eventually became the focus of its attention and the basis for its reformist suggestions. The committee recommended the extension of additional social legislation to Indian peoples, called for greater self-government within Indian communities through the granting of greater powers to band councils, and insisted that the economic betterment of the communities be a priority. Treaty rights also figured prominently in the final report. The IAA linked citizenship to treaty rights, and the committee emphasized that the government had to clearly establish the nature of treaty rights. Citizenship was a concept that embodied more than the right to vote, and, in making the recommendations it did, the committee acknowledged the importance of social rights, and even treaty rights, as the foundation for the political rights associated with it.

Unfortunately, the social rights underpinning the right to vote (e.g., the right to education and access to social welfare funding) fell primarily under provincial jurisdiction, which encouraged the committee to keep its suggestions conservative. When considering Indian education, for example, the committee simply stated, "wherever and whenever possible Indian children should be educated in association with other children,"[55] suggesting that Indian children should be integrated into provincial schools and into a system of education within which all would be trained for responsible citizenship on an equal basis. In order to deal with the potential for conflict between Dominion and provincial jurisdictions, the committee recommended that education, health, fish and game issues, and liquor regulations all be considered at the next Dominion-provincial conference as they "might bring Indians within the scope of such provincial legislation, in order that there be mutual and co-ordinated assistance to facilitate the Indians to become ... citizens."[56]

The committee's final report was not particularly extensive or in-depth. Moreover, since its recommendations were non-binding, its influence was not direct. The work of the committee and its final report were important, however, as a public statement of the government's intention to integrate Indian peoples into the Canadian polity. This represented a major change in Indian Affairs policy direction. Prior to the Second World War, Indian peoples were encouraged to remain separate from Canadian society. Individuals were encouraged to enfranchise through clauses in the Indian Act, but, as a group, Indian peoples were deemed unprepared for full citizenship. The committee's final report represented a change in this line of thinking: as a group, Indian peoples were to be actively prepared for and eased into citizenship.

Contrary to Ian Johnson's conclusion that the work of the Special Joint Committee "revealed the fundamental differences in outlook between Indians and government during the post-war period," and that the committee contemplated assimilation while Indian political leaders argued for self-government, it is clear that the two parties were discussing a shared concern: the nature of Indian citizenship.[57] The committee favoured integrating Indian peoples into Canadian society through providing them with education, increased social assistance, improved health care, and increased self-determination, thus making available to them the long-denied material benefits of "civilized" society. The IAA lobbied hard for this. Through the treaties, Indians became Canadians, which entitled them to the material advantages of life in mid-twentieth-century Canada.

Both the Special Joint Committee, with its reform Liberal outlook, and the IAA desired equal social rights for Indian and non-Indian citizens of the nation. Political rights were a small part of the discussions pertaining to Indian status and equality, primarily because it was recognized that the right to vote did little to address the fundamental social inequalities faced by Indian citizens. Indeed, the IAA membership firmly asserted its rejection of the franchise both before and after the committee hearings.[58] According to the IAA brief, educational and economic liberty preceded the right to vote. As John Laurie remarked in 1949, the year after the committee's report: "The Indian Association respectfully submits that no further nonsense be talked about such matters as access to liquor, or any form of vote. Give our people BREAD not BEER, Blankets not Ballots."[59]

7

Political Pragmatics: Amending the Indian Act, 1948-58

> Mr. Gooderham called to say that he was very pleased to see that you are the new President. He was confident that the relations between his office and the I.A.A. would continue to be pleasant.
>
> – John Laurie to James Gladstone, 1949[1]

The decade between 1948 and 1958 was one in which the Indian Association of Alberta exercised its hard-won position as a recognized Indian political organization within the Canadian political structure, both at the provincial level and at the federal level. As a result of its involvement in the special parliamentary committee hearings, its publicity campaigns, and its government lobbying activities, the IAA had enhanced its credibility. Indeed, it even gained a degree of notoriety, which it subsequently used in attempting to improve conditions for Indian peoples in Alberta.

The relationship between the government and the IAA during this decade saw three new developments. First, where previously the IAA struggled to ensure its credibility and to gain solid political connections in Ottawa while simultaneously seeking to reform existing Indian policy and legislation, it was now solidly established as part of the political machine. Within ten years of its founding, the Alberta association had successfully gained access to the inner workings of the Canadian political system. Surprisingly, this access seems to have compromised the IAA's effectiveness. Between 1948 and 1957 IAA-government relations became routinized and the process of the IAA's entrenchment into the Ottawa routine subsequently encouraged the government to believe that the association no longer posed a significant threat. Second, during this decade the IAA forged a new role for itself as a provincial-federal liaison on behalf of Indian interests. Until the late 1940s, the IAA declined extensive involvement with the Alberta provincial government. After 1948, however, it began to facilitate dialogue between both divisions of government in its attempts to protect Indian treaty rights. Third, IAA-government relations during this period were rooted more in practical than in ideological considerations. In its dealings with the government the IAA rarely pursued any grand vision relating to Indian peoples and their place in Canada; instead, it sought practical solutions to local problems within the scope of the Indian treaties and existing legislation (this at a time when its leadership was fragmented). The IAA had entered into its own era of political pragmatism.

In the twenty-first century, when the relationship between the government and First Nations political groups is so critical to the implementation and recognition of Aboriginal rights, it is surprising that a historical understanding of this relationship is almost non-existent.[2] Gaining analytic insight into this unique interaction in Canadian politics would give greater insight into the practical functioning of First Nations pressure groups. In a paper entitled "The Joint Cabinet/National Indian Brotherhood Committee: A Unique Experiment in Pressure Group Relations," Sally Weaver identified the importance of investigating relations between Indian political groups and the government. She argues that this type of investigation is important for "gaining analytic insight into such relationships and for gaining any practical lessons should the government and Indians in the future seek a similar working forum."[3] Weaver claims that Canadian-Indian pressure group behaviour emerged in the activist 1960s, however, research into the IAA shows that it has a longer history.

Three important events that well illustrate the characteristics of IAA-government relations during this period occurred between the conclusion of investigations into the Indian Act in 1948 and the fall of the Liberal government in 1957. First, the IAA initially focused a great deal of its energy upon monitoring and criticizing federal attempts to revise the antiquated Indian Act. During these years, the association found itself regularly sending comments on proposed revisions to the act to its political connections and the Indian Affairs Branch. Government and IAA interaction during this legislative reform process reveals just how the IAA's involvement with the government became routinized and the extent to which it was drawn into becoming part of government-controlled agendas.

Second, between 1948 and the late 1950s the IAA concentrated its energies on northern issues. In its early years the IAA was primarily a southern movement concerned with problems facing reserves located in the agricultural regions of Alberta. By the end of the 1940s it began to pay more attention to the treaty rights of Alberta's northern bands, whose existence depended upon hunting, fishing, and trapping. The IAA's reawakened interest in treaty rights, as they related to wildlife resource use, led it to act as a liaison between the province and the federal government as it sought to better protect the interests of its expanding northern membership.

Third, a series of critical events that, towards the end of this decade, revealed IAA-government relations were those surrounding the "Hobbema evictions." In 1957 the IAA involved itself indirectly, through its legal counsel, in a court case on behalf of several families threatened with eviction from their reserve community in the Hobbema Agency. The IAA's involvement in this case is important because, in its defence of the evicted families, it employed all of the political and legal strategies it had evolved in the foregoing years. To the association's aging leadership, the *Hobbema* case represented a last attempt to deal with compelling local social concerns.

Overall, the IAA's activities during the 1950s contributed to a general recognition of Indian political groups in Ottawa, and the association no longer had to fight to establish its credibility. Association operations were routinized at the local level, and government officials were frequent guests at IAA general meetings. Although the IAA had vociferously criticized Indian Affairs policy in the past, now it seemed less concerned with the details of new policies and more concerned with addressing specific problems related directly to the Indian Act, to self-government, and to bettering Indian education. Alberta's new economic prosperity, fuelled by a provincial oil boom, encouraged IAA member communities to demand a share in the benefits. Social welfare legislation had been successfully extended to Indian peoples after the Second World War, and now Indian communities sought to improve their conditions by gaining more control over their own resources. In the 1950s, Indian peoples in Alberta turned to the IAA as the venue from which to pursue this greater goal.

National Politics and Federal Indian Policy

In most ways, the national political backdrop to IAA interaction with the federal government after the war until the late 1950s was unremarkable. The federal Liberal party, headed by Mackenzie King, held tightly to the reins of power. The Liberals survived federal elections in 1945, 1949, and 1953 with majority governments and saw a change of leadership, from King to Louis St. Laurent, following King's retirement in 1948. Political scientist Reg Whitaker suggests that the stability of the Liberal party lay primarily in its ability to create an appealing postwar reconstruction program focused upon full employment and domestic infrastructural development. Throughout their postwar reign, the Liberals astutely drew upon the expertise and new ideas of their civil service in order to create a postwar policy with a national housing program, expanded social security plan, family allowances, and government spending initiatives to create full employment.[4] In Whitaker's words, the postwar reconstruction policy initiated "twelve fat but grey years of Liberal party activity."[5] The civil service became the source of most policy ideas and initiatives, and the highly centralized government focused upon national issues rather than regional issues.

The Conservative Opposition had little influence during the years between 1945 and the late 1950s. Conservative leaders Bracken and Drew provided little inspiration to their caucus, and their attacks on the Liberal agendas of the day appeared to lack purpose. As Denis Smith notes, "The

Liberal cabinet was subtly transforming itself from a party government into something more all embracing and permanent – an administration built on wide national consensus ... In the public mind, the prospect of any alternative to a Liberal government grew dim."[6] As a result of the weak Opposition in the House, the civil service was able to press on with its aims of spreading economic growth and with diffusing a spirit of faith in an unlimited future. The mission of nation building, with a centralist bent, offered a stable vision that appealed to the Canadian electorate after the uncertainty of war and could not be undone by the Conservatives. The Conservatives did attempt to undermine the credibility of the civil service, but to no avail.[7]

Although external events like the deepening Cold War and the beginning of the Korean War (1950) did remind Canadians of the spectre of international conflict, between the late 1940s and the late 1950s the Liberals focused squarely upon internal development. One of the more prominent national issues of 1956, for example – and one that undermined the credibility of the Liberal government of St. Laurent – was the attempt by the government to push for the construction of a natural gas pipeline from Alberta to eastern Canada. The Liberals viewed this as one of their last great national projects, one following upon the national housing and other social welfare programs, one that would bring cheap energy to the Canadian heartland and fuel the industrial expansion that was ongoing in central Canada throughout the 1950s. Though the pipeline legislation passed successfully through Parliament during the 1956 session, it was not without tremendous opposition. The involvement of Americans in the project roused Canadian suspicions, as did the attempts by the government to force the legislation through the House. According to Denis Smith, the end of the Liberal grip on power was signalled by this pipeline issue. National development remained a prominent political issue throughout the late 1940s and 1950s, as this issue reveals, but St. Laurent gradually appears to have lost control of his government. The Liberal government was tinged with complacency, and the regime's self-assurance had become troubling to many.[8]

Heavy-handed domestic development projects were certainly a feature of the Liberal Indian policy from the late 1940s throughout the 1950s. Although Noel Dyck suggests that federal initiatives to develop Indian communities did not occur until the 1960s,[9] they were already operating in the 1950s, having been created in conjunction with other national development projects. Liberal ministers responsible for Indian Affairs, Walter Harris (1950-54) and Jack Pickersgill (1954-57), heavily emphasized the reconstruction of Indian communities. In a 1956 speech delivered to the Canadian Club in Ottawa, Pickersgill illustrated that development initiatives such as house building, community development projects, and vocational training programs were products of the late 1940s that were being carried on through the 1950s.[10] Between 1948 and the late 1950s, Indian Affairs policy encouraged the creation of community centres on reserves in order to facilitate local and supervised "wholesome" recreation.[11] As early as 1947, vocational training programs were recognized as key to training Indian workers. Furthermore, by 1957 Indian Affairs had institutionalized an Indian Labour Placement Program aimed at gaining employment for Indian workers in urban settings.[12] Pickersgill, an Oxford graduate who came into the federal Liberal party through the ranks of the civil service, embodied the Liberal focus on giving the highly educated civil service control over policy. During his time as minister, he strove to emphasize employment training, housing, integrated education, and the internal economic development of Indian communities.[13]

National politics and national Indian policy, therefore, intersected during the period after the war. The Liberal government took few initiatives and made few drastic changes to its long-standing policy of making Indian peoples self-sufficient. Between the late 1940s and 1957, the government tinkered with the details of the Indian Act, particularly the critical sections dealing with membership. It attempted to preserve limited hunting, fishing, and trapping rights for Indian communities (in recognition of their continued dependence on these resources), and it tried to integrate Indian workers into the Canadian labour pool. The IAA keyed into this relatively conservative governmental approach to Indian administration as it pursued a handful of causes related to improving the condition of Indian communities and treaty rights. The IAA's interest in the revision of the Indian Act, treaty rights, and the Hobbema trials were a reflection of these concerns. Perhaps because the Liberal government reigned so securely, the IAA was given more attention during this period.

Revising the Indian Act: IAA-Government Relations

At the heart of the IAA presentations before the 1946 Special Joint Committee appointed to review Indian administration and the Indian Act in Canada was the notion that Indian peoples should be granted full citizenship status within Canadian society, in line with the treaties. The arguments pertaining to the relationship between citizenship and the treaties were carefully argued in a lengthy brief presented by the IAA to the committee, and some of the notions of social equality associated with full citizenship were openly argued in person by those IAA representatives who appeared before it. As a result of its intense participation in the committee hearings, the IAA was eager to be involved in the subsequent revision of the Indian Act. When a bill was finally introduced in the House, the IAA closely monitored its progress and helped with its revision. These actions drew the IAA into Ottawa's political routine and effectively co-opted it.

As historian John F. Leslie indicates, revisions to the Indian Act were slow to be introduced in the House of Commons.[14] Between the final report of the Special Joint Committee and the introduction of new legislation to the House, two years elapsed. Following a federal election in 1949 and administrative changes in Indian Affairs in 1950, which saw the Branch transferred from the Department of Mines and Resources to the new Department of Citizenship and Immigration, a draft bill – Bill 267 – was finally introduced in June 1950 by Minister for Indian Affairs Walter Harris. The Liberal government hoped for a hasty passage of Bill 267, and Minister Harris had sufficient confidence in it to avoid drawing attention to its introduction.

Minister Harris gave the clearest expression of the intentions of the bill at its second reading a few weeks later, when he stated: "More emphasis is being laid on greater participation and responsibility by Indians in the conduct of their own affairs ... The ultimate goal of our Indian policy is the integration of the Indians into the general life and economy of the country."[15] This comment reflected the importance the Liberal government placed upon extending full citizenship to Indian peoples. In his remarks on the bill, which all MPs had been able to study, he emphasized that Indian self-government would be increased as a result of the proposed amendments and that the bill represented an amalgamation of the recommendations of the Special Joint Committee as well as the opinions of Indian groups across the country. Harris's views were further reaffirmed when Liberal MP D.F. Brown concurred that "we want the Indians to be assimilated economically."[16]

Interestingly, Bill 267 represented the paradoxical thinking of the government at this time. On the one hand, the Liberals wanted to give Indian peoples increased opportunities within Canadian society, both as citizens with increased political power and as citizens with increased economic power. On the other hand, the Liberals sought to actively limit Indian peoples' self-determining abilities because, "so long as we have Indians requiring the assistance of the government of Canada in the conduct of their affairs, an Indian Act is necessary to give the government the required statutory authority to expend public money and to do other incidental matters."[17] In other words, as long as the government had a fiduciary obligation towards Indian peoples, it was obligated to legislate their existence. At this date, the contradiction between full citizenship and the notion of governmental responsibilities towards Indian peoples had yet to be reconciled.

The reaction of the Opposition members to Bill 267 was not favourable. Upon its introduction and first reading in the House, Opposition members Douglas Harkness, John Blackmore, and even John Diefenbaker attacked the Liberal government for failing to adequately consult Indian peoples as to the contents of the bill. During the ensuing debate, Diefenbaker astutely remarked: "In the building and restoration of a new concept of dealing with the Indians, [we should] give them an opportunity to be the builders."[18] In fact, prior to the introduction of Bill 267 in the House that summer, its contents were a mystery to most Indian peoples. The Opposition continued its attacks on the bill and, time and time again, emphasized that Indian leaders deserved to be closely consulted. During a fiery speech in condemnation of the bill, Harkness stated: "The plain truth is that sufficient time to do that has not been allowed. Many Indians have not seen the bill and have not been able to study it and make intelligent representations in respect to it."[19] Over the course of the debate the Opposition MPs emphasized that Indian peoples deserved improved educational opportunities, increased self-government, and better economic opportunities.

The IAA followed the course of Bill 267 with great interest. It, too, was greatly shocked at the government's failure to adequately consider the perspective of Indian peoples as it was presented to the Special Joint Committee. The bill dashed the great expectations that the hearings had aroused in Alberta's Indian communities. When, under pressure from the Opposition, Minister of Indian Affairs Harris finally relented and agreed to delay the second reading of the bill until the next session of Parliament, the IAA quickly regrouped and prepared detailed critiques of its contents. The IAA executive arranged three meetings for August, at Paget Hall in Calgary and at Hobbema, since the revisions were not available for study at the IAA's annual meeting.[20] At these meetings IAA members from both northern and southern Alberta met to consider their views of the draft legislation. According to Laurie, several communities were relying on the IAA to interpret the new legislation for them.[21]

The IAA meetings were long and intense. Not only did Indian leaders from around the province attend, but so did prominent church leaders, including the Anglican bishop, MPs Blackmore and Harkness, and Senator George Ross.[22] John Laurie also arranged for legal counsel to explain aspects of the Indian Act to the IAA membership. Laurie's friend Ruth Gorman, daughter of respected Calgary lawyer Mark B. Peacock (who had earlier defended Alberta's Stoney in a hunting and fishing case) and a lawyer herself, agreed to work pro bono for the IAA.[23] Gorman recalled the difficulty of explaining the act to the IAA members:

> Laurie takes me to the front and says here is Mrs. Gorman who has come to explain the Indian Act to us and sits down ... and then Laurie says STOP ... we had to translate into four languages ... It was very hard explaining it ... I had to stay three days, which was awful. At the end they never clapped, they just stared at me, which I was getting awful scared of ... This waiting for interpreters ... I had to come back and had to come back.[24]

Unfamiliar with the IAA, Gorman was initially reticent to assist Laurie, but, over time, her friendship with him and her dedication to the IAA cause grew. She continued to act as legal advisor for the association throughout the 1950s, eventually playing a critical role in the Hobbema trial in 1957. At this early date, however, her main function was "to explain the Indian Act" to the IAA membership, and Laurie purposely discouraged her from discussing any other matters, feeling that this might lead to trouble as he attempted to control IAA strategy.[25]

What emerged from the IAA meetings at this time was a detailed analysis of Bill 267. The IAA formulated and presented three central criticisms of it. First, the IAA sought to emphasize the trust relationship between the government and Indian peoples as established by the treaties. Wherever the words "legal title vested in His Majesty" occurred in the bill, referring to Indian lands, the IAA sought to have them revised to read "in trust of the Band."[26] In the same vein, throughout the bill the IAA wanted the word "surrender" to be replaced by the word "entrust." The justification for these changes was not only that this better reflected the true and proper relations between the government and Indian bands, but also that the word "surrender" could not be translated into many Indian languages.

The IAA also criticized the bill for its allocation of arbitrary powers to the minister of Indian Affairs. In its quest for greater self-government for Indian peoples, the IAA rejected the idea that the minister should be granted ultimate power over decisions made by band councils.[27] With the discretionary powers residing ultimately in the minister, the IAA felt that the struggle of Indian peoples for self-government was being hampered. As Secretary Laurie wrote to Minister Harris, "Any arbitrary action, without consent as above [majority of electors of a band], is arousing resentment and fear, if not stronger emotions."[28] The veiled threat was that Indian peoples would not stand to have their self-governing power, as recognized in the treaties, undermined by the government.

In addition to criticizing the bill at this time, the IAA also took the opportunity to demand that Indian treaty hunting, fishing, and trapping rights be recognized and restored rather than limited through provincial legislation. This reflected the IAA's increasing focus upon the concerns of its northern membership, whose economies were rooted in hunting, fishing, and trapping and were threatened by industrial development. The eastern Alberta Peace River region, for example, faced the intrusion of the Alaska Highway and expansion of the oil industry into the region. In addition, in the northwestern areas of the province the plan to establish the Primrose Military Range greatly concerned Indian groups whose interests lay in the land and its resources. The IAA's involvement in the revision of the Indian Act marked an important opportunity for the IAA to emphasize to the government the importance of treaty hunting, fishing, and trapping rights.

Finally, a significant principle in the IAA critique of Bill 267 was the association's insistence that Indian peoples should be recognized as possessing a distinct racial identity. This principle was brought up at the Special Joint Committee hearings, and, in 1950, the IAA took the opportunity to reaffirm it. In many ways, this notion derived from the IAA's fear that the Canadian Liberal government was striving to "integrate" Indian peoples into Canadian society. Reserve communities commonly believed that "integration," or "assimilation," and its accompanying citizenship rights would see Indian peoples lose their treaty rights. Since treaty rights were already compromised by various types of provincial and federal legislation, it was widely feared that a revised Indian Act would simply further erode Indian peoples' special rights. The continued "recognition of an Indian as an Indian" was something the IAA sought to secure for its people, as both a political and a moral right.[29]

Although the IAA presented a united front to the government in criticizing the bill, in reality the association was divided over various specific sections of the proposed legislation. At the Hobbema meeting, the dissension reflected the fear on the Hobbema reserves that the government was working towards the enfranchisement of Indian peoples.[30] Hobbema communities had a long history of being politically influenced by the Saskatchewan Cree leadership. Saskatchewan Cree leader John Tootoosis often visited other Cree leaders in this region, and he aroused suspicion that the IAA supported the enfranchisement of Indian peoples. Tootoosis was particularly suspicious of John Laurie, and this often caused problems for the IAA in that area of the province.[31]

The IAA's detailed and critical analysis of the bill (prepared during its extra summer meetings in 1950) was sent by the executive to every member of the House of Commons, the minister of Indian Affairs, the Senate, and the press. Secretary Laurie himself also wrote popular articles for the press relating the IAA's view of the bill. Laurie minced no words in condemning the bill as "a well-baited trap and nothing else. It is designed to encourage a progressive Indian to assume the status of a citizen and then encroach on the reserves ... the intent is clear. The Indian is to be gradually eliminated."[32] The overall intent in preparing this critique was to educate the public and parliamentarians about the IAA's view of the bill and to seek its revision prior to passage.

Although the Liberals withdrew the bill for further consideration at the end of the June parliamentary session, the federal government did respond to the IAA's protests by attempting to further consult with Indian leaders. Secretary Laurie was busily preparing a united protest with BC Indian political groups when government consultations were announced.[33] Much to everyone's surprise, Indian leaders had successfully influenced parliamentary proceedings, something that had never happened before.

In the ensuing winter months, Minister Harris solicited input pertaining to the bill from his field staff and from Indian leaders. In February 1951, IAA delegates John Laurie, James Gladstone, Albert Manyfingers, and David Crowchild; representatives from other western Indian groups, including Peter Kelly of the Native Brotherhood of British Columbia, Joe Dreaver of the Union of Saskatchewan Indians, and a handful of other representatives from Manitoba and the east met the minister in Winnipeg. Laurie later recalled "sitting a long, long day in conference, analyzing one by one the objections of the Alberta Indians made through their Indian Association of Alberta. Manitoba delegates had done the same a day or two previously. In some groups the feeling was growing that the Minister really meant to listen to the Indians themselves."[34] The minister failed to reveal the contents of a revised bill but did confer personally with IAA leaders in Winnipeg.[35]

However, Indian leaders' feeling of goodwill towards the minister of Indian Affairs did not last. Following this historically unprecedented round of consultations between the government and the Indian leadership, a new all-Canadian round of meetings was called for February 28 in Ottawa to discuss the newly revised Bill, now known as Bill 79. The minister wanted to have Indian leaders present in Ottawa when the reshaped bill received its first reading in the House. At this second round of meetings, Indian leaders from across the country were suspicious of government intentions, and "all were on the defensive." According to John Laurie, however, "Mr. Harris demonstrated his tact and his capacity to hear critical, sometimes bitter opposition, without unchanging courtesy."[36]

Lack of unity was perhaps one of the greatest weaknesses encountered by Indian political groups in their attempts to influence and pressure the government to change the Indian Act. Though all groups shared similar concerns, unified action seemed impossible to attain as regional differences made cooperation difficult. Unified action on the part of the political associations and the independent leaders was also hampered by lack of information about the proposed revisions to Bill 267. When Indian leaders were invited to Ottawa in February, they were made aware of the revised bill only when it was introduced to the House. Minster Harris astutely used the situation to portray his government as sympathetically consulting Indian groups while simultaneously achieving the political goal of pressing the legislation through Parliament.

Somehow the IAA leadership did not share the incongruency of this situation with its membership. It viewed Bill 79 favourably, and, in a memo, commented as follows to its membership: "Please remember the IAA has gained 16 important changes in the new Bill. There is not much danger in Bill 79."[37] To Liberal Don Brown, chairman of the committee on Indian affairs, the IAA wrote, "We feel that Bill 79 has gone a long way to meet the wishes of the Indians in this province."[38] At this point in the debate, the IAA appeared to be satisfied with the gains it had seemingly made. Part of its acceptance of Bill 79 was rooted in the fact that its parliamentary support network, composed primarily of MPs Harkness and Blackmore, doubted that there would be more changes made to the bill. Shortly after the appearance of Bill 79, Laurie confided to IAA president Gladstone: "Harkness was in and altho he is not hopeful about getting further changes, he will carry on the fight during the debate. Blackmore seems to have decided as Mr. Harris is a nice man and sincere, we can trust to his judgement to work the terms sympathetically."[39] Even Senator Ross, whom the IAA had used as a Senate connection, had to leave the battle because of heart trouble.[40]

The revision of the Indian Act was accomplished with the passage of Bill 79 in June 1951, and the new act came into force on 4 September 1951.[41] The major gains made by the IAA through its lobbying of the government included recognition of the treaties, the principle of Indian control over reserves, reserve assets, and trust funds. As a result of the February meetings in Ottawa, the IAA contributed to the removal of Section 112. Most significantly, in the eyes of John Laurie, "it recognize[d], in certain clauses, the right of Indians to appeal to the courts of the land."[42]

The passage of the bill appears to have satisfied Secretary Laurie more than IAA president James Gladstone. Laurie advised Gladstone to focus only upon certain clauses in the battle for revision, especially those in the sections of the act pertaining to reserve funds, lands, and membership. Laurie was also adamant that Indian peoples have the right to appeal certain issues in the courts. Gladstone, on the other hand, was sensitive to the IAA membership's lack of understanding of how the act worked. In a letter to Minister Harris he expressed this concern and indicated that the IAA membership was not united in its acceptance of the changes: "The feeling of the south is that they are satisfied to agree to a trial of the terms of Bill 79, but there is a great need of education and preparation for the carrying out of its provisions. As for the north, they are not at all satisfied with many of its provisions and, perhaps again the answer is lack of education and lack of understanding."[43] The idea that bands wanted more information on the legislation was clearly reflected in the actions taken by the Blood reserve, whose council promptly hired its own lawyer to explain the new legislation to the band.[44]

The IAA's involvement in the revision of the Indian Act represented a significant moment in its history for a number of reasons. Through this process the IAA contributed to the revision of the Indian Act, despite the fact that the statute remained substantively unchanged. The IAA contributed to educating Parliament on Indian affairs, and it represented the Indian perspective on the Indian Act and its revision at a time when no mechanism facilitating Indian representation existed outside the DIA. Through its participation in the revision process and its lobbying of parliamentarians, however, the IAA was drawn into the Canadian political process. As John Leslie notes, Indian organizations participating in this process became a part of Ottawa's "controlled discourse" on Indian affairs.[45] Prior to its involvement in the Special Joint Committee hearings of 1946-48, the IAA simply relied upon petitioning politicians and the civil service of Indian Affairs in its attempts to have its claims attended to. With the revision of the Indian Act, the IAA found that it was one of the few Indian political organizations invited by the Liberal government to participate in government-sponsored discussions. The result of this recognition was the co-optation of the IAA.

In his analysis of Indian-government relations in the United States, Michael Lacy has developed what he refers to as the "threat model" of co-optation.[46] The threat model seeks to circumscribe the dynamic interplay between power holder and resistant elements when the former seeks to absorb the latter through co-optation. According to Lacy, the process of co-optation is unusual in power relations because, in it, "the power holder moves to include persons who are in some sense 'hostile' rather than friendly" in its agenda.[47] The reason for the initiation of the inclusion, or co-optation, process on the part of the power holder is also the defining element in this model: threat. Where the power holder is threatened by resistant elements, it initiates a co-optation process that seeks to grant resistors the ability to participate in power by offering them either legitimacy payoffs or filtering payoffs.[48] In this model, legitimacy payoffs refer to those rewards that confirm the democratic nature of society, while filtering payoffs refer to those rewards that blunt, or channel, the power of the resistors in order to render them ineffective.

Lacy's model is a useful tool in analyzing the relations that evolved between the Canadian federal government and the IAA. The IAA's protests of government activity and policies, in Parliament and through the press, threatened the government's liberal and democratic reputation. Although this threat was neither immediate nor pressing, it was used to advantage by Opposition members of the House of Commons (e.g., Diefenbaker, Blackmore, and Harkness) to embarrass the Liberals at a time when the Canadian public was sensitive to the ideals of democracy and minority rights. In response to the "threat" the federal government moved to initiate dialogue with these organizations and to include them in the process of legislative reform. As part of this co-optation process Minister Harris travelled to western Canada to meet informally with Indian associations and leaders, and he followed this with well publicized formal meetings in February 1951. In 1953, 1955, and 1956 this process of controlled consultation with Indian groups was entrenched in Ottawa politics through follow-up meetings on the Indian Act and a series of regional Indian conferences held across Canada.[49] By the mid-1950s Indian political organizations, including the IAA, had been included in federally sponsored consultation processes. Not surprisingly, Indian Affairs also began publishing its public relations newsletter, entitled "Indian News," in 1954.

The primary incentives offered to Indian political groups to participate in federally orchestrated consensus building represented both legitimacy payoffs and filtering payoffs. By participating with the government in the discussion of Indian Affairs issues, the IAA gained public recognition of its legitimacy; however, the IAA's contributions to the revised Indian Act and its expanded efforts to organize both served to filter its efforts at resisting the federal government into predictable channels with minimal impact on government agendas. In a very crude manner, by acknowledging and encouraging the IAA and other Indian political groups in the late 1940s and throughout the 1950s, the federal government successfully blunted the threat of Indian political resistance by drawing it into the Canadian political system, where the increasing power of band councils, regional differences, and their minority status would minimize the effective action of these fledgling political associations.

This federal strategy is perhaps best revealed by a progressive disregard for the IAA – a disregard that developed within Indian Affairs over the early 1950s. The feeling within Indian Affairs was that the IAA was increasingly undermining and duplicating the role of band councils. As early as 1952, Director D. McKay emphasized to Secretary Laurie that the IAA should limit its activities to matters of general policy rather than to local issues, which were the domain of the band councils: "Departure from such a policy would, I feel, weaken the position of the Band Councils."[50] In essence, Indian Affairs sought to limit and to direct the role of the IAA in order to better facilitate its own plans to empower band government. In 1955 Regional Supervisor R.F. Battle complained openly to Indian Affairs that he felt that the IAA was "useless" since it interfered with decisions being made at the agency level. In his view, band councils deserved more attention. When he complained in this manner to his superiors, the minister in charge of Indian Affairs commented, "Thanks. I think he has something."[51]

The IAA and Treaty Hunting, Trapping, and Fishing Rights

Initially, from 1948 to 1951, IAA relations with the government focused upon the federal level because of the changes in Indian Affairs. Over time the association widened its scope to also include the provincial government of Alberta. In the 1950s, in an attempt to protect Indian hunting, trapping, and fishing rights, the IAA adopted a liaison role between the federal and provincial governments. It was the 1930 Natural Resources

Transfer Act (NRTA) and its effect on treaty rights that provided the IAA with an opportunity to expand its relations with the province. Unlike in Saskatchewan, where Indian peoples developed a formal relationship with the CCF government through the Union of Saskatchewan Indians, such direct provincial support and interest in Indian issues was blatantly absent in Alberta. But Alberta's Social Credit government did not ignore Indian issues. On the contrary, it was quite concerned with Indian use of provincial game resources.

To date the direct relationship between Indian peoples and the Alberta government has not been described. Prior to the Second World War, questions pertaining to Indian peoples were handled through closed provincial/federal negotiations. The constitutional transfer of Crown lands and natural resources to provincial control via the 1930 NRTA, however, increased the frequency of provincial/federal interaction on issues pertaining to Indian hunting, fishing, and trapping. Based on the correspondence between the IAA and the provincial government, and discussions held at the IAA's annual meetings, it seems that the association was eager to directly represent the Indian perspective on hunting, trapping, and fishing problems to the government and to assist in their resolution. Members of the Social Credit government also seized upon this chance to negotiate with Indian communities.

Within the bounds of Alberta, Indian economies were historically founded on hunting, fishing, and (later) trapping. Hunting and fishing provided food, while trapping provided both food and furs. At this time fur represented a source of cash in the fur trade economy. Although the fur trade did somewhat alter Indian subsistence patterns from their precontact form, for most groups the traditional pursuits of hunting, fishing, and trapping continued to supplement their fur trade incomes.[52]

The importance of hunting, fishing, and trapping to the indigenous economy was openly recognized by the Dominion government of nineteenth-century Canada in the text of the treaties it signed with Alberta Indian bands. In Treaties 6, 7, and 8, animal harvesting rights were recognized in some form. Fur trade historians have argued that Indians in the northwestern regions of these treaties were certainly aware that, through treaty negotiations, they could protect their access to natural resources and that this control would have been expressed primarily as a demand for control over wildlife resources.[53] In Treaty 7, hunting rights were acknowledged: "the [said Indians] shall have right to pursue their vocations of hunting throughout the Tract surrendered as heretofore described, subject to such regulations." The text of Treaty 6 recognized both hunting and fishing rights: "the said Indians shall have right to pursue their avocations of hunting and fishing throughout the tract surrendered ... subject to such regulations."[54] Treaty 8 contained perhaps the most generous terms in this regard. Because the government negotiators recognized the special importance of animal harvesting to northern bands, Treaty 8 acknowledged Indian rights to "pursue their usual vocations of hunting, trapping and fishing through the tract surrendered as heretofore described."[55] In Treaty 8, the treaty commissioners even added verbal promises at the time of treaty signing assuring Indian signatories that "only such laws as to hunting and fishing as were in the interests of the Indians and were found necessary in order to protect the fish and fur-bearing animals would be made, and *that they would be as free to hunt and fish after the Treaty as they would be if they never entered into it* [emphasis added]."[56] For the Indian residents of northern Alberta, therefore, the government made it explicit that animal harvesting would continue as before, only now it would be subject to regulation. Surprisingly, only in Treaty 8 was the vocational aspect of this pursuit recognized.

Although agriculture assumed an increasingly important role in Alberta reserve communities in the twentieth century, hunting, trapping, and fishing continued to either supplement income and food derived from farming or serve as the main source of food and cash. In the 1930s and 1940s, Indian families in the Edmonton, Saddle Lake, Athabasca, Lesser Slave Lake, and Sarcee Agencies all relied to some degree upon hunting, trapping, and fishing to feed themselves. Even in Alberta's agricultural belt, seasonal trapping and hunting contributed to the self-sufficiency of farming Indians and reduced their dependence on government assistance.[57] In 1943 the Indian Affairs Branch appointed J.L. Grew to travel throughout northern and central Alberta agencies to register Indian traplines. He specifically noted, "One fact that impressed me greatly in many of my meetings with the Indians was the very keen interest shown by the so-called farming Indians in matters concerning trapping and hunting."[58] Despite the industrialization and agriculturalization of the overall provincial economy, Indian communities in Alberta still retained important links to their traditional economies.

The continuation of Indian peoples' traditional game harvesting was supported not only by the treaties, but also by government policy and legislation. Unfortunately, this support was neither clear nor constant. On the one hand, the federal government encouraged Indian hunting, trapping, and fishing because it provided the Indian population with a livelihood or vocation. In a letter to the Alberta minister of lands and mines, Indian Affairs Branch Director McGill stated the basic federal policy: "It is the wish of this department to work out with you some cooperative plan that will preserve to this population their means of livelihood by hunting and trapping, by which they have heretofore maintained themselves ... fur and game resources of this territory, which is largely unsuited for agriculture, are to be conserved and fostered to a point where they will support even the present population."[59] On the other hand, when Indian hunting, trapping, and fishing rights were compromised, Indian Affairs was slow to defend them.

Until the Second World War, Indian Affairs sought to protect Indian trapping and hunting interests through the creation of exclusive Indian hunting and trapping preserves and areas. In Alberta, for example, special provision for Indian hunting was made within the bounds of Wood Buffalo National Park, and the region around the river deltas near Fort Chipewyan were also restricted to Indian trapping.[60] Other northern areas in Alberta were also under consideration for exclusive Indian use, although after 1930 the federal government was unable unilaterally to assign or to create these preserves without provincial consent, for Crown lands fell under provincial jurisdiction.[61] This notion of exclusive game preserves was something Indian communities also supported.[62]

In addition, when the Province of Alberta began registering traplines in northern Alberta in the early 1940s, the Indian Affairs Branch attempted to protect Indian interests by seeking guarantees that trapline would be assigned only to treaty Indians, paying the registration fees for Indian trappers,[63] attempting to secure communal trapping rights for Indian groups, and initiating fur-restoration projects.[64] The Indian Affairs Branch made these efforts despite lack of cooperation from the provincial government. In fact, the Alberta government actively resisted federal attempts to preserve traditional Indian hunting and trapping practices, claiming: "we are trying our best to show no partiality to any group of individuals ... the Indian has the same right as the white person to a registered trap line."[65] The province did little to support the protective federal policy.

Legislatively, the Branch also tried to support the traditional animal-harvesting economy of the northern Indian bands. According to Frank Tough, in the process of drafting the NRTA the federal government sought to broadly protect Indian treaty hunting and trapping rights from provincial encroachment. In the final text of the agreement, Indian resource use was circumscribed by the following paragraph:

> In order to secure to the Indians of the Province the continuance of the supply of game and fish for their support and subsistence, Canada agrees that the laws respecting game in force in the Province from time to time shall apply to the Indians within the boundaries thereof, provided, however, that the said Indians shall have the right, which the Province hereby assures to them, of hunting, trapping and fishing game and fish for food at all seasons of the year on all unoccupied Crown lands and on any other lands to which the said Indians may have a right of access.[66]

Indian animal harvesting was limited by this agreement to harvesting for food purposes only. In practice, this meant that Indian commercial use of wildlife was limited from 1930 onwards, though Tough contends that this was not the original purpose of the NRTA. In Tough's view, the drafters of the NRTA did not intend to modify the treaty rights granted Indian bands of Alberta, though in practice this did occur.[67]

Paradoxically, despite its policy of working cooperatively with the province to protect Indian harvesting rights, the federal government contributed to the limitation of those rights. At an early date, Alberta Indian peoples were subject to the Migratory Birds Convention Act, 1917, the legislative extension of a treaty entered into by Britain, on behalf of Canada, and the United States to restrict the hunting of migratory birds. This treaty did allow Indian peoples to hunt certain non-game birds for food purposes, but the overall intent of the act was to intentionally and severely limit Indian hunting in favour of conservation. The federal government did not consider its moral, constitutional, and treaty obligations to Indian peoples to be an obstacle to the implementation of this act.[68]

Later, in the 1930s and 1940s, the federal government contributed further to the undermining of Indian treaty harvesting rights by failing to support their assertion. Following the passage of the NRTA, the Alberta government gradually began to regulate Indian animal harvesting through provincial legislation and orders-in-council. By the late 1930s, the province was already informing Indian Affairs that treaty Indian hunters and trappers were to be licensed and subject to all the rules and regulations outlined in the provincial game laws.[69] The province also began to insist upon the equal treatment of Indian and White trappers. By 1944 this "equal" treatment manifested itself in delays in the granting of Indian licences, the slow processing of Indian applications, and the direct billing of Indians for trapline fees.[70] In some cases, the provincial field personnel in charge of trapline registration were giving preference to White trappers because Indians were thought to have too much territory available to them already.[71] Indians were also viewed as inefficient trappers as they worked communally when the province wanted them to work individually, "on the same basis as the white man, making them more independent."[72] Federal Indian Agent Iredale astutely noted: "The Provincial Government officials are not in sympathy with the Indian ... On the surface they may appear to be very much concerned, but only on the surface."[73] Further north, Reuben Bull of Goodfish Lake concurred with Iredale, writing to IAA president Gladstone: "I don't for one moment think that our people are getting equal treatment in their fishing, hunting and trapping."[74]

In these situations, the federal government did very little to assert Indian treaty rights or to intervene on behalf of Indian peoples. Lower-level Indian Affairs civil servants noted the province's disregard for Indian treaty rights, but the Branch in Ottawa did little to challenge the province.

The central fact contributing to this lack of federal intervention was the recognized ambiguity of the law regarding harvesting "for food." From the passage of the NRTA onwards, the federal and provincial governments were locked in a conflict over who should determine what constituted hunting, trapping, or fishing for food. During this period, the provincial government was generally accepted as the judge of this central question and was rarely challenged by the federal government. Indian peoples were not consulted. Fur trade historian Arthur Ray also notes that, up until 1945, the Canadian government was extremely reluctant to take on the issue of Aboriginal relief for fear that this would undermine self-initiative. Unfortunately, this reticence on the part of the government came at a time, after the First World War, when overtrapping, fur conservation measures, and increased competition for animal resources between Indian and White hunters caused great need in Indian communities.[75] Where previously the Hudson's Bay Company had taken on Indian welfare in its own interest, after the Second World War neither the company nor the government seemed to be able or willing to handle the problem.

It was into this atmosphere of federal acquiescence to provincial opinion that, in 1950, the IAA plunged in order to better represent the Indian perspective on animal harvesting. Prior to this date, Indian peoples had relied heavily upon Indian Affairs to represent their needs to the provincial government, clearly to little avail. The IAA concerned itself with hunting, trapping, and fishing issues from its founding through the war;[76] however, it was not until 1950 that it sought to permanently establish itself in a liaison role in order to help resolve those issues.

Before 1950 the IAA was preoccupied with the revision of the Indian Act and with gaining social welfare benefits for Indian peoples. By 1950 the IAA executive began to concern itself with more northern issues and the welfare of northern Indian communities. After the war, the north was more easily accessible, and far northern communities such as Fort Vermilion and others along the Athabaska began to petition for IAA attention.[77] As early as 1949, President Gladstone wrote to Secretary Laurie: "I want to say that we are all in great sympathy with the problems of the northern Indians, and we were all very much in favor of trying to assist in having their plight brought to the attention of the white people, so that more interest may be taken by the Government of Alberta as well as Ottawa."[78] Reuben Bull, at Goodfish Lake, also urged the IAA to take more interest in the northern bands, recommending that it "get our northern friends and Indian people to take an active part in our association. Our Indian people up north are far worse off than we are fur is not plentiful and prices are too low."[79] The north became a new focus for the IAA, and, as a result, treaty harvesting rights increased in prominence in IAA discussions.

Specifically, the IAA publicly supported the case of a group of Indian hunters who were arrested in 1950 for shooting female and calf moose. In this case, in late February a group of thirteen Indian hunters from the Saddle Lake Agency travelled a great distance to Edson country in search of meat for the elders in their community. The assistant agent of the agency gave the Indians a letter of permission, indicating to the provincial authorities that this hunt was intended to generate meat for the old and destitute Indians on the Saddle Lake reserve. The hunt was successful, and the Indians managed to harvest elk, deer, and moose, some cows and some calves. Trouble started for the hunters when the provincial fish and game commissioner received a deluge of complaints from sport hunters throughout the province in connection with the shooting of big game, particularly cows and calves. At this point the province decided to charge the Indians with unlawfully harvesting female and juvenile game as a test case. In the words of the provincial fish and game commissioner: "Indians must obey the game laws of the province but may, throughout the year, shoot big game for food. We are of the opinion that as the shooting of cows and calves of the three species ... is illegal under the [Game] Act, that the continuance of shooting by Indians beyond the regular game season for residents of the province should be confined to the shooting of male animals only."[80] This statement clearly outlines the province's view that it was empowered to determine and to define the right to hunt "for food." Its definition, in this case, was not liberal.

When notified of the charges and the situation, Indian Affairs decided to let the *Edson* case go to court rather than attempt to negotiate a settlement. The regional supervisor of the Indian agencies in Alberta, George Gooderham, opined: "In previous hunts these Indians have been given considerable latitude by the Provincial authorities and it would now appear that they have abused the privilege. However, I believe this is a matter which must be decided by the courts."[81] Indian Affairs, not confident about the meaning of the treaty right, was not eager to assert that right liberally. In order to defend the accused the Department of Justice appointed lawyer Neil Primrose to the case.

Initially, the role played by the IAA in this situation was that of interested observer. Upon notification of the action initiated by the provincial government, the IAA took measures to ensure that the accused would have adequate legal protection by beginning arrangements for IAA legal advisor Ruth Gorman to take over the case on behalf of the accused, should this become necessary. IAA secretary Laurie was worried that the case might represent an attempt by sport hunters in the province to deprive Indians of hunting rights except on reserve. This represented a breach of the treaties, specifically Treaty 6.[82] Laurie contacted Indian agency supervisor Gooderham upon receiving news of the case and immediately volunteered legal assistance to the accused, but Gooderham advised the IAA to wait for a response from Indian Affairs.

The case was tried in a magistrate's court in Edson on 17 June 1950. The judge dismissed the charges against all the Indian hunters involved, ruling that hunting for food was in keeping with the terms of Treaty 6 and that, according to the treaty, animals of either sex or any age could be taken.[83] On this basis he ruled that the province had no claim against the Indian hunters. Despite this seeming victory for the Indian hunters and their treaty rights, however, the province continued to pursue Indian hunters who violated the Game Act in their quest for food, and seizures of meat continued.

As a result of the *Edson* case, the IAA began to monitor the provincial attitude towards Indian harvesting rights more closely. In 1952, following another set of seizures of animal meat, the IAA pioneered its liaison role with the suggestion that tripartite talks be held involving the IAA (as Indian representative), the province, and Indian Affairs. In an unprecedented move, the IAA approached the provincial minister of lands and forests, Mr. Tanner, to support a round-table conference "where each group may speak its own mind openly."[84] In his letter to the minister, in an attempt to win a sympathetic ear, IAA secretary Laurie took a conciliatory tone, saying that game management was a problem in Alberta only because of "unusual friction and misunderstanding between the native people and the administrators" of the province.[85] The letter was also vetted by Supervisor Gooderham in a strategic attempt to bring the federal service on side. Ultimately, however, the IAA challenged the province's right to undermine the rights conferred upon Indian peoples by the Royal Proclamation of 1763, the treaties, the NRTA, and the decision of Magistrate Thomson.

Much to the IAA's credit, both the Indian Affairs Branch and the provincial representatives agreed to tripartite round-table discussion on game management and harvesting issues, although the meeting was not held until the following year, 1953. This represented one of the first opportunities for the two divisions of government to meet directly with Indian representatives to discuss treaty rights issues related to animal harvesting. At this meeting, not surprisingly, the province revealed its view that, since the province paid Indians old age assistance, and that the provision of food to Indian communities was the responsibility of the federal government, the province was correct in its seizure of what it perceived to be illicitly obtained animal meat. At the same meeting the federal representative did not appear willing to consider game management strategies in partnership with the province. The most favourable concession to come out of the meeting was that both provincial and federal representatives agreed to have Indian representatives present at further meetings. The IAA achieved its goal of promoting the Indian perspective at inter-government meetings. Laurie was quietly optimistic that the meeting might give Indian peoples a new advantage in their attempts to assert their treaty rights. After the meeting he wrote as follows to Indian Affairs: "Perhaps if the various Indians were fully taken into the confidence of both province and Branch and the right psychological approach were made, some gentlemen's agreement of a very temporary nature might be made, with every possible assurance being made that the Treaties still stood pre-eminent over any such agreement."[86]

Fishing rights were also a priority for the IAA. Fish continued to be an important food source in many Indian communities, particularly those located on lake shores and those in more northern agencies, including Edmonton, Athabaska, and Saddle Lake. In 1949 the IAA began actively petitioning both the federal and provincial governments for the protection of treaty fishing rights, following a dramatic revision of Alberta's special fishery regulations. The federal Fisheries Act governed fishing throughout Canada, and, in each province, regulations could be added to the act by the respective provincial government; however, these regulations did require the approval of the federal government. In 1949 the new fishing regulations allowed licensed Indian fishers to use nets of no more than 100 yards for domestic food fishing purposes at any time, north of Township 62, with the permission of a game officer. South of Township 62, however, fishing for food in this manner was limited to two days per week.[87] This represented a substantive restriction of fishing times available to the southern Indian communities, who were previously permitted to fish for food on a daily basis.

The IAA vehemently protested this restriction of Indian fishing activity in 1949, calling the regulation "contrary to the spirit of the Treaties" and stating: "we protest also starvation by legislation ... without consultation with the Indians, with Superintendents, with the Regional Supervisor, all of whom are better aware of local conditions and local needs."[88] Again, the province was shown to be in control of defining what constituted harvesting "for food" under the NRTA, and the IAA sought to remedy the situation by encouraging both divisions of government to consider the Indian perspective on this critical issue.

Change to these restrictions was not quick in coming, however. Over the next five years the province, the DIA, and the IAA all wrangled with the question of fishing rights. When confronted with the issue of fishery restrictions, the federal government claimed that it accepted the regulations in the spirit of conservation, although the minister responsible for Indian Affairs openly admitted that the fishing regulations in Alberta were, in some respects, "in contravention of conditions contained in their original treaties."[89] In a concession to the IAA, an interdepartmental committee was set up to study and report on the commitments made to the Indians. When the committee reported that, indeed, in several instances commitments made to Indians through the treaties were being circumvented, both the province and the federal government conceded that the regulations be changed "to comply with commitments made through Indian treaties."[90] Clearly, IAA pressure on both divisions of government helped to achieve some recognition of Indian treaty rights. By involving itself with both governments, the IAA also revealed some of the contradictions in government handling of treaty rights.

From the early 1950s onwards, the IAA was recognized as a source of Indian opinion on local matters, and the organization asserted its new status as a liaison by frequently contacting the provincial government on resource matters. Beginning in 1953, upon invitation, both federal and provincial civil servants regularly attended IAA general meetings. Through IAA meetings, a dialogue between opened up between the DIA and the province pertaining to matters of concern to Indian peoples. Although there is little indication that, as a result of this dialogue, matters of pressing concern to Indian communities were addressed faster then they had been in the past, the IAA did promote the consideration of Indian perspectives in government circles and it did reveal the lack of government consistency in dealing with treaty rights.

The *Hobbema* Case, 1957

Although the IAA increasingly involved itself in government negotiations and facilitated talks between the two divisions of government, it did so from a weakened position. Between 1954 and 1957 the IAA suffered from a lack of strong and directed leadership. Secretary Laurie's progressive heart disease made him frequently tired and unable to fulfill his usual duties. In addition, a leadership struggle within the association pitted southern groups against northern groups.[91] In the mid-1950s Albert Lightning, a founding and influential member of the IAA from Hobbema, and Clarence McHugh, who valiantly struggled to establish a solid IAA local in the Blackfoot reserve community, vied for control of the association. This power struggle limited substantive new action on the part of the IAA and contributed to its focus on local issues.

When Clarence McHugh assumed the IAA's presidency in 1954, John Laurie, who held such central power in the association, took an immediate dislike to him because McHugh failed to fit Laurie's image of a "real" Indian.[92] McHugh, a farmer on the Blackfoot reserve, was also known to be a very serious individual whose approach to political life was not particularly flexible.[93] Laurie, with his romantic sensibilities, had a rather stereotypical image of how Indian leaders should be, and, unfortunately, McHugh failed to live up to it. Subsequently, Laurie did little to support his presidency, eventually taking from 1954 through 1955 off in order to recover his health. Premier Manning of Alberta donated land in Canmore to Laurie, where a small log cabin was constructed by Laurie's Stoney friends. Here Laurie spent the year convalescing in the mountain air.[94] This situation undoubtedly contributed to Laurie distancing himself from McHugh. McHugh remained president from 1954 through 1955 and was replaced in 1956 by Albert Lightning at the annual elections, which were held on the Blood reserve that year. Lightning had been prominent in the IAA since its founding and was eager for a leadership role. A rancher with a great love for horses, he was from the Ermineskin band and was influential in the Cree reserve communities around Hobbema. Thus, he represented a contrast to McHugh, whose connections were focused upon the south of the province. Lightning only held the position of president for a short period. Later he chose to turn his attention to the spiritual needs of his community, eventually leaving the political arena behind.[95] Due to his poor health, Laurie officially retired as secretary that year, and his long-time friend and fellow IAA member David Crowchild took over his duties.[96] Laurie did not abandon the IAA, however, taking on the less strenuous position of treasurer.

Not until late 1956 did the IAA confront a pressing issue that forced it to assert its independence and to challenge the same federal government it had struggled so long to involve in dialogue. The crisis in this case involved the Indian Affairs' decision to remove 122 members of the Samson band from their reserve because, under the Indian Act, they did not qualify as "status" Indians. The IAA challenged the evictions and, with the assistance of Ruth Gorman, it filed an appeal. The Alberta District Court in Edmonton heard the case from late February through March 1957. The question of Samson Band memberships had been raised as early as 1952, however, no final decision was reached until the court delivered its judgment in 1957.

The *Samson* case, as it was known, is significant because it generated a great deal of publicity for the IAA and reveals the extent to which Indian issues were rooted in politics rather than in the law during this period. In the 1950s the IAA had little opportunity to pursue treaty rights or self-government for Indian communities on any grand scale because it lacked either constitutional or statutory support. Moreover, it was locked into a relationship with the DIA whereby negotiations and compromise were the prerequisites for participating in the Canadian political system. The IAA's involvement in the 1957 court case represents a culmination of its efforts to gain access to and experience in the Canadian political system. The strategy the IAA employed in addressing the Samson expulsions was basically an extension of the strategy it had employed in defence of Indian rights in hunting and fishing questions (and in the revising of the Indian

Act). Interestingly, this case was one of the last acts of the original IAA leadership. Following it, the IAA founders, including men like John Laurie, James Gladstone, and David Crowchild, gradually devolved their power to a newer and younger generation who, in the 1960s, chose to pursue questions in a different manner. Where the IAA of the 1950s was drawn into the Canadian political routine, the IAA of the 1960s was not.

In his analysis of the *Samson* case, legal historian Douglas Sanders suggests that it is of interest "for its place in the political re-emergence of Indian questions in post-war Canadian political life."[97] Sanders's remark is strangely general and does little to help us understand the degree of Indian involvement in Canada's political life in the years before the case. With an awareness of the IAA's political involvement prior to the *Samson* case, it is easy to understand why it was fought in the political arena as well as in the courts. The IAA was well versed in political strategy and routine by the time the Samson case went to court. Overall, Sanders's generalization might be refined to suggest that the case shows the degree to which Indian peoples had politicized themselves in order to solve pressing social questions.

The mechanics of the case were fairly straightforward. A new definition of "Indian" was entrenched in the 1951 revised Indian Act, and this concerned the IAA a great deal. Under the new act, legitimate Indians were those who were "legitimate" descendants of individuals who had signed treaties; illegitimate Indians were those who accepted scrip, those who were descendants of those who had accepted scrip, those who were enfranchised, or women married to non-Indians. According to the new act all "Indians" recognized by the government as "status Indians" were registered on a list maintained by Indian Affairs. Under these new rules, the government decided to update the registry lists in 1951, and, in accordance with the Indian Act, the registrar was required to post the existing list of members of each Indian band in a prominent place on the reserve. Individuals had the opportunity to have names added to or removed from the posted lists for six months following their posting. Applications to have names removed from the list were called "protests" and could come from within the community itself. Each protest was investigated by a special commission set up specifically for this purpose. Following investigation by the commission, the final decision to register or de-register any individual lay with the registrar, whose decision was final, subject to an appeal to the courts.

In the case of the Hobbema reserve, 103 individuals from the Johnson and Lightning families who claimed membership in the Samson band were "protested" by other members of the same band in 1952, within the six month period allowed for protests under the new act. Albert Lightning, prominent IAA member, was among those slated for eviction. The protest was based on the allegation that three ancestors of those protested had accepted scrip instead of signing onto treaty. As a result they were considered to be non-treaty Indians. According to the press at the time, the protests were either based purely on greed (the Hobbema reserves received large royalties due to the oil found there) or personal feuds.[98] To members of the Hobbema community, the matter of defining who was considered "registered" and who not was very confusing. In a letter to the Friends of the Indians, members of the Montana band wrote, "as it is now we cannot understand at all which way the Government is driving at. The Government tells the Indians to forget the old times and yet they are digging it up which does not make any sense to the Indians."[99] To members of the community, many of whom spoke no English, the issue of whose ancestors took scrip and whose had not was either irrelevant, unknown, or incomprehensible.

In keeping with Indian Affairs process, a commission was appointed to investigate the question on 19 February 1952, but its findings, which were made public in 1954, were not in favour of the protests.[100] The case was not dropped there, however. Based on the finding of new evidence, another round of hearings was held in July 1955. This time the commission upheld the protests, and, by November 1956, the registrar issued notices for the eviction of the families from the reserve. Those evicted were given three months to either leave the reserve or to appeal the case to a district court.

At this point the IAA became prominently involved in the case. Members of the Hobbema community facing eviction approached John Laurie in 1954, even before the first round of hearings, and, at that time, Laurie recommended Ruth Gorman to act as their counsel. Laurie, however, initially wanted to keep the IAA out of the hearings.[101]Only when the issue became more pressing and the expulsions seemed inevitable did the IAA intervene. Upon notice that the registrar had ruled to evict, the IAA launched a massive campaign aimed at drawing popular attention to the plight of those selected for eviction.

The strategy employed by the IAA in this instance was firmly based in its history of lobbying and influencing both the government and the public. In the late summer of 1956, Gorman presented the issue to the Civil Liberties Section of the Canadian Bar Association. She and John Laurie began a publicity drive that saw them deliver over eighty-one speeches on the subject, gaining the support of a variety of "outside" organizations such as church groups and women's associations interested in Indian matters.[102] Press coverage of the issue was also arranged through IAA connections with the *Calgary Herald*. In a series of articles, this newspaper portrayed the actions of the government in an unfavourable light; relevant sections of the Indian Act were described as having "Star Chamber" attributes, and the impending trial was referred to as a "race trial."[103] In addition, the IAA sent a petition protesting the sections of the Indian Act dealing with band membership and evictions to the Governor General – a petition that was to be forwarded to the Queen.[104] This document emphasized the sacred nature of the treaties and neatly sidestepped the issue of the *Samson* case at Hobbema in the hope that this would prevent it from ending up in the hands of the Department of Justice. The petition asked the Queen to intercede on behalf of the Indians to restore the terms of treaty, which had been broken by the Indian Act.[105] Finally, the IAA requested its usual parliamentary supporters to raise the injustice of the evictions in the House of Commons.[106] In its public statements, the IAA asserted two main principles: (1) the Indian Act was too autocratic; (2) commissioners should not be allowed to concern themselves with band membership.

Using the press, Parliament, and petitions, the IAA brought pressure to bear on the minister of citizenship and immigration (then responsible for Indian Affairs) and the Liberal government. By not filing for appeal through the courts until the last possible minute, the IAA made this pressure last as long as possible. Gorman believed that the only way to win the case was to make it a political issue: "I knew I couldn't win the case so I stirred up public rage ... this got the attention of Ottawa."[107] The negative exposure that the *Samson* case generated for the Liberal government was an embarrassment. Then minister for Indian Affairs, Jack Pickersgill, later recalled that the events made him seem cruel and inhumane:

> I had no legal power to interfere with the decision of the Registrar and the only answer I could give was to advise the complainants to appeal to the courts. Some of the newspapers in Alberta and the Conservative Opposition led by Diefenbaker took up the hue and cry in 1957 ... I was portrayed as arbitrary, arrogant, and inhumane. This abuse was hard to take ... the long agitation had strengthened the impression in Alberta that the government was arrogant and indifferent to human distress.[108]

The IAA's negative publicity campaign was intended to embarrass the minister into reversing the registrar's decision. Unfortunately, the IAA was unsuccessful in achieving this goal. In a February 1957 letter to Reta Rowan of the Friends of the Indians Society, solicitor Gorman noted with despair: "One letter from St. Laurent saying he will personally look into the situation is the only encouraging note – none from Pickersgill."[109] Government procedure and policy remained little affected.

As Sanders points out, however, Gorman and the IAA had little reason to fear the case might be lost. In hindsight band membership cases such as the one at Hobbema, when taken to court elsewhere in the country, were generally won by the complainants on humanitarian grounds.[110] Indeed, when the *Samson* case was finally ruled on by Justice Buchanan of the District Court of Northern Alberta, the expulsion orders were reversed and the Johnson and Lightning families were allowed to remain band members on reserve.

Ultimately, the main results of the case were threefold. First, the case damaged the Liberal's democratic and humane image, and boosted the image of Diefenbaker's Conservative Opposition on the eve of a federal election. On the one hand, it could be argued that the IAA was being conveniently used by an Opposition that, like the federal government, had little interest in Indian issues. On the other hand, the publicity did gain some attention for the IAA: following the judgment on the case, concerned citizens rallied to support the IAA in Calgary by forming a special IAA advisory council to act as a learned resource for the association with regard to legal questions such as those pertaining to the *Samson* case.[111] Clearly, the case affected public sentiment in favour of the IAA and its attempts to improve conditions for reserve communities.

Second, the *Samson* case represented one of the few times the IAA directly confronted the federal government and challenged Indian Affairs through the courts. Prior to this event, the IAA used negotiation as its preferred method of interaction with the government, and this enabled Indian Affairs to actively promote the co-optation of such organizations. In the end the case did not produce any useful legal precedents in favour of Indian rights; the value of the event lay in the public support it gained for the plight of Indian peoples subject to the Indian Act. Only in the 1960s and 1970s would the courts play a significant role in the assertion of Indian rights. With regard to the *Samson* case, it represented a political victory rather than a legal success.

Third, the *Samson* case marked one of the last occasions upon which John Laurie exercised his influence on behalf of the association in which he had participated for almost twelve years. Laurie established much of the strategy employed by Ruth Gorman and the IAA during the Hobbema investigations. His tactics proved successful in reaffirming the effectiveness of Indian political action in the public arena, even if the "politicking" did little to advance the Indian cause within Ottawa and the Branch. After the *Samson* case, Laurie removed himself from IAA activities, resigned from his teaching job, and spent his time documenting Stoney culture for the Glenbow Foundation. Although he served as treasurer through 1957-58, he was soon too ill to work at all. The heart condition that plagued him throughout the 1950s finally forced him to curtail his political involvements and relinquish his position of influence to the next generation of IAA leaders. His death in the spring of 1959 closed a chapter in the history of the IAA – a chapter that emphasized integrating Indian peoples into the Canadian political system.

James Gladstone, who served as IAA president from 1950 to 1954 and from 1957 to 1958, also distanced himself from the daily operations of the

IAA after the Hobbema trial. Gladstone developed a close relationship with Laurie, and together they worked out much of the strategy employed by the IAA in its relations with the government throughout the 1950s. Gladstone attended many of the Indian-government conferences in Ottawa and was a central figure in the negotiations leading up to the revision of the Indian Act. Like John Laurie, Gladstone was well known in Ottawa. When, after the *Samson* case at Hobbema, a federal election was held and Diefenbaker's Conservatives replaced St. Laurent's Liberals, the new government approached Gladstone with a significant appointment. Committed to dealing with Indian issues, Diefenbaker offered the former IAA president a senatorship.[112] Gladstone did not actively seek this appointment, but this event does reveal the extent to which the IAA and its leaders were known in Ottawa. Through this senatorship, the IAA was finally fully integrated into the Canadian political routine.

The *Samson* case marked a turning point in the history of the IAA. With the retirement of two significant leaders, the death of founding president Johnny Callihoo in the summer of 1957, and a new federal Conservative government publicly committed to improving conditions for Canada's registered Indian population, the IAA faced a new set of political agendas with a new set of political leaders. The years from 1948 to 1957 were significant because, during this decade, the IAA was drawn into the Canadian political routine. At the 1958 annual meeting the IAA promoted a set of ideals that reflected its new orientation and that prominently featured the desire "to cooperate with the Federal Government on all matters in which aims do not clash."[113]

In contrast to its first decade of operation, during the 1950s the IAA was less concerned with targeting specific government policies than it was in pursuing a handful of basic issues. During this decade the federal government emphasized Indian education and employment, housing, and leadership programs. The IAA, in turn, was interested in improving not only Indian education and medical services, but also in asserting treaty hunting and fishing rights, protecting the self-determining ability of local communities, and ensuring that the Indian Act protected Indian interests. However, the IAA's interaction with the government continued to be conservative in tone. The association participated in government-arranged conferences and did little to challenge government agendas. This was in keeping with its desire to cooperate with Ottawa, and with its attempts to gain influence within Indian Affairs. The IAA continued to seek reform of Indian Affairs policy, as it had in the first decade of its operations, however, during the 1950s social welfare issues were of less concern than were issues pertaining to the Indian Act and to treaties. By the 1960s the question of treaty rights would gradually assume primary importance in Indian-government relations.

8
Political Visions: Diefenbaker to Trudeau

> Let us all work together. In unity there is strength. Let every person and every Local work for the Association. If we fail, we are failing ourselves.
>
> – IAA President John Samson, IAA annual meeting, 1962[1]

> To us who are Treaty Indians there is nothing more important than our Treaties, our lands and the well-being of our future generation.
>
> – The Indian Chiefs of Alberta, *Citizens Plus* (1970)[2]

The late 1950s marked the end of an era for the Indian Association of Alberta. In the early 1960s it experienced a period of relative weakness, only finding a new direction in 1968. Despite its weak position in the 1960s, between 1939 and 1957 the IAA successfully brought itself and the concerns of status Indian peoples to the attention of the federal government, the provincial government of Alberta, and the Canadian public. It forged a united voice among the varied Indian communities in Alberta, and it gave direction to many of the popular feelings about treaties as well as about the social, political, and economic issues facing reserves in the province. However, by the late 1950s many of the founding members of the association were retiring, and those who carried on the struggle were suffering from ill health. As a result, in order to survive, the IAA was forced to reinvent itself in the 1960s. Not until a young president representing a new generation was successfully elected in 1968 was the IAA able to transform itself and to enter a new era of action.

Between 1957 and 1959, three main events marked the closing of the first phase of the IAA's existence: (1) the end of Liberal rule, (2) the loss of James Gladstone, and (3) the loss of John Laurie. First, the fall of the long-lived federal Liberal government in 1957 marked the end of almost two decades of interaction between the IAA and Liberal ministers. Whereas for many years the IAA relied upon the Conservative Opposition for support in Parliament and for criticism of Liberal policy, suddenly the Conservative party was now in control. Conservative MPs elevated to Cabinet positions, including Douglas Harkness, E. Davie Fulton, and John Diefenbaker, now offered the IAA influential positions from which to press for Indian demands. Second, in 1958 James Gladstone, an original IAA supporter and a long-time executive member, accepted a position in the Senate offered to him by Prime Minister Diefenbaker. Gladstone's move to the Senate marked a great loss to the IAA but further bolstered the legitimacy of the association within the Canadian political system. Third, in 1959 the death of John Laurie, the highly regarded executive secretary of the IAA, truly closed a chapter in the history of the IAA. Laurie infused the association with many of his ideas, and, until 1959, he astutely controlled much of its agenda. His death marked the opportunity for a new and younger generation to assume leadership of the IAA and to take it in new directions. The changeover did not occur overnight, however. For several years the IAA executive struggled to keep the association going. Gradually, the IAA assumed a new emphasis in its politics, increasingly focusing upon treaty rights and changing its constitution to better reflect this new direction. It was not until 1968 that a younger generation of leaders, epitomized by Harold Cardinal, was able to infuse the IAA with new life and openly challenge the government. The presentation of the Red Paper to the government in 1970 marked the end of the old IAA way of operating and initiated a new era of professional politicking in Aboriginal communities.

The Diefenbaker Years: 1957-63

The decline and demise of the federal Liberal government in 1957 ended the IAA's carefully forged relations with Minister Jack Pickersgill. Pickersgill had been involved in the *Hobbema* case and had continued the process of amending the Indian Act in 1955 and 1956. He had also advanced the policy of internal development of Indian communities through vocational training programs, changes to Indian education, housing initiatives, and infrastructural reserve community improvements. Although the minister was never overly friendly with the IAA, he supported the long-standing Liberal policy of cooperating with the association. The change to a Conservative government brought a warming in the IAA's relations with the Indian Affairs Branch.

Following the election of Diefenbaker's Conservatives in 1957, and their achievement of a majority government in 1958, a new minister responsible for Indian Affairs was appointed. This time the minister was a woman: Ellen Fairclough, the first female minister in Canadian history. Unlike her predecessors, Fairclough was very open to the IAA and personally promoted discussions and contact with it. On the surface, this new and friendly relationship appeared to offer the IAA a louder voice in government. Part of Fairclough's positive attitude towards the IAA stemmed from Prime Minister Diefenbaker's personal commitment to Indian issues and civil equality.

Throughout his years in Parliament, Diefenbaker tenaciously supported equal citizenship rights for Indian peoples. While in Opposition, his fiery speeches and sharp arguments were a tremendous asset to the IAA. When he became prime minister in 1957, he carried his support for the Indian community even further. In both his 1957 and 1958 campaigns, Diefenbaker advocated the idea of a bill of rights for Canadians. The draft bill was introduced to the House in 1958 and was meant to entrench equal civil rights for all Canadians into law.[3] An extension of this was initiated by Diefenbaker himself when, in 1960, he granted the federal vote to Indian peoples.

Fairclough had little in her background to connect her to Canada's Indian communities. A well educated middle-class accountant, she was a native of Hamilton and of United Empire Loyalist descent.[4] Fairclough was first elected to the House in 1950, where she quickly took on various important political positions. After 1957 Diefenbaker appointed her secretary of state, and, in 1958, she assumed control over the Indian Affairs administration.[5] Despite her lack of immediate expertise in Indian Affairs, as head of that department Fairclough expressed her appreciation of IAA actions in a letter of greeting sent to the IAA annual meeting in 1959: "I am of course very mindful of the very real contribution already made by your Association towards the progress of Indian citizens in Alberta. These meetings are of value to both the Indian and the administrator and I know that many local problems can be better understood ... by meeting on common ground with the responsible administrators."[6] In the same letter she emphasized how the IAA could contribute to the efficient administration of Indian Affairs as well as to the development of a national Indian point of view. From 1959 onwards, Fairclough directly corresponded with the IAA executive.[7]

The Conservative government endorsed the IAA's past activities and accomplishments by appointing James Gladstone to the Senate in January 1958. Diefenbaker championed the inclusion of an Indian member in the Canadian government system, and, one month after his victory at the polls, John Laurie and Conservative MP Doug Harkness both wrote to him recommending Gladstone for a Senate position.[8] Gladstone was already moving out of IAA politics because of his advanced age and declining health, and he had recently suffered setbacks within the association due to the internal leadership wrangling that plagued the IAA throughout the late 1950s. When Gladstone was offered the Senate position he gladly accepted it and, from that point on, was loyal to the Diefenbaker government.[9] With Gladstone's move to Ottawa the IAA lost an important and seasoned leader. Gladstone continued to promote Indian issues and to monitor IAA activities but never as directly as when he led the association. Interestingly, when, in 1959, the Conservative government further supported the IAA by launching another special joint parliamentary committee to investigate Indian problems, this committee was co-chaired by none other than James Gladstone.[10]

In the late 1950s the IAA not only lost Gladstone, but it also lost John Laurie. As has been said, Laurie suffered severe heart problems for many years, and, in the late 1950s, his health finally deteriorated to the point where he was unable to work. He resigned his public school teaching position in 1956 and drastically scaled back his involvement in the IAA. Gladstone, a long-time friend of Laurie's, was ever concerned about him. In a letter to mutual friend, David Crowchild, Gladstone expressed his feelings: "I got a long letter from Mr. Laurie which made me kind of sad and worried about our dear friend and leader John. He must be quite sick. However I wrote to him and tried to make him feel good. He should not worry too much as that is not helping his health too much."[11] Gladstone and Crowchild tried to help Laurie as much as possible, and they kept him informed of IAA activities when he was ill or hospitalized. In turn, Laurie tried hard to keep involved in the IAA and even wrote letters from his hospital bed. Ruth Gorman recalls that whenever Laurie was hospitalized, crowds of Indian visitors were a common sight in his hospital room. Unfortunately, the IAA finally lost Laurie on 3 April 1959 when, following another bad "spell" with his heart, he died at his apartment.

Laurie's death closed a chapter in the IAA's history. Besides investing a great deal of time, energy, and personal finances in the IAA, Laurie also infused it with a sense of purpose and direction. Although his ideas on Indian issues often differed from those of the membership, he did provide the association with important contacts and credibility in an age when Indian peoples were viewed as politically "inexperienced." At his funeral in Calgary, Indian supporters from around the province crowded into the Anglican cathedral to pay their last respects. Following the service, a procession of some forty cars travelled the old Banff road to the Morley reserve, where a second service was held by members of the Stoney community. Newspaper reports of the proceedings remarked on the crowds that came to acknowledge the work of Laurie. On the reserve, "the little frame McDougall Memorial Church was filled to capacity. An even larger gathering assembled outside in silent mourning. Indian women with their babies in their arms and on their backs sat on the pole fence, and on the steps of the church wiping their tears with their head scarves."[12] Laurie was buried on the reserve, overlooking the Bow River, near his adopted Stoney father Enos Hunter.

A New Generation of Leadership Slowly Emerges: 1959 to 1970

By the early 1960s the IAA had lost a great deal of its original momentum and membership, and sought desperately to maintain itself. Renewal did occur but not before the IAA had changed character and face. The passing of the old IAA leaders, the political instability in Ottawa, and the overhaul of Indian Affairs in the 1960s were all factors that contributed to the transformation of the IAA. Because the political landscape within which it operated was shifting dramatically, the IAA was forced to evolve new methods of operation, new contacts, and new political goals. During these years, the IAA began to turn from its reserve-based roots towards a more urban perspective and to refresh its focus on treaty rights. By 1968 its transformation was complete: in that year a new and dynamic young leader was elected, treaty rights took centre stage, and (almost at the same time) the IAA began to accept federal funds.

In Ottawa many changes to the Indian Affairs and Indian policy were pioneered in the 1960s. One of the most significant events initiating change in Indian policy and within Indian Affairs was the work of the Joint Parliamentary Committee on the Indian Act, of which Senator James Gladstone was the co-chair. The committee was launched in 1959, held hearings from 1959 through 1960, and reported in the summer of 1961. This investigation of the Indian Act and its administration heard representations from Indian leaders across the country, including those from the IAA. The format of the hearings was much the same as that of the hearings held from 1946 to 1948, and virtually all the Indian submissions to the committee reiterated long-standing concerns with social and economic conditions on reserve, Indian Affairs administration, land claims, and treaty rights.[13] Some Indian groups even reintroduced documents they had submitted to hearings in the previous decade. What was remarkable was that the number of associations making representations had increased notably, and established groups (such as the IAA) made very lengthy submissions.

The joint committee made several recommendations, including the refinement of existing Indian administration, the creation of an Indian claims commission, increased community development initiatives for Indian communities, the creation of Indian advisory bodies, and the transfer of Indian services to the provinces.[14] Its overall thrust was to recommend slight reforms in Indian Affairs that would allow the Indian community greater involvement in the management of its own affairs.

The outcome of the final report was the implementation of many of the committee's ideas; indeed, after 1961 the Indian Affairs Branch launched new programs, most of which were aimed at reducing Indian dependence upon the department. These programs encouraged local initiatives in reserve communities and attempts to convince the provinces to deliver social services to Indians within their boundaries. The devolution of Indian education to the provinces was a trend in Indian administration at this time. All in all, this period marked a war on poverty that took the form of community development projects and grants to band councils encouraging Indian self-management.[15] A central goal of the Diefenbaker and Pearson governments (1957-63 and 1963-68, respectively) was to help

Indians move into the mainstream of Canadian life so that they could enjoy the same rights, privileges, and services as were available to all other citizens in Canada.[16] According to the civil servants within the Branch itself, "the reorganization [was] being directed mainly to assisting Indians to achieve self-reliance in the conduct of their affairs, including the social and economic advancement of their communities."[17]

Despite its grand ideals of change, the Indian Affairs Branch was unsuccessful in implementing many of the reforms it was directed to make. The uncertainties of minority government rule characteristic of the mid-1960s appeared to somewhat paralyze the Branch, as its ministers generally held their posts for less than one year, effectively leaving the civil servants within the Branch without political direction.[18] The continuity of senior civil servants in the Branch, on the other hand, was very strong, and Indian Affairs bureaucracy remained rigid. According to Sally Weaver, in her detailed analysis of Indian Affairs between 1968 and 1970, senior officials within the department became discouraged with their work, and their desire for reform diminished by 1967 as the problem of integration versus special rights for Indian peoples came to be seen as intractable.[19] The community development program faltered, and other initiatives such as the Indian advisory boards (which began operations in 1964) were perceived as a waste of time by the Indian peoples who participated in them.[20]

As early as 1964, it had become obvious to those inside and outside Indian Affairs that reform was not occurring at a satisfactory pace. It was believed that major, rather than piecemeal, changes would have to occur in Indian administration if progress were to be made on what the public perceived as the "Indian problem." Indeed, it has been suggested that, by 1964, "from both within and without the IAB [Indian Affairs Branch] progressively lost whatever legitimacy it had possessed" and that, at this time, the branch experienced a breakdown in its authority.[21] From a contemporary perspective:

> Although it is not possible to identify the specific moment at which the existing structure of Indian administration became intolerable in Canada, the years between 1960 and 1964 witnessed the moral collapse of the old order. In 1964, the government gave expression to this general realization by requesting a comprehensive study of the situation as a basis for thorough-going reform [Hawthorn Report] ... climaxed by the Government's New Policy of July 1969, which outlined a policy of termination.[22]

As early as 1967, the federal government recognized that internal reforms within the newly created Department of Indian Affairs (DIA, 1966) would contribute little to its plan of integrating Indian peoples.

Amid increasing public criticism of the department, the government decided that the best solution would be to revise the Indian Act in the hope that this would liberalize relations between the government and its Aboriginal charges. The stage was set for the White Paper of 1969, in which the Liberal government of Pierre Trudeau openly suggested that the Indian Act be repealed.[23]

Against this backdrop of political instability and reform within Indian Affairs, the IAA also struggled. Initially, its main concern was to maintain its position as one of Canada's premiere Indian associations with a close and, it hoped, influential relationship with Indian Affairs officials. In an attempt to remain prominent and to keep involved in Indian Affairs reform, the IAA made a lengthy presentation to the joint committee in 1960, reiterating many of the same concerns regarding reserve poverty and the need for social reform in Indian communities. It also continued its long-standing practice of sending annual petitions and resolutions to Indian Affairs. At the same time, President Howard Beebe assumed a seat on the National Indian Advisory Board, and the IAA involved itself in the new National Indian Council.

Ironically, these IAA initiatives, which were meant to display its strength, also uncovered its weaknesses. Specifically, the IAA leadership was not particularly vital – a fact revealed in a number of realms including, as early as 1960, at the joint committee hearings. The IAA delegation to Ottawa consisted of President Beebe, John Samson, and long-time IAA legal advisor Ruth Gorman. This group was assigned three days in early May in which to bring IAA concerns to the members of the committee. The resolutions to be presented related primarily to self-government, education, and health, and they were drawn together at a special IAA meeting in 1959. They represented resolutions passed in IAA general meetings in the previous sixteen years and were, therefore, a general restatement of the IAA position rather than a new initiative. In addition, the delegates brought with them annotated copies of the Indian Act, a petition containing the signatures of individuals who supported the resolutions, scrap books outlining living conditions on reserves and Indian views on enfranchisement, and separate statements by Ruth Gorman.

When the delegation arrived in Ottawa its president, Howard Beebe of Cardston, relied heavily upon the IAA's legal advisor, Ruth Gorman, to make the representation. Over the course of two days she provided a detailed summary of all the points in the resolutions, significantly opening with a lengthy discussion of treaties, treaty rights, and resolutions on treaty rights. Gorman, an energetic and garrulous individual, also singlehandedly answered all the questions directed to the delegation, speaking on behalf of "the Indians." Beebe spoke on record only a handful of times, yielding to Gorman the opportunity to highlight her point of view at great length. Upon their return home, President Beebe reported at the annual IAA meeting that he felt that "they had made a very successful mission" to Ottawa.[24] At that same meeting he resigned his presidency and took up the post of vice-president, southern region. Two years later, when the recommendations of the joint committee had become public, the IAA protested them in a letter written to Ottawa. The protest was not written by the IAA president, however, but by the honourary secretary, Hugh Dempsey.

The erosion of leadership was also reflected in internal IAA dealings. The long-lived leadership of the previous decades had given way to a leadership within which positions were held for short periods by a number of different individuals. Without judging the personal commitment of the men and women who served on the IAA executive during the 1960s, all of whom appear to have been very dedicated to maintaining the IAA, it seems as though few of them were able to impart their own distinctive vision to the association. President Beebe, for example, continued to lean heavily on the IAA advisory council for direction and appeared often to defer to its expertise. Ralph Steinhauer, in turn, was an individual with strong political skills, but he served as IAA president for only a single term: 1960-61.

The lack of strong leadership was also reflected in a decline in IAA membership during the 1960s. As early as 1961, President Steinhauer, in his opening speech to the IAA general meeting, noted that there had been a drop in membership, and he urged members to work together to build the IAA into a stronger union.[25] By 1964 the membership issue had taken a more critical turn. At the annual meeting, then president John Samson highlighted the weakening of the IAA:

> I have tried to the best of my ability to keep the Indian Association of Alberta moving. I feel that I have failed, especially with the Northern Reserves. I have called three meetings and no one showed up. Membership is on the decline. Maybe the reason is that quite a few new Indian organizations have started up in the last year or so. Perhaps the members feel that these organizations are filling the bill for them, and therefore, are not pushing the Indian Association of Alberta as they should.[26]

Following closely on the heels of the president, Secretary Pauline Dempsey also submitted her resignation, voicing feelings of frustration with the lack of support for the IAA: "I am like the President. I do not feel that I am doing my duties to the fullest for the Indian Association of Alberta. I feel I should retire from this position to let a younger member take over ... I urge you not to let the Association down. It has done us a lot of good."[27]

Last, but not least, at the same meeting even Senator James Gladstone took time to voice his disappointment when he expressed regret that the membership of the IAA was not growing and mentioned the need for bringing in younger members. From the limited sources available, it is not entirely clear what forces were sapping IAA strength in these years; however, the often-changing leadership was most likely a notable factor. Harold Cardinal later suggested that non-Indian supporters of Indian associations, and government initiatives such as the advisory councils, were (albeit indirectly) other significant factors in dissipating the strength of Indian associations at this time.[28]

Despite the challenges facing the IAA, particularly in the area of leadership and membership, it did manage to begin transforming itself into the type of modern political force characterizing contemporary Aboriginal political organizations. Beginning in 1961, it made a start at revitalizing itself: it changed its constitution and, increasingly, turned its attention to the treaties. The revision of the IAA Constitution in 1961 was significant because, for the first time, it limited full membership to treaty Indians. The new constitution opened with a bold statement emphasizing a new direction: "The first constitution and by-laws were passed in 1939. Minor revisions were made during the next few years but in 1961 they were completely rewritten, taking into consideration the changing conditions and responsibilities of the Association."[29]

This revision of membership criteria represented a significant departure from the IAA's original association with Métis peoples. However, such a change was in keeping with the first official "aim" of the IAA: "To maintain Indian treaty rights." The advisory committee was included in the new document, and a new structure was assumed for the executive council. After 1961 the executive council would consist of a president and three vice-presidents (from north, central, and southern regions of the province, respectively). The new executive positions were meant to better reflect the IAA's north/south division as well as underlying treaty differences.

It was not until 1968, however, that the IAA was able to really redirect itself after the inactivity of the mid-1960s. In that year the membership elected a new young president who had long-term family ties to the IAA: Harold Cardinal of Sucker Creek First Nation. Cardinal's father, Frank Cardinal, was a close friend of John Laurie and a founding member of the IAA. The young Cardinal was in his late twenties at the time of his election, and he represented a different generation from that of the previous IAA leaders. Although he was raised on the Sucker Creek reserve, he attended high school in Edmonton and had been to college in Ottawa, where he studied sociology and had worked with the DIA as well as the Canadian Indian Youth Council.

Harold Cardinal proved to be the energetic force needed to propel the IAA back into the national spotlight and to give new voice to its issues.

Cardinal's election to the IAA presidency was heralded by the local Alberta press, with headlines that trumpeted, "Alberta Indians choose leader in Trudeau mold."[30] The election also revealed the old guard's cognizance that new blood and new ways were needed if the association were to survive. Following the younger Cardinal's election, Ralph Steinhauer told the press: "I have been dissatisfied with the way the association has operated. We have to be willing to make some changes. If we don't the association will cease to exist." In turn, the outgoing president Thomas Cardinal admitted: "Our association isn't growing. Something's wrong somewhere. We need young people."[31] Harold Cardinal was an obvious solution to these problems, and, according to news reports, shortly after his election the new leader managed to double IAA membership.[32] Hopes for new directions in Indian politics were evident in both Indian and non-Indian circles.

A final step in changing the IAA from a grassroots reserve-based association to a modern urban First Nations political group was its acceptance of federal funds. Cardinal represented a new approach to Indian political action, and he supported the notion that the work of Indian associations should be handled by full-time professionals in central locations dedicated to the business of negotiating with Ottawa and asserting Indian control over Indian affairs. In his own words:

> The changes over the past five years have posed difficult questions for our leaders. If the organizations are to remain viable as a means through which people can present their grievances for action, then the whole framework of the bodies must be altered ... Much work still can be done on a voluntary basis but the time for purely voluntary assistance has come to an end. Full-time, competent, trained and salaried workers must now carry the bulk of the workload in every office. The problems have increased to the point where the old haphazard, hope-to-get-the-work-done methods are obsolete. This of course means money.[33]

Cardinal represented the first generation of professional First Nations politicians who served on a full-time basis. This represented a significant departure from the former, well established IAA practice of voluntary action. Furthermore, instead of being based within a rural setting, the IAA now held its various meetings in urban locations such as Edmonton, Red Deer, Wetaskewin, and Calgary.

Obviously, few Indian communities in Alberta at this time were able to fund such a professional association on their own. As a result, the IAA began accepting funds from the DIA soon after the department began offering per capita grants to Indian organizations in 1968. Initially, as a form of protest, the IAA turned down a grant from the department. Cardinal objected that the DIA shortchanged the IAA, and he openly wondered whether the reduced funds indicated that the "department wants to stifle the activities of militant native organizations."[34] However, within a year it accepted the federal money in order to cover its operating funds and the salaries of its president and executive.

Initially, Ottawa provided money to Indian associations through two venues. First, the secretary of state sponsored Indian organizations, and, second, the DIA offered per capita funding, starting in 1968. This continued until the summer of 1970, when all grants to Aboriginal organizations were coordinated under the Interdepartmental Committee on Indian Affairs. After 1969, federal funding to Indian groups increased generally. In that year, for example, the IAA received monies from the DIA, the Department of Regional Economic Expansion, the Department of National Health and Welfare, and the Secretary of State – for a total of approximately $320,000. Understandably, this altered the nature of IAA operations, and its budgets quickly doubled and tripled. The funding of regional associations also coincided with the federal government's supporting of a new national-level Indian organization: the National Indian Brotherhood (NIB) (1968), which was created with the support of the IAA to represent the interests of status Indian people across Canada and to advise the federal government on Indian affairs.[35] The bureaucratization of First Nations-State relations was now complete.

Not everyone agreed with integrating Indian associations into the federal budget. In fact, the IAA and Harold Cardinal were singled out as examples of how such close financial ties would corrupt any attempt at improving life for Indian peoples in Canada. William Wuttunee, a Saskatchewan Cree leader who was heavily involved in the National Indian Council (a predecessor of the NIB) launched a vicious attack on Cardinal and the IAA in his book, *Ruffled Feathers: Indians in Canadian Society*, which was published in 1971, shortly after the IAA and other associations began the extensive use of federal funds. Wuttunee directly attacked the salaries of IAA executives under the new government funding scheme, stating: "It seems odd indeed that the hierarchy of the Indian Association of Alberta should pay themselves such exorbitant salaries, bearing in mind the poverty in which so many of the Indian people live."[36] He went on to say: "Although many leaders threaten the federal government by waving verbal tomahawks over their heads in an apparent struggle for better treatment for the Indian, they are in fact exploiting their own people."[37] And Wuttunee was not shy to mark Cardinal as a "bitter person," as a reactionary and a conservative, whose ideas on treaties were outdated.[38] Wuttunee was harsh in his judgment, and he may have been predisposed to criticize the IAA, which had rejected his overtures to have the association involved in the National Indian Council, as early as 1965.

Wuttunee was not the only one who was suspicious of government funding for Aboriginal organizations. In Alberta, Métis leaders such as Adrian Hope chose to leave Aboriginal politics when government funds came into play. Saskatchewan's Maria Campbell, then active in both the IAA and the Métis Association of Alberta, also retreated from politics when government funds began to support Aboriginal political activity. This turn of events corroborates what Joe Sawchuk, historian of the MAA, has noted: "A different type of political candidate began to emerge" at this time, and "leaders who were suspicious of government funding, or who were considered to be backward or old-fashioned by government agents, were shunted aside."[39] It appears that this trend in Métis politics was also echoed in the IAA. Certainly, Cardinal was part of a new generation of leadership that was representing and promoting new ideas.

Despite criticism from individuals such as Wuttunee and others, Cardinal's tenure as president of the IAA is remarkable because it initiated a new approach to First Nations political action. Under his guidance the association very quickly changed its methods of operation and its priorities. Although some have called Cardinal the "*enfant terrible* of Indian politics,"[40] he was a forceful speaker and presence on the national scene at a time when Aboriginal issues were very much in the public eye. In its new incarnation, the IAA adopted yet another constitution, this time basing membership upon bands rather than upon individuals, and, among other things, it began offering service programs for Alberta's First Nations in addition to conducting its political advisory and lobby work. Where previously the IAA and its "outside help" had resisted actively pursuing treaty rights, by the late 1960s the IAA had fully assumed the role of advertising, asserting, and defending treaty rights in the public arena. In his meetings with the press and within other public forums, Harold Cardinal took many opportunities to refer to the treaties. These activities stood in contrast to those of John Laurie and former IAA presidents, who, in the 1940s and 1950s, had resisted making treaty rights an obvious focus, choosing instead to draw attention to social and economic issues facing First Nations communities.

Cardinal's election as president of the IAA came at an auspicious moment in the history of Aboriginal-federal government relations. As mentioned previously, beginning in 1963 the Liberal government had been investigating different options in an attempt to determine how best to update federal Indian policies. In that year the federal government commissioned Harry B. Hawthorn of British Columbia to conduct a national survey of Canadian Indians. The launch of yet another round of investigations into Aboriginal communities was not surprising. Similar large-scale reports were being commissioned on Indian peoples in the United States throughout the 1960s, and, according to Sally Weaver (historian of The Hawthorne Report), public demand and civil service disenchantment with contemporary Indian policy spurred the DIA to authorize the Hawthorn report.[41]

The scope of the Hawthorn Report was to be broad, and its two volumes were complete by 1967. The main conclusions of the report, which was very detailed and yet conducted without Aboriginal input, included the idea that First Nations status within Canada should be recognized as that of "citizens plus." The report was based on the philosophy that Indian peoples, as charter members of the Canadian community, possessed certain rights in addition to the normal rights and duties of citizenship. The report also stressed that Indian political groups should be supported actively by the government and that Indian peoples should be put in charge of decision making that affects their futures.[42] Although the report was considered useful in terms of its data, it was not well received in 1968, when Pierre Trudeau and his new Liberal government took office and sought direction on Indian policy. Despite the detail of the Hawthorn Report, and its many recommendations, the Prime Minister's Office was sceptical of its value because it flew in the face of Liberal notions of equality.[43] Although information from the report was considered noteworthy, its recommendations were not implemented. On the other hand, between 1969 and 1970, the report's conclusions did become important tools for Cardinal and the IAA.

Red Paper and White Paper: Final Steps towards Changing Aboriginal Politics

The actions taken by Trudeau's Liberals between 1968 and 1971 in the realm of Indian affairs are well described in the literature dealing with Aboriginal politics. In fact, these events are probably among the most analyzed and investigated in modern Canadian Aboriginal political history. Not suprisingly, as one of Canada's oldest and most established Aboriginal political organizations, the IAA also played a significant role in the events of this time.

Specifically, in June 1969 the Trudeau government released a proposed new Indian policy in the form of the White Paper. The White Paper on Indian Affairs was the product of a year of meetings and discussions between Indian leaders, members within the civil service, and Trudeau's new ministers. Trudeau had placed Indian policy on the new government's priority list, yet his regime had not prepared any specifics on how the "Indian problem" should be handled at the time of assuming office. In July 1968 the Liberal government issued a booklet entitled *Choosing a Path*, which, for the purpose of future discussions, was meant to outline the government's stance on issues related to the Indian Act and Indian claims. It also contained questions for Indian leaders to consider before meeting with government representatives. Following the issuance of this booklet, across the country the government hosted meetings with Indian leaders and, subsequently, set about formulating new Indian policy in the winter of 1968/69. Sally Weaver's analysis of the policy-making process gives insight into the bristling politics and battles occurring behind closed doors in Trudeau's government during those months. In her view, "by mid-January 1969, 'the problem' was less how to solve the Indian problem and more how to solve the policy-making problem."[44]

The IAA was suspicious of the federal government's consultation meetings throughout 1968, and it resisted pressure to accommodate the desire of federal officials to focus discussions only on the Indian Act. It was also felt that Indian peoples were given little chance to prepare their point of view. Harold Cardinal told the *Edmonton Journal* that he felt that the consultation meetings were "a trap. They are consulting us without giving us a chance of getting together." Other Indian leaders from western Canada, including the head of Canada's only national-level Indian organization, Walter Dieter, believed that suggestions made by Indian leaders would not be implemented.[45] As a result, the IAA requested that the government postpone until December the consultation meetings planned with it for August. By that time, the IAA planned to hire its own lawyer so that it would not to be "out-gunned" by the federal representatives. During this interim period, Cardinal took it upon himself to tour reserve communities in order to prepare band governments for the meetings.[46] Throughout the winter Cardinal's focus was upon negotiation and upon giving a high profile to Indian peoples' positions. His comments to the press in early 1969 revealed his perspective on Canadian society as well as how he felt about working within the system: "I don't agree with Red Power or a violent philosophy ... Strengthening Indian organizations and working closely with non Indians is the only viable alternative ... We are dealing with a very gullible white society."[47]

Finally, after much anticipation, the Liberals released their policy proposal in the early summer of 1969, just before the House of Commons' summer recess. Entitled "Statement of the Government of Canada on Indian Policy, 1969," but known popularly as the White Paper, the short document represented a compromise policy. Generally, it was in keeping with Liberal philosophy and, for the most part, side-stepped Indian peoples' long-standing historic grievances over land and treaties. In a nutshell, the document outlined the rationale behind a government plan to remove what it considered to be those factors keeping Indian peoples "apart" from the rest of Canadian society. The document states: "The road of different status [is] a road which has led to a blind alley of deprivation and frustration. This road, because it is a separate road, cannot lead to full participation, to equality in practice as well as in theory."[48] Thus, the policy proposed measures that would lead Indian peoples away from "different" status towards full economic, social, and political participation in Canadian life. The measures needed to do this included, among other things: folding the DIA; removing the legislative and constitutional bases of discrimination; repealing the Indian Act; devolving to the provinces responsibility for delivering services to Indian peoples; and appointing a commissioner to adjudicate Indian claims. What was perhaps most notable and significant to the IAA was that the policy stated: "The significance of the treaties in meeting the economic, educational, health and welfare needs of the Indian people has always been limited and will continue to decline ... the anomaly of treaties between groups within society and the government of that society will require that these treaties be reviewed to see how they can be equitably ended."[49] Given the history of the IAA's defence of treaty rights, no suggestion like this could be expected to gain its acceptance. The White Paper was clearly an attack on a principle that, since 1939, the IAA had quietly sought to protect: the sacredness of the treaties.

Indian leaders' responses to the policy document were originally mixed but rapidly became negative. At first Harold Cardinal welcomed the demise of the DIA, but he later took a more critical stance. By November 1969 Cardinal and the IAA outlined two major issues that concerned them. First, according to Cardinal, "the Indian people want to renegotiate the treaties to settle once and for all the constitutional bases for their rights and their claims." Second, he pointed out that Indian peoples wanted to "modernize the treaties so that they reflect both the intent of the people who made the treaties and modern social and economic conditions."[50] The Indian Act was also identified as an area of concern; however, the treaties were identified as the priority. For the first time since the Special Joint Committee of 1946, the IAA openly emphasized the significance of the treaties and the rights they conferred.

Following release of the White Paper, the IAA refused to meet or consult with the minister of Indian Affairs, Jean Chrétien, until the following year, at which time it presented the government with its response to the policy document. In September 1969, federal funding was granted to Indian organizations to finance research into such responses. The IAA set about holding meetings on the Blood reserve (in southern Alberta) as well as in Edmonton in order to come up with its response. Not all Alberta bands joined the IAA in rejecting the new federal policy, however. For a time, bands in southern Alberta, including the Peigan and the Stoney, opposed the IAA's stance, but this had little effect on IAA attempts to counter government intentions.

The IAA and Cardinal spent the winter of 1969/70 using government funds to pay for the writing of a response paper. To such ends they employed M and M Systems Research, a research firm established by the former Social Credit premier of Alberta and his son, Preston Manning, for a reputed fee of $25,000.[51] The resulting document, entitled "Citizens Plus," was ready for public consumption in the spring of 1970. Significantly, it was the IAA's position paper that came to be accepted by the NIB as Indian peoples' official response to the White Paper. In the first days of June 1970, leaders from across Canada gathered at Carleton University to plan their strategy for presenting their response to the White Paper to the Trudeau government. After making some revisions to the IAA's document by adding comments on treaties and Aboriginal rights, the NIB took "Citizens Plus" as its own. The Red Paper, as it became known, was presented to the Liberal Cabinet in the Railway Committee Room on Parliament Hill on 4 June 1969. The presenters were IAA members John Snow and Adam Soloway, with Harold Cardinal speaking on the significance of treaty and Aboriginal rights.[52]

The Red Paper promoted two main initiatives: economic development and education. As well, it took as its central theme the significance of Aboriginal and treaty rights, and it hooked into the notion of "citizens plus," which was first brought out by the Hawthorn Report in 1967. Not surprisingly, the red-covered booklet opened with a quote from the Hawthorn Report: "Indians should be regarded as "Citizens Plus"; in addition to the normal rights and duties of citizenship, Indians possess certain additional rights as charter members of the Canadian community." It also opened its discussion by emphasizing, in the first sentence, Indian peoples' treaty rights. For the first time, with the endorsement of Indian peoples across the country, the IAA was able to discuss its longstanding historic concern with treaties at a national level. Where previously the association was expected to focus on social and economic issues first and foremost, by 1970 the focus had switched to treaty rights.

Following the discussion of treaty rights and the critique of Indian policy in Canada, the Red Paper moved into concrete proposals for reserve educational programs and strategies for economic development. Significantly, the section related to economic development promoted a model based on profit and non-profit corporations that would serve reserve communities. Taking a step away from its socialist roots, the IAA had embraced a research company to prepare the Red Paper – a company whose broad goal was "defending capitalism from the socialist threat."[53] The Mannings, who ran M and M Systems Research, believed that supplanting government by private enterprise in as many areas of social life as possible was a good thing, and it appears they felt Indian peoples in Canada would benefit from such a change as well. Such a suggestion was not new – in Alaska Aboriginal peoples were in the process of negotiating a corporate-based settlement to their land claim, and the Red Paper's section on economic development has many similarities to certain aspects of the Alaska Native Claims Settlement Act. The Red Paper, in this sense, did represent a change in political perspective from the IAA's historic socialist orientation, which was originally promoted by Malcolm Norris and the first IAA executive.

According to Cardinal, "Politically, this was our high point; our greatest success, our political equivalent to Little Big Horn."[54] Indeed, through the Red Paper the IAA made a significant mark on the landscape of Aboriginal political action in Canada. It opened an avenue for the discussion of Aboriginal rights and treaty rights apart from their specific relation to social and economic conditions in reserve communities. It caught the Canadian public's attention. Cardinal successfully used the media to broaden the reach of his perspective and of the IAA's activities, and, for the first time in IAA history, the president of the association handled such exposure single-handedly. Cardinal came to represent a new generation of Aboriginal leaders – those who had experienced urban living and had a university education – and he redirected the nature of IAA activity into a more professional, media- and government-savvy operation. Although he freed the IAA from its reliance upon the outside help his father's generation had utilized, he more systematically embraced the Canadian political system by accepting government funding and attempting to turn the IAA into a service-delivery vehicle. Cardinal remained on the IAA executive from 1972 through 1977.

It is true that, by the late 1960s, the IAA was fully integrated into Canada's political system. Some, familiar with the general outlines of Aboriginal political history, argue that this integration has been to the disadvantage of Aboriginal peoples. In the words of analyst Menno Boldt, "the most insidious and perilous assault on Indian special status is concentrated on the institutional assimilation of Indians, that is, the progressive incorporation of Indians into the political, legal, social and economic framework of Canadian society ... institutional assimilation can be regarded as the 'final assault' in the Canadian government's historic campaign to 'civilize' the Indians."[55] Yet, my research suggests that it was precisely the mutual embrace of the federal government and Indian associations such as the IAA that led to the public and very open debate of Aboriginal and treaty rights in Canada. Without some degree of integration the conversation on rights could never have been normalized and would most likely have remained understated and neglected. The current Canadian Constitution reminds Canadians that, indeed, both provincial and federal governments have recognized the unique rights of Aboriginal peoples at the most fundamental level. In many ways the IAA played a significant role in encouraging and fostering government conversations on treaty rights. In the 1940s it brought questions of treaty rights to the Special Joint Committee, and in 1970, through the NIB, it finally forced the topic to the level of a national debate. Over time the IAA demonstrated that it was capable of changing both the form and content of Aboriginal politics in Canada.

9

"Nîkânastêwimâkêwin": Comparing the Political Thought of John Callihoo and John Tootoosis

We're a nation!

– John Tootoosis, 1990[1]

The history of First Nations political activity, including the story of the Indian Association of Alberta, is not only rich in stories of personal commitment and community change, but also in political visions and philosophies. What is most interesting about the decades of Indian political activity prior to the 1960s civil rights movements is the way in which First Nations leaders publicly expressed their political perspectives. The tone and content of their political visions were quite different even within treaty areas. Given the transitions the IAA experienced between its founding and the presidency of Harold Cardinal, a history of the IAA can perhaps be better appreciated if the political and philosophical context of its leaders and their contemporaries is better understood. How did leaders view the role of Indian treaties in postwar Canadian society? What values did they express in their speeches and writings on political issues confronting their communities? This chapter attempts to look beyond the chronological history of the IAA and to analyze the political philosophies grounding one IAA leader and his main rival during the early years of the association's activities.

Different backgrounds, languages, and cultures did not preclude Indian leaders holding similar visions. In fact, if one compares two of the most prominent leaders from the Treaty 6 regions of Alberta and Saskatchewan – namely, Johnny Callihoo and John Tootoosis – their differences are clear. Contemporaries, both men played leading roles in the politics of Indian reserve communities in the 1940s and 1950s. Although Tootoosis had a much longer career than did Callihoo, these men's political visions gained public attention when they were both at the height of their influence as presidents of their respective provincial Indian associations. From 1939 to 1949 Callihoo was the president of the IAA; John Tootoosis was first elected president of the Union of Saskatchewan Indians (USI) in 1946 but had developed a leadership role long before assuming that position. Only by examining the views of these men, as expressed in speeches and the limited set of writings available to date, can the depth and nuance of their opinions and the meaning of western Canadian Aboriginal political action in the mid-twentieth century begin to be appreciated.

To date, the intellectual structures grounding Indian political activity have been little described by mainstream Canadian historians. On the other hand, noted Native American scholar Robert Allen Warrior, in *Tribal Secrets* (1995),[2] has emphasized the importance of investigating the dialogue of American Indian intellectuals in their fight to assert their social, political, economic, cultural, and spiritual rights. In Canada, there is a need to recognize the critical discourses that form the intellectual history of Canadian First Nations. Only by engaging those voices from the past can scholars appreciate the nature of First Nations leaders' commitment to their peoples' futures. The history of Indian political activity in Canada is complex and varied, representing a diversity in thought that goes far beyond mere reactionary "protest" or homogeneous "Pan-Indian" movements.[3] The philosophies underlying Indian political activities, such as those expressed by Prairie Indian leaders in the mid-twentieth century, were complex and varied. A deeper investigation into the nature of Indian political thought during this interwar and postwar period gives insight into a political culture intertwined with belief systems, expressive symbols, and the unique historical experience of specific First Nations cultures and communities.

Studying the political and social visions of Indian leaders in Canada's postwar West is a task requiring special considerations. First, there are few memoirs produced by First Nations intellectuals/leaders from the postwar period that can be used to verify theories of political ideologies. Material of that nature (i.e., published memories from the perspective of the individuals who were politically active) are rare or non-existent. Second, correspondence, speeches, and other standard unpublished documentary sources frequently used by intellectual historians to sketch political histories are equally scarce for many mid-twentieth-century Indian leaders, including Tootoosis and Callihoo. This scarcity can be partly explained by the fact that both men (particularly Tootoosis) were skilled orators who spoke frequently and eloquently in their own languages and did not rely upon prepared speeches. However, what has been passed on to the present, what is accessible, and what does reveal their views are their actual *lives*. Looking at how Tootoosis and Callihoo carried out their political careers is one way of revealing their unique views. Thus, I focus upon their lives as text and context.

Of course, those who have real expertise in this subject are the people who had personal contact with Tootoosis and Callihoo: family members, relatives, friends, and colleagues. What is presented here is a mere reconstruction of their political visions based on preliminary oral history research and the few available documents. Much more oral history research needs to be conducted in order to provide my investigation with long-term value and credibility. What I offer serves as a beginning, as a stimulus to others to attempt more of this much needed work.

In many ways, the rivalry between the Saskatchewan and Alberta First Nations leaders, Tootoosis and Callihoo, respectively, was a result of their differing vision of Indian peoples' place in postwar, reconstructed Canada. On the one hand, both leaders were strongly committed to improving contemporary conditions for their communities as well as for planning for their futures. On the other hand, they differed substantively on the nature of that future. The history of the IAA suggests that Callihoo was particularly concerned with gaining greater rights for registered and non-status Indian people. He also wanted political equality within the Canadian state and the extension of social welfare measures to Indian communities. In essence, Callihoo was eager to break with the oppressive history Indian peoples had experienced as wards of the Canadian state and to forge for them what he viewed as a brighter future.

In contrast, Tootoosis fought hard for his vision of Indian sovereignty. For him, the assertion of treaty rights (rather than civil equality) was the priority. Throughout his lifetime Tootoosis never once strayed from his belief that the treaties represented the future for his peoples. Tootoosis worked to realize a vision of Indian sovereignty in keeping with, and connected to, Cree history.

The 1936 break between Alberta and Saskatchewan in the League of Indians of Western Canada, of which both Tootoosis and Callihoo were members, was perhaps most indicative of the differing philosophies of Treaty 6 communities. This split between Alberta and Saskatchewan movements became the basis for disagreement long into the future. As mentioned previously, Tootoosis's biographers contend that the split between him and Callihoo was based on the former's belligerent behaviour at the Battleford meeting.[4] According to former IAA secretary Hugh Dempsey, the animosity arose over their struggle for political control of the Saddle Lake area, which had its agency office in Saskatchewan.[5] Years later, Tootoosis himself recalled:

> Alberta helped us; we were all in one. All of a sudden they [Alberta reserves] left the organization because of a chief, by the name of Joe Calahoo [sic], from Calahoo Reserve, as it was called. When this chief spoke, he spoke half in English and half in Cree. The people did not like it, at a meeting at Battleford as they didn't speak English. They were lost when he spoke English; they didn't know what he talked about. So we took a vote on this question. I was a chairman then. They said he should speak Cree, all the way through, or be interpreted if he spoke English. He

> didn't like it, and it was too bad. That's when the Alberta Association [IAA] came into being. That's when he took away his fellow Albertans ... He blamed us, saying that they only spoke for themselves in Saskatchewan. And for other reasons, he persuaded them to depart.[6]

Investigating Tootoosis's views further shows that the league failed for reasons more complex than a disagreement over language at a meeting. Indeed, as Tootoosis suggested, there were "other reasons."

Ultimately, during the postwar decades, two main perspectives concerning the future of Indian peoples within Canada came to be expressed and embodied by, respectively, Saskatchewan's John Tootoosis and Alberta's John Callihoo. Seemingly similar, their philosophies were rooted in different understandings of the value of Indian history and treaties. Callihoo was forward-looking, interested in new and untried visions of society offered by socialist politics and traditional Cree teachings. His vision of the future was only cursorily linked to the past. Tootoosis, in stark contrast, was an individual whose raison d'être was rooted in the treaties and the Cree experience of those solemn agreements. The visions these two men had for Indian peoples formed a dialectic that lasted until well into the era of modern politics.

John Callihoo

The history of the IAA and Callihoo's leadership between 1939 and 1949 shows that Callihoo emphasized that Indian peoples should be on an equal footing with non-Indian Canadians. Callihoo had a long-range vision that involved Indian peoples eventually assuming full citizenship within Canada, no longer being held in "wardship" by the federal government, and enjoying the same social benefits enjoyed by all other citizens. In his drive to improve life in reserve communities in Alberta, he allied himself with activists who strove for social justice. Although few of his speeches are available for study, and his surviving correspondence is sparse, Callihoo's associations, his presentations before government, and his actions all reveal that he was less interested in asserting the unique history of Indian peoples than he was in gaining for them the benefits of a more humane Canadian society.

Callihoo's "progressive," or socially oriented, approach to problems facing Indian peoples both before and after the Second World War had two main characteristics. First, it emphasized improved education and increased social welfare measures for Indian communities. Second, it lacked any extensive reference to treaty rights. This view stemmed directly from his own background and life experiences. His familial connections to the non-registered French Métis community residing near his reserve, his work experience as a freighter, and his close ties to Métis leader Malcolm

Norris gave him a perspective unlimited by narrow definitions of treaty rights and Indian status. Adrian Hope, who knew Callihoo and his position in the community, recalled that language very much determined Callihoo's place. He recalled that Callihoo's strength lay in his ability to speak French, not Cree, and this undoubtedly influenced Cree perceptions of him.[7]

Furthermore, it appears that many of the ideals promoted by the Métis Association of Alberta leader, Malcolm Norris, were shared and carried forward by Johnny Callihoo. Fluent in both Cree and English, Norris was a master orator and an activist whose colleagues recalled him being "a whirlwind ... you didn't dare brush him the wrong way."[8] Norris believed ardently in the value of democracy and was solidly opposed to emphasizing "special" rights for Indian peoples, something he equated with "petty nationalism," and he believed that Indian and Métis peoples should be treated in the same manner.[9] It is no surprise that Norris, who was widely respected for his intellect and who shared with Callihoo a passion for politics, would have a strong influence on Callihoo's political vision.

Last but not least, it appears that some of those involved in the IAA viewed politics as a spiritual as well as secular endeavour; for them, improving the lives of Indian peoples generally was something of a moral imperative. Specifically, founding IAA members Albert Lightning and Peter Burnstick, both publicly and privately, actively promoted traditional Cree values. According to Métis historian Maria Campbell, unlike many of the leaders in the Treaty 6 region, Lightning and Burnstick were not under the influence of the Christian church, and traditional spiritual teachings formed the foundation of their political ideals. Politics and spirituality were taken together and presented as being "for the good of the people," and both Lightning and Burnstick spent much time emphasizing this message to younger generations. In Campbell's view, this perspective permeated IAA politics in Alberta into the 1960s, while in Saskatchewan Native politics was primarily secularized. The spiritual dimension of the IAA's political vision is important because it supposed a unity in the Aboriginal community based upon a humanitarian vision rooted in traditional teachings rather than treaty boundaries or ancestry. It was also a vision that meshed well with socialist philosophy. During his time in the IAA, Callihoo worked closely with Lightning and Burnstick, both of whom held prominent positions in the IAA executive.[10] Taken together, these factors in Callihoo's background encouraged him to emphasize improving social and economic conditions on reserve rather than treaty rights, and they oriented him towards the needs of Métis and treaty peoples alike.

Documentary sources further support the idea that, throughout his career as president of the IAA, Callihoo consistently promoted the "advancement" of Indian communities through improved education, additional social welfare, and access to the full range of citizenship rights. For example, Callihoo endorsed the "Memorial on Indian Affairs, 1944," which listed the IAA's priorities. In its opening paragraphs it clearly emphasized "that the authorities cannot but look favorably upon the extension of democratic rights and privileges to the Indian people ... they will not be overlooked in any discussion on Reconstruction."[11] This opening statement highlighted (1) the IAA's dissatisfaction with Indian peoples' lack of participation in Canadian society and (2) the hope that Canada's postwar reconstruction plans would see the extension of more rights to Indian peoples. Furthermore, it called upon "the Federal Government to extend to Indians the benefits of Old Age Pensions, Widows' and Mothers' Allowances, Aid to the Blind, Indigent Relief, and all other social legislation as may be provided from time to time by legislation and on the same basis as white citizens."[12] Emphasizing the participation of Indian peoples in the mobilization process, and as subject to indirect taxes, the memorial demanded the extension of full rights to Indian peoples based upon the principles of democracy and fairness that Canadian society had come to appreciate as a result of the Second World War. Only at the very end of the document were treaty rights mentioned, and then only within the context of the Indian Act.

Later, in 1946, Callihoo again endorsed this same vision through his in-person presentations to the Special Joint Parliamentary Committee of the Senate and the House of Commons to investigate the Indian Act. As one of a handful of Indian leaders to testify before the committee, Callihoo had an unusual opportunity to directly explain to the government his hopes for the future of Indian peoples. He emphasized the need for Indian equality with non-Indian citizens through better education, the extension of social welfare programs, and increased band self-government within the system established by the Indian Act.

Callihoo never challenged the authority of the Indian Act, nor did he challenge the authority of the Department of Indian Affairs and its system of Indian administration; instead, Callihoo promoted open cooperation with, and acceptance of, federal authority. Not surprisingly, in his drive to gain greater benefits for Indian peoples, he went along with the DIA's idea of revisiting the concept of Canadian citizenship and its relationship to Indian peoples. In the same year that Callihoo presented his petitions before the Special Committee, the Citizenship Act was passed. An astute politician, Callihoo played into existing governmental concerns rather than challenging them.

Significantly, Callihoo's vision of cooperating with the government in order to increase the citizenship rights of Indian peoples within the state structures of his time was further emphasized in a short essay he produced for an adult education seminar hosted by the IAA (found in one of his surviving notebooks, held by Hugh Dempsey). In this rare essay on the meaning of Treaty 6, Callihoo took the opportunity to re-establish the primacy of the treaties for Prairie Indian peoples. Although he did say that the Indian Act undermined the treaties, he still saw them as a route to equality, not to a separate existence, for Indian peoples:

> Now the Indians feel that what was said on August 18, 1876 [the signing of Treaty 6] was never open to the whole people. The Indians feel that it has been hidden to this very day and that it was never fulfilled and if we are of the same blood and if the same God made us, and the same Queen ruled over us *why then are the Indians treated so much different?* [emphasis added] ... Now what does the Indian Act provide for all this? The Indian Act, it appears, is strictly against all the promises made during the negotiations, and it is gradually taken away all the Indian rights [sic]. It has taken unto itself dictated powers ... I will leave this to your own judgement but for me it seems there was no justice and no Christianity. Do you not think it would be better to help the poor than to covet what little they have?

Callihoo's personal life was lived within the context of Treaty 6; however, in his political life, he chose to extend himself beyond his treaty rights and to search for a future for his community. In doing so, he allied himself with those who offered insights into the workings of the Canadian state and those who struggled to improve conditions for both non-treaty, non-status, and treaty Indian peoples. During his IAA presidency, Callihoo forged close relations with various kinds of "outside help" – individuals and groups concerned with minority rights. He and his wife were active members of Edmonton's Friends of the Indians Society,[13] the service club led by the Fabian socialist Rita Rowan. Among other things, this society wanted "to promote a better understanding between Indians and the Canadian public, to improve living conditions on reserves, to raise the educational level of the Indian communities, ... to press for changes to the Indian Act."[14] It noted treaty rights but never pursued them as a priority. This hesitancy to press for treaty rights was a long-standing characteristic of Callihoo's political career. He was clearly optimistic about the future offerings of Canadian citizenship but perhaps downplayed the significance of the treaties because he saw them as hampering unity in Indian communities. Indeed, his own family was divided into treaty and non-treaty fragments.

Ultimately, Callihoo was optimistic about life outside the treaties, and this optimism carried over into his own community: on 31 March 1958 his band enfranchised, liquidating their reserve and Indian status. This occurred one year after Callihoo's death.[15]

John Tootoosis

In contrast to John Callihoo, John Tootoosis saw the treaties as fundamental to his vision of an Indian future. Although Tootoosis shared much with Callihoo in terms of life experience – they shared Cree ancestry, were farmers, were from leading families within their respective communities, and were members of the League of Indians – unlike Callihoo, his political thinking was firmly rooted in the historical experiences of his people. Tootoosis's aim was to build on that heritage and to revisit it as a basis for future decision making. Just as Callihoo sought to break with the past in the hope of asserting a better future, Tootoosis emphasized the importance of Cree history. For Tootoosis, there was no future for Indian peoples outside the treaties. A man of incredible strength, vision, and constitution, Tootoosis, in his years of travelling widely in western Canada, may have had more opportunity to express his views than did Callihoo. His long political career may also be why there is more documentary evidence of his political life than of Callihoo's.

Born in 1899 John B. Tootoosis was one of eleven children, and his family were descendants of Yellowmud Blanket, whose brother Poundmaker was one of the leaders to sign onto Treaty 6 in 1876. Poundmaker and his band, including the family of Yellowmud Blanket, finally settled on their reserve near Battleford, Saskatchewan, in 1879 when their migratory hunting lifestyle became impossible to continue. In the early 1880s farming proved difficult on the reserve, and many families in the band endured tremendous hardship, depending increasingly on government rations for survival. Despite the Treaty 6 promise that adherents to the treaty would be provided with rations, many reserve residents found the government's distribution of rations less than generous. They also found their own autonomy increasingly undermined by an Indian Agent who controlled the food hand-outs. Even Yellowmud Blanket found his attempts to provide for his family intercepted by the government when he and his sons were arrested for what the local Indian Agent claimed was illegal fishing.[16]

Within the first ten years of their residency on reserve, Poundmaker's band came into direct conflict with the Canadian government. In the complex set of events surrounding the Métis Resistance of 1885, some Indian leaders sought to remind the federal government of its failure to honour its treaty promises. In northwestern Saskatchewan violence ensued in a handful of locations, and Canadian government troops were sent in to "subdue" what were perceived to be the Indian "troublemakers" on Poundmaker's reserve. Oral history accounts of Colonel Otter's attempt to attack Poundmaker's people recall how Poundmaker urged restraint and emphasized the importance of the treaty promises to his people.[17] Despite his desire to maintain the peace, Poundmaker was arrested for his actions and imprisoned in Manitoba. Yellowmud Blanket, in turn, was also briefly incarcerated in Regina. Eight other Indian men were sentenced to hang at Battleford before Indian school children who were taken from their residential school to witness the event.[18]

The memories of these events in the Poundmaker community were part of John B. Tootoosis's history and reflected his community's deep commitment to the treaty. As a young man, Tootoosis was already singled out by the elders in his community to pursue the treaty and its promises. As early as 1927, Tootoosis was already aware of the shortcomings of government administration of Indian Affairs, and he strove to educate himself on the Indian Act and the treaties. Later, he recalled:

> Back in 1927, I locked horns with the Department of Indian Affairs. I was on my own, working for myself. I did not get along with the officials at Battleford because I didn't want them to tell me what to do, while I was trying to become independent. Then it was that I studied the Treaty; I studied the Indian Act; I studied the administration of Indian Affairs. I went across the country. I knew what was going on in Alberta.[19]

During the same time period, Tootoosis fought the lease of reserve lands to neighbouring farmers of the Poundmaker reserve, and he experienced first hand the inability to sell his calves because of the "permit" system implemented by Indian Affairs.

Tootoosis was very sensitive to what he perceived to be the incongruency between the treaty, which promised land, education, and government assistance, and government policy, which appeared to interfere in almost every aspect of Indian peoples' lives. As he mentioned in 1947 to the same Special Joint Committee that Callihoo testified before: "The Indians of Saskatchewan are treaty Indians. We made a treaty with Great Britain in the first place, and the trust was given to the Canadian government to live up to our treaties. Ever since the first treaties the Indians have felt that the officials have not complied with those treaties."[20]

As a result of his concerns, Tootoosis took up the task of educating his community, and it supported him in his attempts to do so. In 1921 he was sent with his father to attend one of the first western meetings of the League of Indians, and, by 1932, he was voted to replace his father on the league's executive. He later remembered his desire to help:

> These old people that made these agreements [treaties], they had to do everything through interpreters after they settled down on reservations, they had no interpreters to express themselves with ... I had to explain everything to people, it was much harder to organize people in my time because they were illiterate and so damn used to being dominated ... they had no hope at all ... the Elders depended on me.[21]

Chosen by his community to pursue the needs of the people, Tootoosis took his mission very seriously. His commitment was in part fuelled by his membership in the "Okichitawak," or Cowboy society, a Cree institution designated to safeguard the welfare of the community. He travelled extensively throughout the Prairies, promoting the importance of the treaties. His journeys were occasionally hampered by government interference, but he was adamant in his determination to communicate with other reserve communities. In 1932, for example, he travelled to northern Alberta to discuss treaty rights but was threatened with arrest by the RCMP. This threat did not deter Tootoosis. His persistence and dedication is revealed in his recollections: "I kept on going knowing that the day would come when Indian conditions would have to be changed if the Indians would keep on hammering away for better health conditions, better education." Tootoosis was well known for his extensive organizing and travelling. In 1947, on a trip to the Poundmaker reserve, Assistant Superintendent W.L. Falconer noted: "at the Sun Dance I met Tootoosis, a grandson of Poundmaker a representative of Saskatchewan at the Parliamentary inquiry held in Ottawa recently. When visiting the reserve I saw his home which is a log and mud shack about 8 x 10. He has 8 children, but apparently spends his time travelling about Saskatchewan organizing the Indians."[22]

One of the central differences between Tootoosis and Callihoo was rooted in the former's focus upon Treaty 6. Tootoosis insisted that there were simply too many differences between Indian peoples and the Métis (or non-status, non-treaty Indians) for their causes to be linked. Callihoo was fighting for a future that included better living conditions for all Aboriginal peoples, while Tootoosis believed that the treaty promises demanded priority for treaty peoples. In his view, Métis peoples would simply complicate the cause of treaty people. Second, he believed that pursuing the issues affecting non-treaty Indians would serve only to draw all Indian peoples closer into the Canadian political system, since he believed that the Métis were far more prone to consult and rely upon White advisors than were Indians. From the start, this affected the nature of Tootoosis's vision of the future.

Closely linked to his desire to distance himself from non-treaty people was Tootoosis's reticence to cooperate with "outsiders." Later in life Tootoosis was more vocal about his opposition to outside help. He frequently criticized the IAA for its reliance upon non-Indian advisors, whom he believed were distracting people from the primary issue: treaty rights. His critique of the IAA is reflected in the fact that, as early as 1944, the IAA's organizer Malcolm Norris wrote Tootoosis a blistering letter, insisting upon the importance of gaining non-Indian assistance and emphasizing that "this policy has been justified in the progress which has already been made." Norris continued: "This state could not have been brought about by any attempt to segregate ourselves, as an Indian race (not nation) within Canada ... We are certain that the day of small segregated groups is past."[23] Norris's ideas stood in stark contrast to Tootoosis's powerful statements: "We want to hold our land. We want to hold our language ... We are a nation within a nation."[24] Tootoosis did not believe in gaining help that encouraged the integration of Indian peoples into mainstream Canadian society through cooperation with the government.

Tootoosis was adamant about keeping Indian political organizations "Indian," and when the IAA organized itself as a separate body, Tootoosis was terribly suspicious of its goals. Tootoosis was distrustful of the IAA's Métis connections, and he was also aware that the first IAA executive secretary was a non-Indian. As his biographers point out, Tootoosis feared that the IAA was promoting enfranchisement and assimilation for Indian peoples, and he "wrote to the Alberta chiefs and all the councillors he knew by name, warning them against the possibility of being separated from their land and treaty rights."[25] Norris and Laurie were well aware of Tootoosis's suspicions of "citizenship," and, in their correspondence, they frequently mentioned Tootoosis as a threat to the IAA. Writing to a supportive Parliamentarian in 1945, Laurie warned: "We have had trouble with this man before and our executive knows his tricks very well, and what his character is ... he wrote to Hobbema and to Gleichen charging that we had asked for citizenship, and urging them to leave the Alberta Association and join him."[26]

In keeping with his reticence to associate with outside assistance, Tootoosis discouraged Indian political organizations from working to achieve provincial-level unity. In the 1940s and 1950s he supported either a national-level association striving for *all* treaties and Indian nations or local treaty-level unions. These ideas were played out in his alliance with British Columbia Indian leader Andrew Paull, founder of the North American Indian Brotherhood in 1944. Paull wanted a national-level Indian union to represent Indian concerns to the government, and Tootoosis supported him. At the same time, Tootoosis resisted the IAA and similar provincial unions, as was illustrated in 1946 by his initial lack of enthusiasm for a union of Saskatchewan movement. When, in meetings with Indian leaders that year, Premier Tommy Douglas encouraged Tootoosis to form a provincial-level organization, he resisted, instead promoting the NAIB and emphasizing that he was "against the franchise."[27] In the early spring of 1946, when provincial organization became a reality for Indian people in Saskatchewan, Tootoosis continued to resist and insisted (albeit symbolically) that Cree be spoken at the organizational meeting of the USI. At that time, when government officials irritated him, he pointedly remarked: "I understand that when the meeting was called in Saskatoon that it was to be a purely Indian conference."[28] This event also revealed one of his primary concerns: that Cree peoples involved in these political events must fully understand the implications of what was being communicated to them in English. Throughout the 1940s and 1950s, he wrote many letters and travelled widely to Cree communities, his main aim being to explain the treaties and the Indian Act to Cree speakers. In 1953 he wrote as follows to IAA supporter Frank Cardinal: "I can translate that Act in Cree better than any Indians in Saskatchewan and Manitoba, and wouldn't hesitate to compete with any Cree speaking Indians in Alberta ... I'll give you any way of understanding the Indian Act in conjunction of our Treaties Rights. You have to act quick because I am a busy man, doing a lot of traveling in explaining the Act and our Treaties."[29]

Unlike Callihoo and the IAA, Tootoosis did not see Indian peoples' inclusion in the Canadian political system as advantageous; rather, he viewed it as a threat to their treaty rights. The history of Poundmaker and his reserve served as a metaphor for Tootoosis, exemplifying what could and had happened to Indian nations within Canada: once they joined into a relationship with the Canadian state, the latter actively undermined their separate existence. He continued to press home this point well into his old age, and, in a speech to Saskatchewan Indian students in 1990, he perhaps expressed his position most clearly and passionately:

> We're given the vote ... one door for the provincial vote, one door for the federal vote ... why? That wasn't to help us ... that is to *destroy* and abandon our status, in time if you people continue to vote for the government running another country that is no more yours you're gonna be out there with them ... we haven't got anymore to go vote outside ... we're a nation ... they want us to automatically abandon our rights ... how can we be citizens? We're a *nation!*[30]

For Tootoosis the treaty was the reason for being – it was the future and the past. His place as a chosen protector of the treaty and his community was something he took seriously throughout his life.

Given these fundamental differences between Callihoo and Tootoosis, it is not surprising that the two leaders could not support the same organization. Because of their differing views of the future for Indian peoples, their ways parted in 1937. Over the course of subsequent decades they continued to disagree publicly and struggled to convince the communities of the Prairies of the merits of their respective views. Tootoosis crusaded for the treaties; Callihoo struggled to negotiate fuller Aboriginal inclusion in the Canadian social welfare system. Tootoosis saw his role as linked to the traditions and history of his people, while Callihoo viewed his work as an extension of the democratic process as embodied by the state and extended to Indian peoples. For Callihoo, learning the "White man's ways" was a priority; for Tootoosis, Cree ways were of central significance. He would have agreed with the Cree spiritual leader Albert Lightning: "When we finish learning about Cree behaviour, Cree hopes, Cree in-depth understanding, then we will all understand discussions on Cree."[31]

The influence these men had on Indian political activity was tremendous as both achieved substantive improvements for Indian peoples through the revision of federal Indian policy and administration. Although they were political rivals, their relationship was symbiotic, and, over the course of the 1940s and 1950s, each served as a "watchdog" over the political moves of the other. Disunity in Prairie Indian politics functioned as a powerful and creative force; in effect, the different political views of each strengthened Indian political action.

Characterizing the indigenous thought of these men is difficult if one analyzes their politics apart from their historical-cultural context. Is it sufficient to label the views of Callihoo and Tootoosis as "liberal" and "conservative," respectively? Perhaps it is more insightful to consider Tootoosis a sovereigntist: as someone who spoke for a community that never surrendered its sense of nationhood. Callihoo, in turn, believed he saw freedom within the Canadian political system. In both cases, these men were "nîkânastêwimâkêwin" – attempting "to put things into the future for others."

10
Final Thoughts

Sifting through the many files, documents, photos, and accounts related to the Indian Association of Alberta's past is the quickest way to begin understanding the depth of its history. Produced by a variety of people, this material represents the many different strands of thought the association encapsulated. Not that the material was always clear and consistent. Documentation relating to the IAA's past is frequently incomplete, and oral histories are difficult to come by. The fact remains, however, that the IAA's story is rich in ideas and ideals. Its history encompasses a complex set of interactions between a vast array of people, world and local events, laws and policies, social attitudes, and economic realities. The association was made up of a handful of individuals who founded and directed it from its birth through its institutionalization in 1959; it was an expression of community desires, of individual hopes, of relations between Indian and non-Indian peoples, and of the power of government policy and legislation over individual lives. Between 1939 and 1970, the IAA embodied all these factors as it gradually emerged from being an obscure provincial Indian political group to take the role of one of Canada's premier Aboriginal political unions – one with a national reputation and capable of effecting change.

So many different people played important roles in this organization that it is not surprising that the IAA's history has multiple voices. These voices emphasize that the IAA was significant to its members in different ways. Leaders like John Callihoo viewed it as a mechanism to further equality for Indian peoples, status or non-status. Others, like James Gladstone, saw the IAA opening doors for Indian communities in government circles. Harold Cardinal used the IAA as a tool for community development, as a vehicle to assert Indian peoples' treaty rights, and, in doing so, he exposed the Department of Indian Affairs' policy-making process to public scrutiny. Obviously not all IAA leaders' dreams for their association and its members were realized; many IAA resolutions were never acted upon. However, the IAA did change how Indian peoples moved within

Canada's political system. Until 1970 the IAA operated as a union based upon grassroots concerns, was run within the bounds of Canada's political structure, drew upon outsider experience, and sought government cooperation on all levels. This enabled it to draw public attention to Indian issues in Canada in a way that, to this point, had been limited to special government inquiries. In addition, the IAA created a generation of Indian leaders who were not connected to the Indian Act system of governance, and it forced new conversations on Aboriginal and treaty rights into the public sphere.

The change in Native political action pioneered by the IAA had humble beginnings. Not until the interwar years did social, political, and economic conditions shift sufficiently to allow Alberta Indian leaders, working in conjunction with Métis and other non-Indians, to form a new union – one that rapidly gained government recognition. In 1939 poor economic conditions in reserve communities; the erosion of Alberta treaty rights; the alienation of reserve lands; the dissatisfaction of Indian communities with the state of health care and education; and, finally, problems with hunting, trapping, and agriculture spurred a handful of individuals from some of Alberta's poorer reserve communities to form a political union. In short, local, everyday experiences and concerns played a primary role in the establishment of the IAA.

The first leaders of the IAA were not all neophytes in the realm of politics and power. From the start, the IAA was a product of the political experience, charisma, and savvy within the Aboriginal communities that supported it. Malcolm Norris, Johnny Callihoo, Peter Burnstick, Joe Dion, and the others who helped forge the association drew upon their collective past involvement with radical political groups, farmers unions, the Métis Association of Alberta, and the older League of Indians of Western Canada.

The structure of the newly formed IAA reflected its leaders' desire to launch a modern organization that would work within the existing Canadian political system and would be flexible enough to expand and accommodate Indian communities around the province. The result was that its structure mirrored that of Alberta's farm unions and the MAA. It was composed of a series of locals, each of which was governed by a local council. A provincial executive oversaw these locals. Meetings were held regularly within reserve communities, and an annual summer general convention allowed all locals to share their concerns before presenting petitions to Ottawa. Whereas it started as an Edmonton-based association, by the late 1940s the IAA had successfully expanded its range into the northern and southern reaches of the province, from Fort Chipewyan to the Blood reserve. Men and women participated eagerly in many aspects of the IAA's meeting and organization processes, and, in the first two decades of its operations, its conventions were well attended and were viewed as enjoyable social occasions.

Early IAA leadership also acknowledged the significance of accepting "outside help" and not closing the association off from developments outside reserve communities. As it turned out, in the long run "outsiders" were very important with regard to shaping the IAA's activities. The first IAA constitution opened IAA membership to any individual claiming Indian ancestry (not just treaty Indians). IAA organizer Malcolm Norris actively encouraged the IAA to use outside help, a point upon which he differed with Saskatchewan Indian leader John Tootoosis. The IAA's openness to outside help facilitated its establishing and maintaining contact with important non-Indian service groups who worked to advance the IAA cause. It also gave it special DIA recognition.

Most prominent among those representing outside help was Calgary schoolteacher John Lee Laurie. Laurie became acquainted with the condition of reserve communities through his visits to the Stoney reserve, near Calgary. His Stoney connection eventually led to his appointment as provincial secretary of the IAA at the 1944 annual convention in Hobbema. Over time, Laurie evolved his role far beyond its official parameters. Not only did he control and manage much of the IAA's official correspondence, but he also infused the association with many of his own ideas. Laurie believed that the IAA represented an opportunity for Indian peoples to learn the principles of democracy, to improve their moral standing, and to educate the Canadian public about the problems facing reserve communities. Interestingly, he also viewed the IAA as an organization that would facilitate the integration of Indian peoples into Canadian society. His view stood in contrast to those held by other IAA members, who believed that the IAA's primary function was to assert Indian peoples' unique treaty rights. Laurie wielded great influence within the IAA, provided it with many important contacts in Canada's political world, and invested it with substantial personal resources. Laurie's goal was to reform Indian Affairs and administration through existing channels. Finally, as a respected citizen of average means involved in an Indian cause, Laurie provided the IAA with legitimacy in an era when those in government circles still viewed Aboriginal political groups with suspicion.

Other sources of outside help in the late 1940s and 1950s included various service groups and influential individuals, such as the Edmonton-based Friends of the Indians Society, the Calgary Home and School Association, and Laurie's acquaintances Anne Downe, lawyer Ruth Gorman, and politicians Douglas Harkness and Aylmer Liesemer. Together, these connections provided the IAA with valuable links to Ottawa's political circles and generated significant publicity for the IAA cause. Like Laurie, however, these organizations and individuals emphasized the importance of Indian communities gaining access to political power rather than the assertion of treaty rights. The down-playing of the treaties and treaty rights revealed the outside help's fundamental belief in the state as a model of political and social power. And the state was something that Indian communities were perceived as lacking. Ultimately, outside help influenced the IAA in a conservative manner, encouraging it to work *within* the system of Indian administration rather than to challenge that system's racist and paternalistic foundations. It encouraged the IAA to seek change through existing formal organizations, rules, and regulations. In the end, the IAA's reliance upon assistance from these well intentioned middle-class individuals gave the association its moderate political stance.

Relations between the IAA and the federal government ran smoothly from the association's founding in 1939 through the mid-1960s. Contrary to the belief that, until the 1960s, the federal government actively discouraged Indian political activity, the government initially accepted and later even formally encouraged the IAA. IAA relations with the federal government, and specifically with the Indian Affairs Branch, seemed to evolve through two phases: (1) the period prior to the sitting of the 1946 Special Joint Committee of the Senate and House of Commons on Indian affairs and (2) the period after the release of the committee's final report. Prior to 1946 the IAA's primary form of contact with Indian Affairs came through its submission of memorials to Ottawa. The memorials of 1944 and 1945 were products of IAA annual conventions and represented membership concern with sections of the Indian Act, retaining reserve lands, improving reserve health and education standards, and seeing social legislation extended to treaty Indian peoples. During this early period, the IAA emphasized "bread-and-butter" issues over the promotion of treaty rights. It is important to note that the moderate tone of the memorials gave the IAA credibility with the civil service and played into existing Indian Affairs policies. The timing of these two memorials was also important as it enabled Indian peoples to be involved in government discussions relating to postwar reconstruction.

Following its involvement with the Special Committee on Indian affairs, the IAA entered the second phase of its relationship with the government. Between 1948 and 1959, the IAA exercised its hard-won position as a legitimate Aboriginal political organization within the Canadian political system. During this decade, Ottawa came to view the IAA as a valued source of information on Indian issues and opinions. Gradually, as social and economic conditions improved due to Canada's postwar boom, the question of treaty rights began cropping up with increasing frequency. Over these years, in its attempt to better support Indian needs, the IAA successfully positioned itself as a liaison between the federal and provincial divisions of government. Since, after the 1930 passage of the Natural Resources Transfer Act, many of the hunting, fishing, and trapping issues confronting Indian peoples fell under provincial jurisdiction, the IAA saw it as imperative that Indian peoples have a voice in provincial politics.

Another way the IAA forged closer relations with the federal government was through its active participation in government-sponsored conferences and consultation sessions dealing with Indian administration issues. Attendance at these gatherings further bolstered the political credibility of the association. Unfortunately, participation in these meetings did more to coopt the IAA into the Canadian political system than to accomplish substantive gains for reserve communities. Early on, the federal government recognized the IAA as a threat to its liberal democratic reputation and, by entering into dialogue with it through conferences and promised legislative reform, the Indian Affairs Branch blunted the threat of Indian political resistance. In many ways, this government tactic was very successful. Throughout the 1940s and 1950s only once did the IAA directly attack the government, and this was over the question of band membership. Not until the late 1960s did the amiable relationship between the IAA and the government change.

An early and significant IAA action was its participation in the hearings and proceedings of the 1946 Special Joint Committee of the Senate and House of Commons. Empowered to investigate the Indian Act and Indian administration in Canada, the Special Committee accepted briefs from Indian groups across Canada. (To date, specific Indian representations have received little attention by scholars.) The IAA brief attempting to reconcile treaty rights with the liberal democratic notion of citizenship rights was one of the most extensive briefs presented to the committee. The question of applying citizenship rights to Indian peoples was of central concern to the committee, and the IAA submission attempted to justify the granting of full citizenship rights on the basis of the treaties, which, it held, were originally intended to give Indian peoples full equality with non-Indian citizens. In making its presentations before the committee, the IAA revealed its concern with treaty rights and its unique political vision, which was focused upon achieving educational and economic liberty for Indian peoples. The IAA made significant contributions to the committee and drew public attention to the condition of reserve communities. Contrary to the assertions of scholars who argue that the work of the committee revealed the conflicts between Indian and government interests, the IAA's involvement in the committee proceedings shows that both parties were concerned with one central issue: the nature of Indian citizenship.

Finally, through its actions in the late 1960s, the IAA changed the nature of modern Aboriginal political activity. Under the leadership of a young, well educated, and politically experienced Harold Cardinal, the IAA began exercising more control over how Canadians perceived Aboriginal issues and how government would deal with those issues. It launched publicity campaigns and used the press to its advantage in ways the older generation of leaders had never managed. It also accepted government funding, thereby actively professionalizing Aboriginal politicians. Under Cardinal's leadership these funds were employed to support full-time IAA employees and to stimulate and disseminate research on solutions to the "Indian problem." In 1970 the IAA was able, for the first time, to actively and opening challenge the federal government as it had never done before: with a well constructed plan of action employed at the national level in the public view.

The accomplishments and failures of the IAA in the first three decades of its operations reveal certain significant developments in mid-twentieth-century Indian politics and leadership. First, it was through this association that a generation of leaders emerged outside the framework of government-sponsored and government-sanctioned band councils. IAA leaders were elected democratically and were able to take control because they were able to deal with collective concerns and because they had a grassroots appeal. The IAA leadership faced the same hurdles as did band councils when it came to battling Indian Affairs administrators; however, unlike band council leaders, IAA leaders could use the media to draw public support to their cause and raise collective concerns such as treaty rights (which were beyond the jurisdiction of band councils). Until 1968 their voluntary position also gave them a certain idealist freedom to pursue causes they felt had priority.

Second, through the IAA, treaty Indian communities in Alberta began to generate a shared understanding of what was possible within the Canadian polity. The IAA functioned as a new and important venue for the expression of a collective will and shared ideas. Previously, leadership was limited to the community level; the IAA presented an ongoing opportunity to transcend such boundaries. This kind of experience was a vital precursor for the emergence of the successful national-level Indian political movements of the late 1960s. The IAA was one of the first Indian associations in western Canada to extend itself beyond treaty boundaries.

Third, IAA history challenges the notion that Indian political activity on the Prairies has been a primarily contemporary phenomenon. In Alberta the IAA was an early and effective force representing a large number of communities throughout the province. The IAA asserted a place for the Indian "voice" within the existing political system, brought basic Aboriginal issues to the attention of the Canadian public, and contributed to a sense of collective identity. The IAA's early years reveal the historical depth of issues such as treaty rights, Indian education, and community improvement. It shows how Indian peoples and their supporters strove to have these issues acknowledged.

Last, the IAA's history indicates the extent to which Indian peoples were connected to the social history of non-Indians. Obviously, Indian communities in Alberta did not exist in isolation, nor were they disconnected from the non-Indian population. The actions of the IAA illustrate how social reform ideas and other political movements operating in the province in the pre- and postwar decades influenced its leaders and members. Rather than viewing the IAA as a product of all-embracing impersonal forces of colonialism, the history of IAA reveals that this movement possessed deeply personal roots. Indian leaders in Alberta had distinct opinions on issues they shared with Indian peoples in the other western provinces.

The IAA story certainly has significance for the contemporary Canadian reader. Today, conversations on Aboriginal rights and their place in Canada's political landscape are common, and the IAA's history indicates that these conversations are part of an intellectual history. Older ideas on the nature of treaty rights and their relationship to Canadian citizenship, such as those presented by IAA leaders to the Special Committee in the late 1940s, may have continued relevance in the present. Furthermore, the IAA's history shows that the issues relating to Indian peoples in Alberta have never been the exclusive concern of those communities. In fact, they have always involved and interested a concerned, supportive non-Indian population. Contemporary discussions of Aboriginal rights, although part of a changed context, still bring out many of the same themes and questions originally raised after the war by organizations such as the IAA. It seems that royal commissions and special committees have done little to answer these well entrenched questions. The IAA story also illustrates and corroborates conclusions reached by the most recent royal commission on Aboriginal peoples: that there has been no pan-Aboriginal voice in Canadian discussions on Aboriginal and treaty rights and that, indeed, the government has always recognized and accommodated differences between Aboriginal peoples.[1] The royal commission's conclusions were focused specifically upon an investigation of the years between 1965 and 1992, but the IAA's history reveals that they are valid for a greater period of time. Thus, it seems obvious that the histories of Aboriginal political associations such as the IAA are relevant to contemporary politics and questions.

Western Canadian First Nations have been part of Canada's political scene for some time; the history of their political thought is rich and should be acknowledged not as deriving from non-Indian help but, rather, as being personally formulated and deeply held. The history of First Nations political action reveals the many shades of meaning pertaining to such complex issues as Aboriginal and treaty rights. And it is only through studying the individual leaders and their ideas that a better understanding of those concepts can arise. It would be particularly interesting should future investigations give attention to a comparison between American and Canadian interpretation of Aboriginal and treaty rights.

In the end, the IAA's history is most compelling for its activism. Prior to the advent of government funding for Aboriginal political associations, voluntary groups such as the IAA gave the communities they represented a cumulative sense of power and strength. In addition, such organizations have highlighted, for outside observers, the different interests of various Aboriginal communities in Canada and their need for support. Through associations such as the IAA, Indian communities helped themselves. The IAA predates the publicly funded Indian friendship centres and other social service support institutions. In fact, political unions such as the IAA pioneered much of the support work that was later taken over by the Canadian welfare state. Although, starting in the late 1960s, government funding changed the nature of Aboriginal political activism, and although many still argue that government funding negatively affected Aboriginal political power, the story of the IAA reminds us that Aboriginal activism long predated the advent of the pay-cheque politician.

Appendix A
Indian Association of Alberta Executive Members, 1939-71

Year (June Election)	Executive Members
1939-40	Johnny Callihoo, President Joe Dion, Vice-President Malcolm Norris, Provincial Organizer
1944-45	Johnny Callihoo, President Joe House, Vice-President Joe Dion, Vice-President Sam Minde, Treasurer John Laurie, Secretary
1945-46	Johnny Callihoo, President John Laurie, Secretary
1946-47	Johnny Callihoo, President John Laurie, Secretary
1947-48	Johnny Callihoo, President John Laurie, Secretary
1948-49	Johhny Callihoo, President Bob Crow Eagle, Vice-President John Rabbitt, Vice-President Sam Minde, Treasurer John Laurie, Secretary
1949-50	James Gladstone, President Bob Crow Eagle, Vice-President Phillip Soosay, Vice-President Sam Minde, Treasurer John Laurie, Secretary
1950-51	James Gladstone, President John Laurie, Secretary
1951-52	James Gladstone, President

▶

Year (June Election)	Executive Members
	Bob Crow Eagle, Vice-President Albert Lightning, Vice-President Sam Minde, Treasurer John Laurie, Secretary
1952-53	James Gladstone, President Joe Scott, Vice-President, South Albert Lightning, Vice-President, North John Laurie, Secretary
1953-54	James Gladstone, President Clarence McHugh, Vice-President, South Victoria McHugh, Treasurer John Laurie, Secretary
1954-55	Clarence McHugh, President (John Laurie takes a leave as Secretary)
1955-56	Clarence McHugh, President John Laurie, Secretary
1956-57	Albert Lightning, President James Gladstone, Honourary President John Laurie, Treasurer David Crowchild, Secretary
1957-58	Albert Lightning, President John Laurie, Treasurer David Crowchild, Secretary
1958-59	Howard Beebe, President John Samson, Vice-President John Laurie, Treasurer Ed Hunter, Secretary David Crowchild, Secretary
1959-60	Howard Beebe, President Ralph Steinhauer, Vice-President, North Narcisse Pipestem, Vice-President, South Peter Burnstick, Northern Organizer Steve Mistaken Chief, Southern Organizer Jacob Twoyoungmen, Central Organizer Ed Hunter, Recording Secretary David Crowchild, Corresponding Secretary (treasurer position to go to chartered accountant)

Year (June Election)	Executive Members
1960-61 (revision of IAA constitution begun)	Ralph Steinhauer, President John Samson, Vice-President North Howard Beebe, Vice-President South Peter Burnstick, Northern Organizer Steve Mistaken Chief, Southern Organizer Johnny Bearspaw, Central Organizer Daisy Crowchild, Treasurer Pauline Dempsey, Recording Secretary David Crowchild, Corresponding Secretary
1961-62 (revised constitution adopted, 1961)	Howard Beebe, President Peter Burnstick, Vice-President, North Judea Wesley, Vice-President, Central Matthew Melting Tallow, Vice-President, South Ralph Steinhauer, Northern Organizer George Labelle, Central Organizer Steve Mistaken Chief, Southern Organizer Pauline Dempsey, Recording Secretary David Crowchild, Corresponding Secretary Daisy Crowchild, Treasurer
1962-63	John Samson, President Peter Burnstick, Vice-President, North Judea Wesley, Vice-President, Central Howard Beebe, Vice-President, South Joe Giroux, Northern Organizer Wallace Snow, Central Organizer Steve Mistaken Chief, Southern Organizer Pauline Dempsey, Recording Secretary David Crowchild, Corresponding Secretary Daisy Crowchild, Treasurer
1963-64	John Samson, President Daisy Crowchild, Treasurer Pauline Dempsey, Secretary
1964-65	Howard Beebe, President Bert Crane, Vice-President, North

▶

Year (June Election)	Executive Members
	Wallace Snow, Vice-President, Central Adam Solway, Vice-President, South Phil Thompson, Recording Secretary David Crowchild, Corresponding Secretary Ernest Ennow, Northern Organizer Mike Divine, Central Organizer
1965-66	Thomas Cardinal, President Peter Burnstick, Vice-President, North Adam Solway, Vice-President, South Wallace Snow, Vice-President, Central Joyce Matchatis, Recording Secretary David Crowchild, Corresponding Secretary Daisy Crowchild, Treasurer Stan Laboucan, Northern Organizer Ed Hunter, Central Organizer Adolphus Weasel Child, Southern Organizer
1966-67	John Samson, President
1967-68	Thomas Cardinal, President
1968-71	Harold Cardinal, President

Appendix B
Supervisors of Local Department of Indian Affairs, Alberta, 1939-69

Year	Supervisor of Indian Agencies, Alberta
1939	C.P. Schmidt (Inspector of Indian Agencies)
1940	C.P. Schmidt
1941	C.P. Schmidt
1942	C.P. Schmidt
1943	C.P. Schmidt
1944	C.P. Schmidt
1945	C.P. Schmidt
1946	George Gooderham (Regional Supervisor of Indian Agencies, Alberta)
1947	George Gooderham
1948	George Gooderham
1949	George Gooderham
1950	George Gooderham
1951	George Gooderham
1952	George Gooderham
1953	George Gooderham
1954	George Gooderham
1955	R.F. Battle
1956	R.F. Battle
1957	R.F. Battle
1958	R.F. Battle
1959	R.F. Battle
1960	R.F. Battle
1961	L.C. Hunter
1962	L.C. Hunter
1963	L.C. Hunter
1964	L.C. Hunter
1965	R.D. Ragan
1966	R.D. Ragan
1967	(Unavailable)
1968	(Unavailable)
1969	(Unavailable)

Note: At the time of publication information for the years 1967-69 was not available through the National Archives of Canada or the Indian Affairs archives.

Appendix C
Indian Affairs Administration, 1939-68

Year (March year end)	Department responsible for Indian Affairs	Minister responsible for Indian Affairs	Director of Indian Affairs
1939-40	Mines and Resources (since 1936)	T.A. Crerar	H.W. McGill
1940-41		T.A. Crerar	H.W. McGill
1941-42		T.A. Crerar	H.W. McGill
1942-43		T.A. Crerar	H.W. McGill
1943-44		T.A. Crerar	H.W. McGill
1944-45		T.A. Crerar	R.A. Hoey (acting)
1945-46		J. Allison Glen	R.A. Hoey
1946-47		J. Allison Glen	R.A. Hoey
1947-48		James A. Mackinnon	R.A. Hoey
1948-49		Colin Gibson	D.M. McKay
1949-50	Citizenship and Immigration	Walter Harris	D.M. McKay
1950-51		Walter Harris	D.M. McKay
1951-52		Walter Harris	D.M. McKay
1952-53		Walter Harris	D.M. McKay
1953-54		J.W. Pickersgill	H.M. Jones
1954-55		J.W. Pickersgill	H.M. Jones
1955-56		J.W. Pickersgill	H.M. Jones
1956-57		E.D. Fulton (acting)	H.M. Jones

Year (March year end)	Department responsible for Indian Affairs	Minister responsible for Indian Affairs	Director of Indian Affairs
1957-58		E.D. Fulton (acting)	H.M. Jones
1958-59		Ellen Fairclough	H.M. Jones
1959-60		Ellen Fairclough	H.M. Jones
1960-61		Ellen Fairclough	H.M. Jones
1961-62		Ellen Fairclough	H.M. Jones
1962-63		R.A. Bell	H.M. Jones
1963-64		G. Favreau	R.F. Battle
1964-65		R. Tremblay	J.H. Gordon (acting)
1965		J.R. Nicholson	R.F. Battle
1965-66	Northern Affairs and National Resources	J. Marchand	R.F. Battle
1966-67	Indian Affairs and Northern Development	A. Laing	J.W. Churchman
1967-68		A. Laing	J.W. Churchman (acting)
1968		J. Chrétien and R. Andras (minister without portfolio)	J.W. Churchman (director)

Appendix D
Alberta Reserve Land Surrenders

Reserve number	1914 reserve name	Original area, 1914 (acres)	Surrendered to 1914 (acres)	Surrendered 1915-1930 (acres)
120	Makaoos	9,030	0	0
121	Ooneepowhayos	21,120	0	0
122	Puskeeahkeewenin	25,600	0	0
123	Keheewin	20,531	0	0
125	Saddle Lake and Blue Quill	73,600	0	18,720
125A	Cache Lake	8,960	0	0
128	Whitefish Lake	11,200	0	0
132	Michel	25,600	9,905	10,114
133	Alexis	14,720	24	39
133B	White Whale Lake	20,928	6,034	0
134	Alexander	26,240	9,438	9,489
135	Stony Plain	28,480	15,537	15,580
136	Papachase	25,536	25,536	25,536
137	Samson	39,360	7,400	9,680
138	Ermineskin	39,360	14,517	255
138A	Pigeon Lake	4,979	0	220
138B	Louis Bull	13,760	5,308	5,351
139	Montana	20,160	13,155	13,179
142	Bearspaw	69,760	1,583	1,852
143	Jacob	0	0	0
144	Chiniquay	0	0	0
145	Sarcee	69,120	6,247	6,281
146	Blackfoot	300,800	12,5845	126,014
147	Peigan	116,096	22,944	23,102
148	Blood	350,390	543	1,105
149	Cold Lake	46,720	10,412	132
149A	Cold Lake	177	0	0
149B	Cold Lake	10,268	0	0
153	Beaver lake	13,696	0	0

▶

Reserve number	1914 reserve name	Original area, 1914 (acres)	Surrendered to 1914 (acres)	Surrendered 1915-1930 (acres)
150	Driftpile River	15,964	0	82
150A	Sucker Creek	15,189	0	209
150C	Halcro	51	0	0
150B	Freeman	73	0	0
150D	Pakashaw	964	0	18
150E	Swan RIver	11,528	0	151
150F	Assineau River	175	0	0
150G	Sawridge	2,263	0	16
151	Peace River Crossing	3,520	0	3,520
151A	Peace River Crossing	5,120	0	0
151B	John Felix Tustavits	294	0	294
151C	Tavish Moosewah	126	0	126
151D	Aluie Kweenay	91	0	91
151E	Duncan Tustavits	118	0	118
151F	David Tustavits	134	0	134
151G	Gillian Bell	5	0	5
151H	Louis Cardinal	160	0	160
151K	William McKenzie	960	0	961
152	Beaver	15,360	0	15,040
152A	Neepee Chief	260	0	260
154	Sturgeon Lake	21,555	0	0
154A	Sturgeon Lake	649	0	0
154B	Sturgeon Lake	240	0	0
155	Metikoomah Lake	8,160	0	0
155A	Metikoomah Lake	2,592	0	0
155B	Mink Lake	1,241	0	0
162	Fox Lake	17,775	0	0
163	Beaver Ranch	2,080	0	0
164	Boyer River	10,560	0	0
164A	Child's Lake	7,040	0	0
166	Wabiskaw Lake	21,040	0	0
166A	Wabiskaw Lake	1,563	0	0
166B	Wabiskaw Lake	6,094	0	0
166C	Wabiskaw Lake	8,620	0	0

Notes

Introduction

1 Robert Allen Warrior, *Tribal Secrets: Recovering American Indian Intellectual Traditions* (Minneapolis: University of Minnesota Press, 1995), xvi.

2 Paul Tennant, "Native Indian Political Organizations in British Columbia, 1900-1969: A Response to Internal Colonialism," *BC Studies* 55 (Autumn 1982): 8. See also Peter Kulchyski, "A Considerable Unrest: F.O. Loft and the League of Indians," *Native Studies Review* 4, 1 and 2 (1988): 95-117.

3 Elizabeth Cook-Lynn, "American Indian Intellectualism and the New Indian Story," in *Natives and Academics: Researching and Writing About American Indians*, ed. Devon A. Mihesuah (Lincoln: University of Nebraska Press, 1998), 111-38 (quote, 111).

4 Cook-Lynn, "American Indian Intellectualism," 125.

5 Ibid., 129.

6 Personal communication with Hugh Dempsey, 20 February 1995, Calgary.

7 See James M. Pitsula, "The CCF Government and the Formation of the Union of Saskatchewan Indians," *Prairie Forum* 19, 2 (Fall 1994): 131-52; Olive Patricia Dickason, *Canada's First Nations* (Toronto: McClelland and Stewart, 1992), 328-29; E. Brian Titley, *A Narrow Vision: Duncan Campbell Scott and the Administration of Indian Affairs in Canada* (Vancouver: UBC Press, 1986), 101.

8 Richard G. Fox, "For a Nearly New Culture History," in *Recapturing Anthropology*, ed. Richard G. Fox (Santa Fe: School of American Research Press, 1991), 93-113 (see, esp., 95).

9 Michel Foucault, *The Archeology of Knowledge* (New York: Pantheon Books, 1972), 5.

10 John Comaroff and Jean Comaroff, *Ethnography and the Historical Imagination* (Oxford: Westview Press, 1992), 39, 45.

11 Comaroff and Comaroff, *Ethnography*, 16, 34.

Chapter 1: A General Setting

1 See James M. Pitsula, "The CCF Government and the Formation of the Union of Saskatchewan Indians," *Prairie Forum* 19, 2 (Fall 1994): 131-52; J.R. Miller, *Skyscrapers Hide the Heavens: A History of Indian-White Relations in Canada* (Toronto: University of Toronto Press, 1989), 220-21.

2 Robert Bothwell, Ian Drummond, and John English, *Canada, 1900-1945* (Toronto: University of Toronto Press, 1987) 373.

3 Donald Creigthon, *The Forked Road: Canada, 1939-1957* (Toronto: McClelland and Stewart, 1976) 50; Drummond, Bothwell, and English, *Canada*, 353-55

4 Bothwell, Drummond, and English, *Canada*, 355.

5 Ibid., 370.

6 Howard Palmer and Tamara Palmer, *Alberta: A New History* (Edmonton: Hurtig Publishers, 1990), 286.

7 Canada, *Sessional Papers*, Report of the Department of Mines and Resources, year end 1941, Director McGill, 161.

8 See Ronald F. Laliberte, "The Canadian State and Native Migrant Labour in Southern Alberta's Sugar Beet Industry" (MA thesis, University of Saskatchewan, 1994) for a discussion of the sugar beet industry. The annual reports of the DIA contained in the sessional papers mention road building, farm work, and bush work as being significant in the later years.

9 In his investigation of the end of agrarianism in Alberta and Saskatchewan, David Monod has shown how, in Alberta, the push towards farm mechanization drove many small farmers out of business. In his view, "because of higher labour costs, they could not compete with the mechanized producers without machinery, and they could not use machinery because their smaller acreage still meant higher area costs" (141). Not only did mechanization undermine the small farmer, but it also undermined the seasonal demand for farm labour that many Indian workers depended on for income. After the Second World War, the change in Alberta's agricultural industry was dramatic: small farms declined in number by 25 percent. Indian communities, in turn, found it increasingly difficult to participate in the new urban-industrial order from the isolation of their reserves, especially given the inadequate social and educational services offered them. See David Monod, "The End of Agrarianism: The Fight for Farm Parity in Alberta and Saskatchewan, 1935-48," *Labour/Le Travail* 16 (Fall 1985): 117-43.

10 See Dennis Guest, *The Emergence of Social Security in Canada*, 2nd ed. (Vancouver: UBC Press, 1991), chap. 8, which describes the discussions concerning this social legislation.

11 Frank James Tester and Peter Kulchyski, *Tammarniit (Mistakes): Inuit Relocation in the Eastern Arctic, 1939-63* (Vancouver: UBC Press, 1994), 94; Guest, *Social Security*, 145.

12 Tester and Kulchyski, *Tammarniit*, 94.

13 Guest, *Social Security*, 145; Tester and Kulchyski, *Tammarniit*, 97.

14 Bothwell, Drummond, and English, *Canada*, vol. 2, 174, 91.

15 Reginald Whitaker, *The Government Party: Organizing and Financing the Liberal Party of Canada, 1930-1958* (Toronto: University of Toronto Press, 1977), 140.

16 J.W. Pickersgill, *The Liberal Party* (Toronto: McClelland and Stewart, 1962), 37-53.

17 Alvin Finkel, *The Social Credit Phenomenon in Alberta* (Toronto: University of Toronto Press, 1989) 28.

18 Palmer and Palmer, *Alberta*, 244, 255, and 305-6.

19 Ibid., 286-91. As historian Alvin Finkel explains, between 1935 and 1945, the Social Credit "transformed from a mass, eclectic movement for social reform led by monetary reformers to a relatively small government party that enjoyed considerable support from various sectors of the Alberta population for its judicious combination of right-wing rhetoric and social service and road-building programs. The gas discoveries, and the U.S. inspired Cold War allowed Social Credit to maintain successfully a combination of mild social reformism and strident anti-socialism" (Finkel, *Social Credit*, 99).

20 A survey of the annual reports of the DIA indicate how little oil development was contributing to Indian reserve economies.

21 See John J. Barr, "The Impact of the Oil Boom on Alberta: Retrospect and Prospect," in *The Making of the Modern West: Western Canada since 1945*, ed. A.W. Rasporich (Calgary: University of Calgary Press, 1984), 97-103; Peter J. Smith, "Urban Development Trends in the Prairie Provinces," in *The Making of the Modern West: Western Canada since 1945*, ed. A.W. Rasporich (Calgary: University of Calgary Press, 1984), 133-43.

22 Finkel, *Social Credit*, 102, 146.

23 Ibid., 146.

24 For a more extensive overview of Aboriginal political groups, see Don Whiteside, *Efforts to Develop Aboriginal Political Associations in Canada, 1850-1965* (Ottawa: Aboriginal Institute of Canada, 1974); or Richard R.H. Lueger, "A History of Indian Associations in Canada, 1870-1970" (MA thesis, Carleton University, 1977).

Chapter 2: The Origins of the Indian Association of Alberta

1 Malcolm Norris to Ben Calfrobe, 13 September 1944, Murray Dobbin private collection.

2 Paul Tennant, "Native Indian Political Organizations," *BC Studies* 55 (Autumn 1982): 3-49, 8.

3 James M. Pitsula, "The CCF Government and the Formation of the Union of Saskatchewan Indians," *Prairie Forum* 19, 2 (Fall 1994): 131. Pitsula, cited in Norma Sluman and Jean Goodwill, *John Tootoosis: A Biography of a Cree Leader* (Winnipeg: Pemmican Publications, 1984), 185.

4 E. Brian Titley, *A Narrow Vision: Duncan Campbell Scott and the Administration of Indian Affairs in Canada*, (Vancouver: UBC Press, 1986), 101.

5 Jaqueline O'Donnell's thesis is one of the few to note the contribution of local factors to the founding and rise of a political group. See Jacqueline P. O'Donnell, "The Native Brotherhood of British Columbia, 1931-1950: A New Phase in Native Political Organization" (MA thesis, University of British Columbia, 1985).

6 Jacqueline O'Donnell (ibid.) suggests that, "without just cause, even a group of natives possessing the predisposition and potential to organize will not necessarily do so" (75). In her view, a "distinct historical experience" is necessary as it acts as a triggering factor, stimulating action within Indian communities. She uses this perspective to explain why, unlike other Indian groups in Canada, Indian peoples in British Columbia became politically active early on.

7 Titley, *Narrow Vision*, 101; Pitsula, "CCF Government," 131.

8 The task of writing the history of Indian political activity from a locally rooted perspective is hindered by the fact that many of the related documents and recollections are neither in public archives nor published in political memoirs. At this time, the Glenbow Archives, Calgary, holds a large body of papers relating to the IAA. Local concerns are not always reflected in the archival records on the subject, however. In the case of the IAA's history, important papers and photographs revealing the early years of IAA activity are still held privately, and many of the elders who participated in political activities in the 1930s and 1940 have died. Luckily, a few important individuals contributed to this account of the IAA. Stan Cuthand, Hugh Dempsey, Murray Dobbin, Willie Norris, Gordon Crowchild, and Harold Cardinal all provided private papers and memories that informed my assessment of the IAA's founding, thereby adding much to information derived from the limited archival sources. A great deal more oral history research must be done in the field of Indian political movements; this book represents a preliminary inquiry into the subject as it relates to Alberta. I hope that publishing some of this material will make it available to a larger audience and will contribute to a more specific understanding of Indian political action during the 1930s and 1940s.

9 Kerry Abel, *Drum Songs: Glimpses of Dene History* (Montreal: McGill-Queen's, 1993), 173.

10 Paul Tennant, *Aboriginal Peoples and Politics: The Indian Land Question in British Columbia, 1849-1989* (Vancouver: UBC Press, 1990), 112. Oral history on the Prairies supports this notion.

11 See Treaties and Historical Research Centre, *Indian Acts and Ammendments, 1868-1950* (Ottawa: Department of Indian and Northern Affairs, 1981).

12 Alexander Morris, *The Treaties of Canada with the Indians* (Saskatoon: Fifth House Publishers, 1991), 250. For a detailed discussion of Treaty 7, see Treaty Seven Elders and Tribal Council with Sarah Carter, Walter Hildebrandt, and Dorothy First Rider, *The True Spirit and Original Intent of Treaty 7* (Montreal: McGill-Queen's University Press, 1996).

13 Abel, *Drum Songs*, 168-69. As Abel points out, "Because of the strength of the opposition to the creation of reserves, the treaty commissioners decided to leave the reserve question in abeyance. Although they duly reported that the Natives did not want reserves, the clause stipulating that they were to be created was left in the text of the treaty" (171). Unlike in the southern regions of Alberta, in the northern regions reserve lands were less of an issue within Indian communities as the local economy was firmly based on hunting, trapping, and fishing.

14 Stan Cuthand, "A Sacred Treaty," unpublished manuscript, 1997. In author's collection.

15 Hugh Dempsey, *Treaty Research Report: Treaty Seven* (Ottawa: Treaties and Historical Research Centre, 1987), 37-39; John Leonard Taylor, *Treaty Research Report: Treaty Six* (Ottawa: Treaties and Historical Research Centre, 1985), 22-24. See also Richard Price, ed., *The Spirit of the Alberta Indian Treaties* (Edmonton: Pica Pica Press, 1987).

16 Abel, *Drum Songs*, 170-72.

17 Personal communication with Muriel Manywounds, September 1996. The relationship between the treaties and the Indian Act was a continual subject of discussion both in IAA meetings and amongst the leadership.
18 Ibid.
19 Joe Dion, *My Tribe the Crees* (Calgary: Glenbow-Alberta Institute, 1996), 145.
20 See Indian Agent monthly reports, National Archives of Canada (NAC), RG 10, vol. 4046, f. 353,647 (reel C-14257). Although these reports are for the early 1920s, the pattern was not reversed during the Great Depression.
21 NAC, RG 10, vol. 4046, f. 353, 647, annual report of Agent T. Graham, 31 March 1920.
22 Claudia Notzke, *Indian Reserves in Canada: Development Problems of the Stoney and Peigan Reserves in Alberta* (Marburga: Geographischen Instituts der Universitat Marburg, 1985), 17.
23 Hugh Dempsey, *The Gentle Persuader: A Biography of James Gladstone, Indian Senator* (Saskatoon: Western Producer Prairie Books, 1986), 78.
24 NAC, RG 10, vol. 10414, box 47 (reel T-10071). A.G. Smith to Agent Laight, 23 December 1938; Agent Laight to P.J. Bristow, 1 December 1938.
25 Personal communication with Muriel Manywounds, September 1996.
26 NAC, RG 10, vol. 10414, f. 47, Indian Agent Laight to Secretary, Indian Affairs Branch, 20 March 1939.
27 See NAC, RG 10, vol. 10414, f. 47, which contains many letters between Indian agents regarding the travels of reserve members.
28 Personal communication with Harold Cardinal, 20 February 1997.
29 Ibid., 114, 202.
30 Ibid., 202-3.
31 See NAC, RG 10, vol. 10414, f. 47. This file contains correspondence between the Edmonton Agency Indian agent and various provincial and federal administrators regarding fishing issues.
32 NAC, RG 10, vol. 10414, f. 47, 1 August 1939, Alberta fishing regulation report.
33 NAC, RG 10, vol. 6732, f. 420-2B, Agent Gullion report, 1 March 1931.
34 NAC, RG 10, vol. 10414 f. 47, Phil. J. Power, Hudson's Bay Company to Battleford Indian Agent, 25 November 1939.
35 Ibid. Translated letter from Alphonse Pichie to the Indian Agent, Portage La Loche, 25 November 1939.
36 John Leonard Taylor, *Canadian Indian Policy during the Interwar Years, 1918-1939* (Ottawa: Department of Indian Affairs, 1984), 30. The relatively small size of reserves in Canada is analyzed by Robert White-Harvey, "Reservation Geography and the Restoration of Native Self-Government," *Dalhousie Law Journal* 17, 2 (Fall 1994): 587-611.
37 See Appendix D for a list of reserve land-base changes over time.
38 See David Lupul, "The Bobtail Land Surrender," *Alberta History* 26, 1 (Winter 1978): 29-39. Lupul gives a good indication of the interests in reserve lands in the early twentieth century.
39 *Calgary Albertan*, 29 May 1911, in the Glenbow clipping file, Blackfoot – Lands and Natural Resources.
40 George Gooderham, "Twenty Five Years as an Indian Agent to the Blackfoot Band," in Gooderham Fonds, M3974, f. 1, Glenbow Archives, Calgary.
41 Notzke, 43. See also NAC, RG 10, vol. 4093, f. 600,107, which contains Indian complaints against the Peigan leases.
42 Ibid., 44.
43 NAC, RG 10, vol. 4046, f. 353, 647. List of Alberta reserve lands for sale in 1924.
44 See Howard Palmer and Tamara Palmer, *Alberta: A New History* (Edmonton: Hurtig Publishers, 1990), 244-46 on population, 252 on low grain prices; see also John J. Barr, "The Impact of Oil on Alberta: Retrospect and Prospect," in *The Making of the Modern West*, ed. A.W. Rasporich (Calgary: University of Calgary Press, 1984), 97-103, especially 98-99.
45 Roger Gibbins, "Regionalism in Decline: 1940 to the Present," in *Riel to Reform: A History of Protest in Western Canada*, ed. George Melnyk (Saskatoon: Fifth House Publishers, 1992), 215-23, 220-21.
46 See the Indian Act, R.S.C. 1924, sec. 141.

47 The *Regina Post* reported the meeting of Indian leaders in Fort Macleod in June 1925 to form an association known as the Allied Tribes of Western Canada. Many of those who attended this meeting (including Walking Buffalo, Teddy Yellowfly, Mike Mountain Horse) were later active in the League of Indians of Western Canada and in the IAA. See *Regina Post*, 8 June 1925. Hugh Dempsey, private papers.

48 Titley, *Narrow Vision*, 101.

49 Kulchyski, "A Considerable Unrest," 99. See also Sluman and Goodwill, *John Tootoosis*, 128-36.

50 See Stan Cuthand, "The Native Peoples of the Prairie Provinces in the 1920s and 1930s," in *One Century Later: Western Canadian Reserve Indians Since Treaty 7*, ed. Donald B. Smith and Ian A.L. Getty (Vancouver: UBC Press, 1978), 32.

51 NAC, RG 10, vol. 3211, f. 527, 787, pt. 1 (Reel C-11340). Letter from J.L. Laverne, O.M.I. to Fred Loft, 18 January 1922. Laverne was sending money, collected by members of the Peigan reserve, to Loft for use by the league.

52 See Sluman and Goodwill, *John Tootoosis*, 172.

53 Cuthand, "Native Peoples," 33.

54 The history of the UFA is well described. See C.B. Macpherson, *Democracy in Alberta: Social Credit and the Party System* (Toronto: University of Toronto Press, 1962); W.K. Rolph, *Henry Wise Wood of Alberta* (Toronto: University of Toronto Press, 1950); Carl F. Betke, "Farm Politics in an Urban Age: The Decline of the United Farmers of Alberta after 1921," in *Essays in Western History*, ed. Lewis H. Thomas (Edmonton: University of Alberta Press, 1976).

55 Glenbow clipping file, Agricultural Societies, "Alberta's First Farm Group Formed Provincially in '09," no source, 26 November 1953.

56 M1749, UFA Fonds, Glenbow Archives, 1936 convention minutes, microfilm.

57 See Alvin Finkel, "Populism and Gender: The UFA and Social Credit Experiences," *Journal of Canadian Studies* 27, 4 (Winter 1992-93): 76-94.

58 Personal communication with Muriel Manywounds, September 1996.

59 Personal communication with Pauline Dempsey, September 1996; Muriel Manywounds, September 1996; Sheldon Cardinal, October 1996; Johnny Callihoo's AFU membership card is in the private collection of Hugh Dempsey.

60 Murray Dobbin, *One and a Half Men: The Story of Jim Brady and Malcolm Norris, Metis Patriots of the Twentieth Century* (Vancouver: New Star Books, 1981), 63.

61 Ibid., 64.

62 Personal communication with Willy Norris, March 1995; see also Dobbin, *One and a Half*, 34-41.

63 Ibid., 31-33.

64 Ibid., 57-58; Joe Dion, *My Tribe, the Crees* (Calgary: Glenbow Museum, 1979), 156-63. In this section, Dion recalls his teaching days, which give some insight into his concern with the well-being of the Kehewin community.

65 Dobbin, *One and a Half Men*, 69.

66 Ibid., 92.

67 Ibid., 88.

68 Saskatchewan Archives Board, Don Nielson interview with Murray Dobbin, tape No. IH-399, transcript disc 96, 10 August 1977.

69 Ibid., 84. The extent to which Norris involved himself in Indian questions is difficult to document since his personal papers are still privately held.

70 *Calgary Albertan*, 7 January 1915; *Calgary Herald*, 12 December 1924.

71 *Lethbridge Herald*, 14 November 1924, in RG 10, vol. 4093, f. 600, 107 [reel C-11063].

72 NAC, RG 10, vol. 4093, f. 600,107, 24 January 1925, Mike Mountain Horse to the Minister of the Interior.

73 Ibid., 3 February 1925, Indian Affairs Branch letter, no author.

74 Cuthand, "Native Peoples," 33-34.

75 M 331, Joe Dion Papers, Glenbow Archives. Joe Dion in correspondence with Hugh Dempsey, 12 November 1960.

76 Personal communication with Stan Cuthand, spring 1995. Cuthand mentioned that it

was difficult to travel distances to attend meetings and that people would travel by horse and wagon. Travel is also mentioned in Joe Dion, *My Tribe*, 173. Hugh Dempsey confirms that people found it difficult to travel during the Depression, and he suggests that this led to the founding of an Alberta branch of the League of Indians of Western Canada in 1932. Personal communication with Hugh Dempsey, 20 February 1995.

77 Hugh Dempsey, private papers; Callihoo Papers; Augustine Steinhauer, Saddle Lake, to Johnny Callihoo, 15 March 1937. See also Sluman and Goodwill, *John Tootoosis*, 156.

78 Hugh Dempsey, private papers; Callihoo Papers; Peter Gladu of Beaverlake Reserve to Johnny Callihoo, 3 August 1937.

79 Sluman and Goodwill, *John Tootoosis*, 154 and 173.

80 The activities of Tootoosis during this period are described in Sluman and Goodwill, *John Tootoosis*, 148-50, 157-63.

81 Hugh Dempsey, *Gentle Persuader*, 108-9. For a short account of this meeting see the *Edmonton Journal*, 5 August 1937. The meeting was well attended, and it included delegates from Manitoba as well as the infamous Grey Owl.

82 Sluman and Goodwill, *John Tootoosis*, 172-73.

83 Ibid., 182.

84 Victoria Callihoo, "The Iroquois in Alberta," *Alberta Historical Review* 7, 2 (Spring 1959): 17.

85 See also K. Dalheim and M. Kerr, eds., *Calahoo Trails* (The Calahoo Women's Institute, 1976); John Laurie, "One of the Greatest Indians Ever Born in Alberta," *Camsell Arrow* 9, 3 (September/October 1955): 9-11.

86 Personal communication with Willie Norris, March 1995.

87 Ibid.

88 See Dobbin, *One and a Half Men*, 150. The first constitution of the IAA cannot be located, but a copy seems to be attached to the application for society status that the IAA submitted to the Alberta provincial government in 1940. This document is used in this book.

89 Hugh Dempsey contends that the first IAA constitution was an adapted copy of the MAA constitution (Hugh Dempsey, personal communication, 20 February 1995 and 25 July 1995). To date, it is impossible to tell to what extent the constitution was adapted or changed for the IAA. I assume that it was left virtually intact.

90 Personal communication with Hugh Dempsey, 25 July 1995.

91 Hugh Dempsey, private papers; Callihoo Papers. The letters written to Johnny Callihoo between 1937 and 1939 reflect this range of issues. This is also confirmed by a letter from Joe Dion to Hugh Dempsey concerning the founding of the IAA. Clearly, the issues pertaining to war veterans were not part of the agenda; treaty issues were the primary concern. See M331, Joe Dion Papers, Glenbow Archives, f. 19, Joe Dion to Hugh Dempsey, 12 November 1960.

92 M656, John Laurie Papers, Glenbow Archives, f. 22, "The Indian Association of Alberta," by John Laurie. The meeting is described in John Laurie's account of the IAA, 31.

93 Hugh Dempsey, private papers, Hugh Dempsey's private notes.

94 Murray Dobbin, private papers, Norris to Dion, 21 July 1944. This letter is addressed to Dion as vice-president of the IAA.

95 According to Murray Dobbin, "A common feature of the Alberta and Saskatchewan Leagues was their loose structure and undemocratic methods" (Dobbin, *One and a Half*, 150).

96 Murray Dobbin, private papers, letter from Norris to Joe Dion, 18 April 1945.

97 Ibid.

98 Ibid., Norris to J.B. Tootoosis, 8 July 1944.

99 Ibid.

100 Though the 1939 constitution document cannot be located, it seems that a 1944 copy, with revisions, is assumed to be a copy of the original. See Hugh Dempsey, private collection.

101 Hugh Dempsey, private papers; Callihoo Papers, letters written to Callihoo from 1937 to 1939.

102 Murray Dobbin, private papers, Norris to Ben Calfrobe, 13 September 1944.

103 Hugh Dempsey, private papers. See IAA application for society status.

104 Ibid.

105 Ibid.

106 Donald B. Smith, private papers, newspaper clipping, *Ottawa Citizen*, 28 February 1938.

Chapter 3: Structure and Expansion

1 Hugh Dempsey, private papers; Callihoo papers, John Callihoo to Chris Shade, March 1944.

2 Murray Dobbin, *One and a Half Men: The Story of Jim Brady and Malcolm Norris, Metis Patriots of the Twentieth Century* (Vancouver: New Star Books, 1981), 150.

3 Hugh Dempsey, private papers. See IAA Society status application.

4 Ibid.

5 Murray Dobbin, private papers, John Laurie to Andrew Paull, 12 October 1944.

6 Joe Dion, *My Tribe, the Crees* (Calgary: Glenbow Museum, 1979), 174.

7 See M331, Joe Dion Papers, Glenbow Archives, file 19, Joe Dion to Hugh Dempsey, 12 November 1960.

8 Hugh Dempsey, private papers; Callihoo Papers, file 1940-49. Based on a letter from W.H. Steinhauer to Johnny Callihoo, 1941 (this letter mentions the resolutions).

9 NAC, RG 10, vol. 10414, box 48, pt. a, Secretary, Indian Affairs Branch, to Indian Agent G.C. Laight, Winterburn, 17 March 1941.

10 Hugh Dempsey, private papers; Callihoo Papers, William Okemaw to Johnny Callihoo, 2 April 1944.

11 Hugh Dempsey, private papers; Callihoo Papers, 1940-49 file. Callihoo was paid by the Alexis band to visit.

12 M331, Joe Dion Papers, Glenbow Archives, Joe Dion to Hugh Dempsey, 12 November 1960.

13 Personal communication with Jim Tootoosis, Poundmaker Reserve, September 1996; see also NAC, RG 10, vol. 10414, box 48, pt. d, Indian Agent G.C. Laight to A.J. Charnetski, Supervisor Farm Labour Service, Department of Agriculture, 19 April 1943; C. Pant Schmidt, Inspector of Alberta Agencies, Circular Letter, 18 April 1943.

14 M1825, Hobbema Agency Fonds, Glenbow Archives, agent's daily journals, Agent Lewis, 24 May 1944.

15 See Indian Act, R.S.C. 1927, S. 16, c. 98(2), which states: "No half-breed head of a family, except the widow of an Indian or a half-breed who has already been admitted into a treaty, shall, unless under very special circumstances, which shall be determined by the Superintendent General or his agent, be accounted an Indian or entitled to be admitted into any Indian treaty." When coupled with section 18 (1) – "The Superintendent General may, from time to time, upon the report of an officer, or other person specially appointed by him to make an inquiry, determine who is or who is not a member of any band of Indians entitled to share in the property and annuities of the band" – the preceding section allowed the government to de-register Indians deemed to be half-breeds. Half-breeds were identified on the basis of their acceptance of scrip – a system of payment in land and money granted by the Dominion government to the Métis peoples upon the extinguishment of their land rights (after 1867 and 1885). For a full discussion of the intricacies of the scrip system, see Douglas Sanders, "The Queen's Promises," in *Law and Justice in a New Land: Essays in Western Canadian Legal History*, ed. Louis A. Knafla (Calgary: Carswell, 1986), 101-27, 107-12.

16 The reduction of band memberships was a goal of the DIA's Malcolm McCrimmon, who challenged dozens of memberships during the war years. Communities in the Lesser Slave Lake Agency, and also around Hobbema, saw this bureaucrat strike many of their community members from the membership lists. In 1942, McCrimmon struck 640 people from band lists. For a detailed discussion of this activity, see John Goddard, *Last Stand of the Lubicon Cree* (Vancouver: Douglas and McIntyre, 1991), 21-31. See also M 656, John Laurie Papers, Glenbow Archives, f. .22, "The Indian Association of Alberta," 14-15.

17 See NAC, RG 10, vol. 10414, box 48, Laight to T.R. Blaine, Government of Alberta, 22 January 1942.

18 The practical workings of this policy are illustrated by a case on the Stoney Plain reserve,

as reported by Indian Agent Laight in 1941: "This man and his family have been ordered to leave the reserve on several occasions during the past five years, in fact he has been off this reserve four times during 1941. When ordered to leave the man goes away but leaves his wife and children on the reserve, they move to another part of the reserve and live in the bush where they cannot be seen." See NAC, RG 10, vol. 10414, box 48, Laight to T.R. Blaine, Government of Alberta, 22 January 1942.

19 NAC, RG 10, vol. 6826, f. 496-3-3, Dr. Harold W. McGill to John Laurie, 3 August 1944.

20 M7155, IAA Papers, Glenbow Archives, IAA Memorial on Indian Affairs, 1944, 2. As a result of the IAA petition, the DIA allowed Hodgson and Ward to remain on the reserve. See also Sanders, "Queen's Promises," 112.

21 Hugh Dempsey, private papers; Callihoo Papers, list of locals as of 14 October 1944. The reason for Stoney interest in the IAA related directly to the extreme poverty of their reserve. The lack of suitable agricultural lands around Morley, and the shrinking Stoney hunting territories as a result of the establishment of Banff National Park caused much of their hardship. Through membership in the IAA, Stoney leaders sought to gain social assistance for their people.

22 Malcolm Norris noted the reason for this change in the constitution in a margin note on the original IAA constitution. Hugh Dempsey, private collection.

23 Hugh Dempsey, private papers, Albert Lightning interview with Hugh Dempsey, Blood Reserve, May 1959.

24 M1825, Hobbema Agency Fonds, Glenbow Archives, Agent's Daily Journal, 29 May 1944.

25 Personal communication with Hugh Dempsey, September 1996; personal communication with Gordon Crowchild, September 1996.

26 Personal communication with Gordon Crowchild, September 1996.

27 Dempsey, *Gentle Persuader*, 108.

28 M100, John Blackmore Fonds, Glenbow Archives, file 130. Jim White Bull to John Blackmore, MP, 14 March 1944.

29 M100, John Blackmore Fonds, Glenbow Archives, file 130. Other letters in this file expand on the issues that concerned the Blood community.

30 Murray Dobbin, private collection, Johnny Callihoo to Chris Shade, March 1944.

31 Hugh Dempsey, *Gentle Persuader*, 109-10.

32 Personal communication with Hugh Dempsey, 20 February 1995.

33 According to Hugh Dempsey, John Cotton and Dick Soup were part of these meetings, and they were involved with John Blackmore a year or two earlier.

34 M656, John Laurie Papers, Glenbow Archives, file 2, Rev. B.S. Green to John Laurie, 15 March 1945.

35 M656, John Laurie Papers, Glenbow Archives, file 2, John Laurie to Johnny Callihoo, 9 April 1945.

36 Reta Rowan Papers, University of Alberta Archives, IAA 1945 annual meeting minutes, 4-5.

37 M3974, George Gooderham Papers, Glenbow Archives, file 1, "Twenty-Five years as an Indian Agent to the Blackfoot Band," 1.

38 Valerie K. Jobson, "The Blackfoot Farming Experiment" (MA thesis, University of Calgary, 1990), 120.

39 Ibid., 23.

40 Ibid., 121.

41 As early as 1935, the Blackfoot chiefs had requested a meeting with DIA officials to discuss their band funds and surrendered lands; however the DIA vetoed the council resolution that the chiefs visit Ottawa and, as a result, the trip was cancelled. Teddy Yellowfly was one of the chiefs who participated in this protest. See NAC, RG 10, vol. 7142, f. 772/3-7, 25 November 1935; and A.F. McKenzie to Agent Gooderham, 17 December 1935. Interestingly, Jobson suggests that the failure of farming and the loss of autonomy drove the Blackfoot "back to Blackfoot traditional ways" (Jobson, "Blackfoot Farming," 127). The response of some Blackfoot was decidedly opposite: they chose to join a progressive political organization – the IAA.

42 M8078, Hanks Papers, Glenbow Archives, file 300/9, interview with Ben Calf Robe.

43 Ibid., file 300/22, interview with Indian Agent Gooderham.

44 M7655, James Gladstone Papers, file 328, Glenbow Archives, John Laurie to James Gladstone, 15 May 1951

45 Personal communication with Hugh and Pauline Dempsey, September 1996. See also Frances Weaselfat and the Indian Association of Alberta, "Our Legacy: 50 Years in Unity, 1943-1993, Indian Association of Alberta 50th Annual Assembly and Anniversary Commemoration brochure," September 1993. See Appendix A.

46 Hugh Dempsey, "David Crowchild," unpublished manuscript, Hugh Dempsey, private collection.

47 Personal communication with Harold Cardinal, 20 February 1997.

48 M656, John Laurie Fonds, Glenbow Archives, file 11, bulletin, 1 May 1954.

49 Personal communication with Gordon Crowchild, September 1996.

50 Personal communication with Hugh and Pauline Dempsey, February 1995.

51 NAC, RG 10, vol. 8476 (reel C-13813), D.M. McKay memo, approves of spending of Blackfoot band funds to feed IAA delegates meeting on the Blackfoot reserve, 29 May 1952.

52 Personal communication with Pauline Dempsey, September 1996.

53 See photographs on pages 101-6. These photographs reveal aspects of IAA meetings.

54 Personal communication with Hugh and Pauline Dempsey, September 1996.

55 M7155, IAA Papers, no file, Glenbow Archives, IAA Annual Meeting, minutes for 12 and 13 June 1952, Mrs. Dan Minde.

56 It seems there could be a relationship between the role of women in the IAA and the role of women in the farm unions. Since Indian farmers held membership in farm unions, it makes sense that their partners would take on the same roles in the IAA as they did in the unions. Further research needs to be done in the area of gender and Indian political activity. See Alvin Finkel, "Populism and Gender: The UFA and Social Credit Experiences," *Journal of Canadian Studies* 27, 4 (Winter 1992-93): 76-94.

57 Reta Rowan Papers, University of Alberta Archives, "Mrs. Crowchild," *Calgary Herald*, n.d., file 17/1/1-69.

58 M656, John Laurie Papers, Glenbow Archives, file 11, IAA annual meeting, 1953, meeting minutes, 13.

59 M656, John Laurie Papers, Glenbow Archives, file 11, IAA annual meeting, 1953, meeting minutes, 7.

60 NAC, RG 10, vol. 8476, f. 1/24-2-1, pt. 2 (reel C-13813), D.M. McKay to G. Gooderham, 16 July 1952. This was a reiteration of policy from previous years.

61 Gooderham may have been an exceptionally tolerant Indian agent as he had a life-long association with Indian peoples. Born on Poor Man's reserve in Saskatchewan, and raised on Piapot's reserve, he spoke Cree and was intimately familiar with the traditions of Plains First Nations. He succeeded his father as Indian agent at Gleichen, Alberta, in 1920 at the young age of thirty-one. Biographical material on Gooderham can be found in the George Gooderham Papers in the Glenbow Archives as well as in Donald B. Smith, *Long Lance: The True Story of an Impostor* (Toronto: Macmillan, 1982), 59-60.

62 NAC, RG 10, vol. 8476, f. 1/24-2-1, pt. 3, "Confidential" letter, R.F. Battle to Col. Jones, 27 June 1955.

63 NAC, RG 10, vol. 8476, f. 1/24-2-1, pt. 3, R.F. Battle to Col. Jones, 30 December 1955.

64 Before 1951, Indian Act, R.S.C. 1927, c. 98, s. 126-37 forbade Indian people from purchasing or possessing liquor, and it dealt with the details and charges applying to liquor possession. These sections on liquor were repealed in 1951 by subsection 123(2), c. 29, of the Indian Act, 1951.

65 NAC, RG 10, vol. 8476, f. 1/24-2-1, pt. 3, Constable Neil McLeod to Superintendent of Indian Agencies, Regina, 16 June 1951.

66 Personal communication with Hugh and Pauline Dempsey, September 1996; personal communication with Gordon Crowchild, September 1996; personal communication with Muriel Manywounds, October 1996.

Chapter 4: "Outside Help"

1 M656, John Laurie Papers, Glenbow Archives, f. 2, John Laurie to Pat Lalonde, 7 September 1945.

2 Interestingly, French political anthropologist Pierre Clastres has written eloquently about the tendency of the Western world to view "primitive societies" as devoid of power. This line of thinking suggests that these societies are unable to attain a state of civility beyond subsistence because the West has arbitrarily tied the state of civilization to the acquisition of institutionalized instruments of power and coercion; that is, it has tied it to the acquisition of statehood. With the help of ethnological theory, the absence of any visible and effective organ of power has led many to deny non-Western societies, including Aboriginal societies, even the function of power. Access to political power, according to this perspective, assumes access to social change. See Pierre Clastres, *Society against the State* (New York: Zone Books, 1989), 189-218.

3 R.M. Galois, "The Indian Rights Association," *Native Studies Review* 8, 2 (1992): 1-34, 8-9; Darcy Anne Mitchell, "The Allied Tribes of British Columbia: A Study in Pressure Group Behaviour" (MA thesis, University of British Columbia, 1977), 105-6; Philip Drucker, *The Native Brotherhoods: Modern Intertribal Organizations on the Northwest Coast*, Smithsonian Institution, Bureau of American Ethnology Bulletin No. 168 (Washington: Government Printing Office, 1958), 81

4 J.R. Miller, *Skyscrapers Hide the Heavens: A History of Indian White Relations in Canada* (Toronto: University of Toronto Press, 1989), 220, 221. See also James M. Pitsula, "The CCF Government and the Formation of the Union of Saskatchewan Indians," *Prairie Forum* 19, 2 (Fall 1994): 132; John Tobias, "Protection, Civilization, Assimilation: An Outline History of Canada's Indian Policy," in *Sweet Promises: A Reader on Indian-White Relations in Canada*, ed. J.R. Miller (Toronto: University of Toronto Press, 1991), 127-44, 139.

5 Hugh Dempsey, private collection, interview with Albert Lightning, 22 May 1959.

6 Personal communication with Ruth Gorman, 5 July 1992.

7 *The Crescent Bugle* (Crescent Heights yearbook), Glenbow Archives, 1928 edition, 54.

8 Donald B. Smith, personal research notes in collection of author, information provided by the Calgary Public School Board.

9 Dean H.T. Coutts, "Presentation of John Lee Laurie," *New Trail* 14, 3 (1957): 6.

10 See John Morgan Gray, *Fun Tomorrow: Learning to Be a Publiser and Much Else* (Toronto: Macmillan, 1978), 191. Ruth Gorman also believed he was a war veteran.

11 Personal communication with Ruth Gorman, July 1992.

12 Murray Dobbin, private collection, John Laurie to Dorise Neilsen, 25 March 1944.

13 M656 John Laurie Fonds, Glenbow Archives, file 25, Autobiography dictated to Marjorie Bond.

14 M656 John Laurie Fonds, Glenbow Archives, file 25, Autobiography dictated to Marjorie Bond, 2-5.

15 A.H. Young, *The War Memorial Volume of Trinity College* (Toronto, Toronto: Printers Guild Ltd., 1922). M656, John Laurie Papers, Glenbow Archives.

16 An excellent description of Laurie's life can be found in Donald B. Smith, "A Good Samaritan: John Laurie," in *Citymakers: Calgarians after the Frontier* (Calgary: Historical Society of Alberta, 1987), 263-74. Many people believed that Laurie had served overseas and had sustained some war injuries. In the *Calgary Herald*, 27 February 1953, Ken Liddell stated: "He saw service in Europe and on patrol work."

17 Smith, "Good Samaritan," 266-67; Coutts, "Presentation," 6; A.H. Young, *The War Memorial Volume of Trinity College*, in M656, John Laurie Papers, Glenbow Archives; *Calgary Herald*, n.d., Glenbow Clipping file, 1959.

18 Smith, "Good Samaritan," 267. According to Liesemer, John Laurie was little affected by the politics of Aberhart, though he did respect his work as principal of the school. Interview by Donald B. Smith with Aylmer Liesemer, 1985.

19 Donald B. Smith interviews with Laurie's students Jack Dunn and Shelagh Jameson; see also Smith, "Good Samaritan," 267.

20 *The Crescent Bugle* (yearbook), 1928-1940 editions, Glenbow Library.

21 Smith, "Good Samaritan," 267; personal communication with Ruth Gorman, July 1992; According to Cynthia Downe, Laurie was not a "party man." Politically, however Harkness and Liesemer were his political connections (Cynthia Downe, personal communication, December 1994). According to Hugh Dempsey, Laurie met Norris at a CCF meeting

in Calgary (personal communication February 1995). According to Dorothy Gowan, Crescent Heights was a politicized school.

22 Laurie's introduction to the Stoney is described in his manuscript, "The Indian Association of Alberta," M656, John Laurie Papers, Glenbow Archives, file 22, 1-3; see also Smith, "Good Samaritan," 267-68.

23 Personal communication with Dorothy Gowan, August 1995.

24 Ibid.

25 Personal communication with Ruth Gorman, July 1992.

26 M656, John Laurie Papers, Glenbow Archives, file 22, "The Indian Association of Alberta," by John Laurie, 2.

27 Douglas Sanders, "The Queen's Promises," in *Law and Justice in a New Land: Essays in Western Canadian Legal History*, ed. Louis A. Knafla (Toronto: Carswell, 1986), 101-27, 104-6. Very interestingly, in 1932 R.B. Bennett himself had inquired into the poor state of the Stoney reserve. See RG 10, vol. 7101, f. 772/3-1, pt. 1, Duncan Campbell Scott to R.B. Bennett, 15 January 1932.

28 M656, John Laurie Papers, Glenbow Archives, file 22, "The Indian Association of Alberta," 3.

29 Apparently Laurie was speaking publicly on Indian issues and writing newspaper articles on the poverty of reserve communities during the war years. See M656, John Laurie Papers, Glenbow Archives, file 22, John Laurie manuscript, 5-6; see also Murray Dobbin, private collection, John Laurie to George H. Ross, 12 February 1944.

30 Murray Dobbin, private collection, John Laurie to George H. Ross, 12 February 1944. Laurie appears to have joined the League of Nations of North American Indians in early 1944. This international organization, headed by Lawrence Two Axe, sought to promote the shared concerns of American and Canadian First Nations. Little information is available on the relationship between Laurie and this organization; however, a few samples of letters from this league have been found in Laurie's correspondence. One of these letters is in the possession of the author.

31 Hugh Dempsey, private papers, Norris to Callihoo, 10 February 1944. No other information on this association exists. It seems that it strove for political equality for Indian peoples.

32 Murray Dobbin, private collection, John Laurie to George H. Ross, 12 February 1944 (in response to questions from Ross about issues Laurie raised publicly in 1943).

33 M656, John Laurie Papers, Glenbow Archives, file 22, "The Indian Association of Alberta," 4; see also the *Minutes of Proceedings of the Special Committee on Reconstruction and Re-establishment* (Ottawa: King's Printer, 1944).

34 *Minutes of Proceedings of the Special Committee on Reconstruction and Re-establishment*, Thursday, 18 May 1944, 254, 258-59; see also 24 May 1944.

35 Ibid., 310.

36 Murray Dobbin, private collection, John Laurie to G.H. Castleden, 26 February 1945.

37 Murray Dobbin, private collection, John Laurie to Dorise Nielsen, 25 March 1944 (in response to inquiries made by her in 1943). See also Margaret Conrad and Julie Landau, "Dorise Nielsen, 1902-1980: A Tribute," *Atlantis* 6, 2 (1981): 138-46. Dorise Nielsen was elected to Parliament in 1940 as an independent. She was originally a supporter of the CCF but was expelled from the party in 1940 because of her campaign strategy. According to historian Margaret Conrad, "She saw her role as spokesperson for the poor and oppressed of Canada" (138). Her central political concerns included full employment for both men and women, equal pay for equal work, and other social causes. These concerns easily carried over to First Nations in Canada and were perfectly compatible with the IAA's focus upon the economic development of reserve communities. Disillusioned with Canada's political left, Nielsen went to China in 1957 and became a Chinese citizen in 1962. She died in Peking in 1980.

38 Murray Dobbin, private collection, John Laurie to Dorise Neilsen, 25 March 1944 (in response to inquiries made by her in 1943).

39 Laurie, "Indian Association of Alberta," 4; see also Fred Kennedy, "Personality of the Week," in the *Calgary Herald*, n.d. Glenbow Clipping file, John Laurie; Smith, "Good

Samaritan," 268. According to Smith, Ed Hunter was the first Stoney to attend high school in Calgary.

40 Murray Dobbin, private collection, John Laurie to John Bracken, 8 May 1944. The emphasis in this letter was on improving education for Indian children, and it called for the extension of social legislation to Indian people.

41 Personal communication with Hugh Dempsey, September 1996.

42 Department of Indian Affairs, in-house correspondence, RG 10, vol. 7101, f. 772/3-1 pt. 1.

43 Hugh Dempsey, private collection, Norris to Callihoo, 10 February 1944.

44 Ibid.

45 Hugh Dempsey, private collection, Norris to Callihoo, 24 March 1944.

46 Personal communication with Gordon Crowchild, September 1996.

47 M7655, James Gladstone Papers, Glenbow Archives, file 328, John Laurie to James Gladstone, 26 January 1951.

48 Hugh Dempsey, private papers, IAA by-laws, 1944.

49 M7655, James Gladstone Papers, Glenbow Archives, file 328, John Laurie to the Blood Reserve IAA Local, 25 February 1946. Laurie's duties as secretary are outlined in this letter.

50 Murray Dobbin, private collection, John Laurie to Sam Minde, 3 July 1944.

51 Murray Dobbin, private collection, John Laurie to G.H. Castleden, 26 February 1945.

52 House of Commons, *Debates*, J.A. Glen, 24 October 1945, 1457.

53 Ibid., 1446-47.

54 Ibid., 1448

55 Ibid., 1450-51.

56 Murray Dobbin, private collection, John Laurie to Castleden, 22 February 1945.

57 House of Commons, *Debates*, 14 December 1945, 3514.

58 Ibid., 11 July 1947, 5486-89; 14 December 1945, 3514-15; 26 June 1947, 4727.

59 Ibid., 11 July 1947, 5487; 13 May 1946, 1464.

60 Ibid., 11 July 1947, 5488.

61 Ibid., *Debates*, 14 December 1945, 3516.

62 Personal communication with Cynthia Downe, 14 December 1994.

63 M7155, IAA Papers, Glenbow Archives, no file, Alberta Home and School News newsletter, May and June 1945, 4.

64 M7155, IAA Papers, Glenbow Archives, no file, Crescent Heights Home and School Association resolutions.

65 Personal communication with Cynthia Downe, 14 December 1994.

66 Ibid.

67 See also *Calgary Albertan*, 23 December 1970; *Calgary Herald*, 18 December 1970; *Foothills Review* (Winter/Spring 1977).

68 Canada, Special Joint Committee of the Senate and the House of Commons Appointed to Examine and Consider the Indian Act, *Minutes of Proceedings and Evidence*, 1947, no. 5, Appendix CC, 199.

69 Personal communication with Harold Cardinal, 20 February 1997.

70 Hugh Dempsey, private papers, Callihoo Papers.

71 Reta Rowan Papers, University of Alberta Archives, file 17/1/1-1.

72 Ibid., file 17/1/1-57. Membership lists of the Friends of the Indians Society show the following to have been members: N.E. Tanner; Professor A. Mardiros; Father Rousell, OMI; Father Rheaume; Mr. Forsland; Mr. Coldwell; Dr. Stone; and Mr. Pitcher.

73 Reta Rowan Papers, University of Alberta Archives, file 17/1/1-1, contains cards identifying the aims of the Friends of the Indians Society.

74 Reta Rowan Papers, University of Alberta Archives, contains an outline of Friends of the Indians Society's activities over the years.

75 NAC, RG 10, vol. 6826, f. 496-3-3, pt. 1, R.A. Hoey to John Laurie, 8 April 1947.

76 Reta Rowan Papers, University of Alberta Archives, no file, meeting minutes, 7 February 1951.

77 Ibid., file 17/1/1-11 Johnny Callihoo to Reta Rowan, 11 February 1946.

78 Ibid., no file, IAA meeting minutes, 19 June 1946.

79 Ibid., IAA meeting minutes from 1948, 1949, 1950 reveal this, as do materials taken from the society's education classes.
80 Ibid., IAA meeting minutes, 1948, 1949, 1950.
81 Ibid., speech for Mission Circle Rally, 16 April 1956.
82 Ibid., speech for Mission Circle Rally, 16 April 1956.
83 Ibid., speech for Mission Circle Rally, 16 April 1956.
84 M8078, Hanks Papers, Glenbow Archives, file 300/22, interview with George Gooderham.
85 In his diaries, Gooderham notes Laurie coming to his office. See M4738, Gooderham Papers, Glenbow Archives, box 3, diaries for 1948, 1949. The DIA instructed Gooderham to function as the link between it and the IAA. See NAC, RG 10, vol. 8476, file 1/24-2-1, 2, (reel C-13813), D.M. McKay to Gooderham, 16 July 1952. In this letter McKay reaffirms the standard procedure for dealing with the IAA.
86 Personal communication with Hugh Dempsey, September 1996.
87 T.N. Brewis, H.E. English, Anthony Scott, Pauline Jewett, and J.E. Ganders, eds., *Canadian Economic Policy* (Toronto: Macmillan, 1961), 147.
88 C.A. Ashley, ed. *Reconstruction in Canada* (Toronto: University of Toronto Press, 1943), 17.
89 Ibid., 107.
90 Ibid., 119.
91 Ibid., 119-20.
92 Ibid.
93 See T.N. Brewis, H.E. English, Anthony Scott, Pauline Jewett, and J.E. Ganders, eds., *Canadian Economic Policy* (Toronto: University of Toronto Press, 1961). In this work Brewis examines the Keynesian nature of Canadian postwar economic policy and how Keynesian theory provided Canada with the concepts that made possible the administrative implementation of an economic policy that supported the new social ideals of combatting idleness and providing welfare for all.
94 Canada, *Employment and Income* (Ottawa: King's Printer, 1945), 23.
95 House of Commons, *Debates*, G.H. Castleden, 13 May 1946, 1464.
96 Personal communication with Hugh Dempsey, 10 September 1996. John Laurie and other legal experts believed that the treaties should be ignored lest they be undermined. Since they had no place in the law they were perceived as too difficult to pursue.
97 *Rex* v. *Commanda* (1939), *Canadian Native Law Reporter* 5 (1987), 372.
98 Frank Tough, "A Review of the History of Indian Resource Rights and Conservation Regulations in Ontario ca. 1880-1945," Unpublished manuscript, 1995, 60-76.
99 Murray Dobbin, private collection, John Laurie to Johnny Callihoo, 18 June 1945.
100 M7655, James Gladstone Papers, Glenbow Archives, f. 329, John Laurie to James Gladstone, 29 May 1953. See also John Laurie to James Gladstone, 21 November 1949, where Laurie makes similar suggestions regarding IAA actions.
101 See M656, John Laurie Papers, Glenbow Archives, f. 1, 2.
102 Ibid., f. 2, Laurie to Rod Callihoo, 15 February 1945.
103 See M656, John Laurie Papers, Glenbow Archives, f. 2, John Laurie to Johnny Callihoo, 11 April 1945.
104 Laurie explained his position on how the Friends of the Indians Society could assist Indian peoples with what he referred to as the "acculturation" process in a speech found in the Reta Rowan Papers, University of Alberta Archives, no file, "For Mission Circle Rally," 16 April 1956. He expressed similar views in a report submitted to the Joint Planning Commission of the Canadian Association on Adult Education, M656, John Laurie Papers, Glenbow Archives, b. 1, file 11, page 1, where Laurie mentions how the IAA has helped treaty Indians "overcome ancient animosities."
105 M7655, James Gladstone Papers, Glenbow Archives, no file, n.d. John Laurie designed this adult education class poster on IAA letterhead.
106 Hugh Dempsey, private papers, newspaper clipping, n.d., shows photo of men bandaging each other and outlining some of the course content. This was probably a Calgary paper as the class was held at Paget hall.
107 Murray Dobbin, private papers, John Laurie to Reverend G. Laviolette, OMI, 20 November 1944.

108 M7655, James Gladstone Papers, Glenbow Archives, f. 328. John Laurie to James Gladstone, 11 October 1951. Laurie included this as copy for a bulletin.
109 M7655, James Gladstone Papers, Glenbow Archives, f. 328, f.329. Speech by John Laurie for James Gladstone, dated 1954.
110 M656, John Laurie Papers, Glenbow Archives, f. 26. John Laurie's speech, February 1956. This speech was delivered to Knights of the Round Table, Calgary, and the Rotary and Lions Club, Red Deer.
111 M656, John Laurie Papers, Glenbow Archives, f. 5, Gooderham memo cc to John Laurie.
112 Personal communication with Hugh Dempsey, March 1995.
113 Ibid., September 1996. Dempsey noted Laurie's suspicious nature and dislike of large-scale government activities; Laurie's critique of government power comes through in various *Cattlemen* articles. See *Canadian Cattlemen*, May 1951, "The Ottawa Conference"; "General Meeting 1951," August 1951; "The Indians Organize" June 1950.
114 M656, John Laurie Papers, Glenbow Archives, f. 22, speech on the integration policy of government.
115 Ibid., f. 26, YMCA panel discussion, 22 November 1956.
116 Personal communication with Harold Cardinal, 20 February 1997.

Chapter 5: The IAA and the Indian Affairs Branch, 1939-46

1 M656 John Laurie Papers, Glenbow Archives, f. 2, John Laurie to Johnny Callihoo, 11 April 1945.
2 Murray Dobbin, private papers, Malcolm Norris to John Tootoosis, 8 July 1944.
3 This idea is promoted in John L. Tobias, "Protection, Civilization, Assimilation: An Outline History of Canada's Indian policy," in *As Long as the Sun Shines and Water Flows,* ed. Ian A.L. Getty and Antoine Lussier (Vancouver: UBC Press, 1983), 39-55 (quote, 51). Canadian historians of the 1930s also paid scant attention to Aboriginal history. Among five Canadian academics participating in the conference, only one, George F.G. Stanley, was a historian.
4 Donald B. Smith, "Now We Talk – You Listen," *Rotunda* (Fall 1990): 48.
5 T.F. McIlwraith and C.T. Loram, eds., *The North American Indian Today* (Toronto: University of Toronto Press, 1943), x.
6 Diamond Jenness, *Indians of Canada* (Ottawa: King's Printer, 1932), 264.
7 McIllwraith and Loram, eds., *North American Indian,* 160. In his presentation at the conference D.J. Allan stated: "Possibly the mistaken theory that the Indian was a vanishing race was held too long. Realization that their race will persist and will increase is of fairly recent acceptance" (McIllwraith and Loram. *North American Indian*, 196-97).
8 Tobias, "Protection, Civilization, Assimilation," 51.
9 Ibid., 48, 50-51.
10 E. Brian Titley, *A Narrow Vision: Duncan Campbell Scott and the Administration of Indian Affairs in Canada,* (Vancouver: UBC Press, 1986), 201-3.
11 F.L. Barron, "A Summary of Federal Indian policy in the Canadian West, 1867-1984," *Native Studies Review* 1, 1 (1984): 28-38.
12 These elements are derived from the parameters of the Indian Act, which outline the specific duties and responsibilities of the DIA. The interpretation of these duties naturally varied over time, and, by the late 1930s, achieving self-sufficiency for Indian peoples on reserve was seen as a priority.
13 See M742, H.W. McGill Papers, Glenbow Archives, Calgary.
14 McGill in McIlwraith and Loram, *North American Indian,* 132-33.
15 MacInnes in McIlwraith and Loram, *North American Indian,* 161.
16 D.J. Allan in McIlwraith and Loram, *North American Indian,* 184.
17 Ibid., 186.
18 Ibid., 187.
19 Ibid., 198.
20 Ibid., 188; see also John F. Leslie and Ron Maguire, *The Historical Development of the Indian Act* (Ottawa: Treaties and Historical Research Centre, Indian and Northern Affairs, 1978), 127. The revolving loan fund was derived from a revolving fund voted by Parliament

expressly for the purpose of making money available to deserving Indians. Repayment of such loans had to occur in order for other individuals to borrow money.

21 D.J. Allan in McIlwraith and Loram, *North American Indian*, 188.

22 Ibid., 191.

23 J.F. Woodsworth in McIlwraith and Loram, *North American Indian*, 266, quoting a United Church report; see also Sessional Papers, *Annual Report for the Indian Affairs Branch*, year ended 1939, 186, where the DIA states: "There is a growing realization on the part of our Indian population of the direct relationship between worth-while secondary school courses – academic and vocational – and the ability of the members of the younger generation to establish themselves on a self-supporting basis."

24 In 1939 the schools delivering Indian education in western Canada were primarily residential schools. In fact, Alberta was one of the Prairie provinces in which residential schools were virtually the only available educational facility for Indian students. Woodsworth conceded publicly that residential schools were less than ideal enviroments for many children who longed for their homes and parents; however, he felt that the efficiency of the residential school system was unparalleled. Unlike day schools, residential schools were able to provide a religious and cultural atmosphere as well as vocational training. It is revealing, however, that Woodsworth commented: "I believe that a partial return to the Day school system in ultimately inevitable," for "we must not sacrifice the spirits and souls of these people ... upon the altar of efficiency." Woodsworth's comments foreshadowed a trend in Indian education that was to occur during and after the Second World War. This trend emphasized the creation of new day schools and, in many ways, was encouraged and pioneered by the IAA. See Woodsworth in McIlwraith and Loram, *North American Indian*, 270.

25 Ibid., 271.

26 E.L. Stone in McIlwraith and Loram, *North American Indian*, 242.

27 Ibid., 244.

28 See Canada, Sessional Papers, *Annual Report for the Indian Affairs Branch*, year end 1939, 185-86 for a basic description of DIA activities in the field of health. See also Laurie Meijer Drees, "Reserve Hospitals and Medical Officers," *Prairie Forum* 21, 2 (1996): 149-76.

29 See NAC, RG 10, vol. 10414, f. 47-48, for specific examples.

30 See B.M. Greene, ed. *Who's Who in Canada, 1945-1946* (Toronto: International Press), 756.

31 Ibid.., 536.

32 R.A. Hoey, in McIlwraith and Loram, *North American Indian*, 206.

33 Ibid., 202.

34 Ibid., 202-4.

35 Allan Harper, "Canada's Indian Administration," *Americana Indigena* 5, 2 (1945): 126.

36 D.C. Scott, *The Administration of Indian Affairs in Canada* (Toronto: Canadian Institute of International Affairs, 1931), 10, 13.

37 Ibid., 17-18. Interpretation of Scott's writing, 24-25.

38 D.C. Scott in T.R.L. MacInnes, "The History of Indian Administration in Canada," *Canadian Journal of Economics and Political Science* 12 (1946): 389.

39 John Collier in McIllwraith and Loram, *North American Indian*, 140-51 (quote, 145). Collier did not attend the conference in person, but the Americans were represented by his assistant, J.C. McCaskill.

40 Bureau of Indian Affairs, Office Files of John Collier, Memorandum for Mr. Collier, 23 September 1939.

41 Ibid.

42 Hanks Papers, Glenbow Archives, box 301, folder 15, interview with Teddy Yellowfly, possibly 1941 (date unclear on manuscript).

43 Scott, *Administration of Indian Affairs*, 27.

44 Leslie and Maguire, *Historical Development of the Indian Act*, 127.

45 Ibid.

46 See Claudia Notzke, *Indian Reserves in Canada: Development Problems of the Stoney and Peigan Reserves* (Marburg: Universitat Marburg, 1985). Notzke outlines how the special

problems faced by the Stoney community were greatly influenced by the poor condition of the land upon which the bands were situated following treaty signing.

47 John Snow, *These Mountains Are Our Sacred Places* (Toronto: Samuel Stevens, 1977), 44, 45, 46. Regarding the battle to enlarge the reserve to improve agriculture, see pp. 66-68, 83-8.
48 Notzke, *Indian Reserves in Canada*, 14-15.
49 See Snow, *These Mountains.*
50 "Tribe Needs Government Assistance," in the *Calgary Herald*, 1 August 1936, Glenbow clipping file, Stoney Indians – Industry and Development.
51 "Young Stoneys Being Trained to Raise Mink," unidentified newspaper source, February 1931, Glenbow clipping file, Stoney Indians.
52 "Indians as Well as White Men Benefit by Oil Development," *Calgary Herald*, 31 July 1929, Glenbow clipping file, Stoney Indians.
53 *Calgary Herald*, Glenbow clipping file, Stoney Indians, 1 August 1936.
54 Ibid., 12 July 1935.
55 Ibid., 1 August 1936.
56 NAC, RG 10, vol. 10414, file 48, pt. a. G.C. Laight to Secretary Indian Affairs, 17 March 1941. The agent's letter contains aspects of the petition made by Johnny Callihoo to Ottawa. The DIA director responded by simply addressing the most pressing concerns. No further discussion of issues confronting Indian peoples came out of this presentation.
57 NAC, RG 10, vol. 6826, file 496-3-3, McGill to John Laurie, 8 August 1944; John Laurie to Dr. H.W. McGill, 9 July 1944.
58 Ibid., Citizens to T.A. Crerar, 7 July 1944.
59 Ibid., type copy of names sent to T.A. Crerar by groups endorsing the 1944 IAA Memorial on Indian Affairs, 7 July 1944. See also Murray Dobbin, private collection, John Laurie to G.H. Castleden, 26 February 1945; NAC, RG 10, vol. 2686, file 496-3-3, Daisy Millar to Mackenzie King, 3 August 1944.
60 Murray Dobbin private collection, John Laurie to Sam Minde, 3 July 1944.
61 M 7155, IAA papers, Glenbow Archives, Calgary, no file, Indian Association of Alberta, IAA Memorial on Indian Affairs, 1944, 1.
62 Ibid., 4.
63 Ibid., 3.
64 Ibid.
65 Reginal Whitaker, *The Government Party: Organizing and Financing the Liberal Party of Canada, 1930-58* (Toronto: University of Toronto Press, 1977), 137, 143-44. See also Robert Bothwell, Ian Drummond, and John English, *Canada, 1900-1945* (Toronto: University of Toronto Press, 1987), 329.
66 J.W. Pickersgill, *The Liberal Party* (Toronto: McClelland and Stewart, 1962), 37.
67 See M656, John Laurie Papers, Glenbow Archives, f. 1, John Laurie to Manley J. Edwards, MP, 12 August 1944.
68 Ibid.
69 Ibid., John Laurie to James Ward, and John Laurie to Fred Hodgson, 7 August 1944.
70 Ibid., John Laurie to Manley J. Edwards, MP, 12 August 1944.
71 Canada, House of Commons Debates, 6 June 1944, 3567.
72 NAC, RG 10, vol. 6826, file 496-3-3, John Laurie to T.A. Crerar, 9 July 1944.
73 Ibid., H.W. McGill to John Laurie, 8 August 1944.
74 Richard Leuger, "A History of Indian Associations in Canada, 1870-1970" (MA thesis, Carlton University, 1977), 6-7.
75 Peter Kulchyski, "A Considerable Unrest: F.O. Loft and the League of Indians," *Native Studies Review* 4, 1 and 2 (1988): 95-117, 109.
76 NAC, RG 10, vol. 6826, file 496-3-3, P.E. Moore to H.W. McGill, 6 September 1944.
77 Ibid., R.A. Hoey to H.W. McGill, 12 September 1944.
78 Ibid., W.J.F. Pratt to John Laurie, 7 October 1944.
79 Murray Dobbin, private collection, Malcolm F. Norris to Ben Calfrobe, 13 September 1944.
80 Ibid.

81 M7155, IAA Papers, Glenbow Archives, no file, IAA Memorial on Indian Affairs, 1944.
82 Canada, Sessional Papers, *Annual Report for the Indian Affairs Branch*, 1942-43, 144. See also NAC, RG 10, vol. 10414, Shannon box 48, part d. This file contains correspondence between the provincial agricultural extension service and the Edmonton Agency, requesting the use of Indian workers during the harvest because, during the war years, other workers were scarce. Throughout the war yeas, the DIA encouraged Indian labourers to use the National Selective Service to gain wage labour positions.
83 Canada, Sessional Papers, *Annual Report for the Indian Affairs Branch*, year end 1943, 145.
84 Ibid., 151.
85 Howard and Tamara Palmer, *Alberta: A New History* (Edmonton: Hurtig, 1990), 283.
86 Canada, Sessional Papers, *Annual Report for the Indian Affairs Branch*, year end 1944, 153.
87 Ibid., 156.
88 Ibid., 1945, 168-69.
89 Ibid., 168.
90 Palmer, *Alberta*, 286. See Canada, Sessional Papers, *Annual Report for the Indian Affairs Branch*, 1942-45.
91 M656, John Laurie Papers, Glenbow Archives, f. 22, "The Indian Association of Alberta," by John Laurie, 20.
92 Ibid., 21.
93 See NAC, RG 10, vol. 6826, file 496-3-3, R.A. Hoey to John Laurie, 15 October 1945, where Hoey hopes to hear IAA perspectives on a variety of issues: "There are so many matters to discuss with respect to the administration of Indian Affairs at the moment and Indian Rights Associations, which appear to be multiplying rapidly throughout the Dominion, and I would appreciate very much indeed an opportunity to discuss a number of matters with you."
94 NAC, RG 10, vol. 6826, file 496-3-3, memo possibly sent December 1944.
95 Ibid., R.A. Hoey to C. Schmidt, 20(?) May 1945.
96 See NAC, RG 10, vol. 10414, file 48, part a. T.R.L. McInnes to Agent Laight, Edmonton Agency, 9 May 1941.
97 M7155, IAA Papers, Glenbow Archives, no file, IAA Memorial on Indian Affairs, 1945, 13.
98 Ibid.
99 Ibid., 10.
100 Ibid., 6, 8.
101 NAC, RG 10, vol. 6826, file 496-3-3, IAA memo to Acting Director R.A. Hoey. In this document the IAA officially but privately called for the revision of the Indian Act. See M7155, IAA papers, Glenbow Archives, no file, IAA Memorial on Indian Affairs, 1945, 1.
102 NAC, RG 10, vol. 6826, file 496-3-3, Hon. T.A. Crerar to Mr. George Ross, 27 March 1945.
103 Ibid., newspaper clipping, Elmore Philpott column entitled "Indians Awake," 18 September 1945, no source. See also a speech used at a political rally, M7155, IAA papers, Glenbow Archives, no file, 1945.
104 House of Commons, *Debates*, 24 October 1945, 1445.
105 M7155, IAA Papers, Glenbow Archives, Circular sent by Laurie to all IAA members, 6 December 1945.
106 NAC, RG 10, vol. 6826, file 496-3-3, R.A. Hoey to John Laurie, 15 October 1945.
107 Ibid., 25 October 1945.
108 M656, John Laurie Papers, Glenbow Archives, f. 11, John Laurie speech to IAA delegate, 1945.
109 Ibid., John Laurie to J.A. Glen, 7 March 1946.
110 Ibid., n.d.

Chapter 6: Reconciling Citizenship and Treaty Rights

1 A version of this chapter was published in *Great Plains Quarterly* 20, 2 (Spring 2000).
2 House of Commons, *Debates*, 13 May 1946, 1446.
3 Indian people's review of Bill 14 has received little scholarly attention. See NAC, RG 14, vol. 666, Appendix 3 (reel T-14571), "Indian Act Amendment Bill, Report of Evidence," 1920. These original documents were never printed and were recently transferred to

microfilm thanks to the efforts of Paul Lemieux, Reference Archivist, National Archives of Canada. At this time, in the words of Fred Loft, the Indian spokespersons from Ontario and Quebec had "opposed the measure because of its compulsory features and because it meant to them denationalization and the eventual disintegration of their peaceful tribalism, together with the absorption of their lands and homes by white people." The bill passed but was amended by the Liberals, who came to power in 1921, leaving choice of enfranchisement to each male Indian by formal application as prescribed by the Indian Act. See undated letter from F.O. Loft, published in the *Toronto Star,* in possession of Donald B. Smith, History Department, University of Calgary.

4 Ian V.B. Johnson, *Helping Indians to Help Themselves – A Committee to Investigate Itself: The 1951 Indian Act Consultation Process* (Ottawa: Treaties and Historical Research Centre, Indian and Northern Affairs, 1984).

5 John Leslie and Ron Maguire, *The Historical Development of the Indian Act* (Ottawa: Indian and Northern Affairs, Treaties and Historical Research Centre, 1978), 133-45; John F. Leslie, *A Historical Survey of Indian-Government Relations, 1940-1970* (Ottawa: Claims and Historical Research Centre, 1993).

6 Jim McMurtry, "The 1946-1948 Special Joint Committee on the Indian Act and Educational Policy" (MA thesis, University of Alberta, 1985). McMurtry's thesis focuses upon the educational policy that emerged from the Special Joint Committee. Of interest in this work is his questioning of Indian participation in the consultation process. See also Peter Kulchyski, "Anthropology in the Service of the State: Diamond Jenness and Canadian Indian Policy," *Journal of Canadian Studies* 28, 2 (Summer 1993): 21-50. Kulchyski discusses the role of Diamond Jenness in the formation of Indian policy in Canada and gives some insight into the workings of the committee. See also John L. Tobias, "Protection, Civilization, Assimilation: An Outline History of Canada's Indian Policy," in *Sweet Promises,* ed. J.R. Miller (Toronto: University of Toronto Press, 1991), 127-54, for a mention of the committee and its works in the context of the history of Indian policy. Tobias gives little insight into either the stimuli behind the establishment of such a committee or of the presentations made at its hearings.

7 Report of the Special Committee on Reconstruction and Re-establishment, *Minutes of Proceedings and Evidence* (Ottawa: King's Printer, 1944), 238.

8 Ibid., 243.

9 Ibid., 253.

10 Ibid., 259, 256.

11 J.R. Miller, *Skyscrapers Hide the Heavens* (Toronto: University of Toronto Press, 1989), 220-21.

12 Tobias, "Protection, Assimilation, Civilization," 139.

13 NAC, RG 10, vol. 6811, f. 470-3-6, part R, (reel C-8534), *Newsweek,* 15 April 1946.

14 Ibid., *St. John Telegraph Journal,* 15 July 1946.

15 Ibid., *Vancouver Sun,* 15 May 1946, David Spencer Inc. Poll.

16 Ibid., *Edmonton Bulletin,* 15 December 1945.

17 Ibid., *Saturday Night,* 30 March 1946.

18 Ibid., unidentified Victoria clipping, 15 March 1946.

19 House of Commons, *Debates,* J.A. Glen, 13 May 1946, 1447.

20 See C.E.S. Franks, *The Parliament of Canada* (Toronto: University of Toronto Press, 1987). Chapter 8 of this book offers insight into the functioning of Parliamentary committees and the process of government.

21 Franks, *Parliament of Canada,* 162.

22 Ibid., 164, 166.

23 Ibid., 167, 169.

24 The North American Indian Brotherhood (NAIB) was given an early hearing because it was in Ottawa in June 1946 for an NAIB conference. In order to accommodate the NAIB, the committee agreed to hear from two of its delegates, Andrew Paull and Thomas Jones. Peter Kelly of the Native Brotherhood of British Columbia was also heard at this time. British Columbia Indian groups were, therefore, among the first to be recognized and to represent their claims to the government.

25 See Franks, *Parliament of Canada*, 161-85.
26 Canada, Special Joint Committee of the Senate and the House of Commons Appointed to Consider the Indian Act, *Minutes of Proceedings and Evidence* (Ottawa: King's Printer, 1946-49), 14 June 1946, 217.
27 Ibid., 21 June 1946, D.F. Brown, 266.
28 Ibid., 9 July 1946, Mr. Case.
29 Canada, Special Joint Committee of the Senate and the House of Commons Appointed to Consider the Indian Act, *Minutes of Proceedings and Evidence* (Ottawa: 1946-49), 9 July 1946, 483-94. During this meeting there was a great deal of debate as to why Indian representation on the committee was deemed not necessary by certain members of the committee. Castleden was in favour of having Indian representatives; however, his motion to institute this was defeated.
30 See J.M. Barbalet's discussion of T.H. Marshall in J.M. Barbalet, *Citizenship: Rights, Struggle and Class Inequality* (Milton Keynes: Open University Press, 1988), 45-51.
31 Special Joint Committee of the Senate and the House of Commons Appointed to Consider the Indian Act, *Minutes of Proceedings and Evidence*, 1946, 141. There was an error in the minutes, and Case was noted as saying "I *cannot* understand." Case later revised his statement to read "I *can* understand." See 218 of Minutes, 1946.
32 Norman Lickers studied law at Osgoode Hall in Toronto and, in 1951, acted as a consultant to the federal government on ammendments to the Indian Act. In 1969 he participated in protesting the Liberal's white paper on Indian Affairs. See the *Brantford Expositor*, 16 March 1987; *Tekawennake*, 19 March 1987.
33 Hugh Dempsey, *The Gentle Persuader: A Biography of James Gladstone, Indian Senator* (Saskatoon: Western Producer Prairie Books, 1986), 114-15.
34 McMurtry, "1946-1948 Special Joint Committee," 40.
35 The histories of the IAA and of the USI are intertwined. Both organizations originated with the League of Indians in Western Canada, and, though their relationship was not close in the 1940s, the founding of the USI re-established bonds between Indian leaders in both provinces. For a history of the USI see articles by James Pitsula, 1994; Rauncie Murdoch, "The Union of Saskatchewan Indians," unpublished manuscript, 1995. For more information on the CCF's involvement with Aboriginal peoples, see F.L. Barron, *Walking in Indian Moccasins: The Native Policies of Tommy Douglas and the CCF* (Vancouver: UBC Press, 1997).
36 R834, f.37, Saskatchewan Archives. Meeting minutes of the USI, 4 January 1946.
37 Murray Dobbin, private collection, president's message, 7th general meeting of the IAA. It is clear from the style of this speech that it was written by Secretary John Laurie. Laurie frequently wrote speeches for the president, and the content of this speech clearly reveals information that Laurie had gathered over the course of the winter of 1945-46 as a result of his involvement with the USI and his communications with various MPs.
38 M7655, James Gladstone Papers, Glenbow Archives, f. 329 (?), Laurie to Gladstone, 9 August 1946.
39 Ibid.
40 Murray Dobbin, *One and a Half Men: The Story of Jim Brady and Malcolm Norris, Metis Patriots of the Twentieth Century* (Vancouver: New Star Books, 1981), 161. The contribution of Norris to the submission is not clear either. According to his own accounts, Norris was away in the Northwest Territories working as a prospector until October 1946 and had been there since April of that year. He may have made a contribution over the winter months. Thus far, no known documentation of his participation exists, except as held in Dobbin's collections. See Murray Dobbin, private collection, Norris to Joe Dion, 14 November 1946, where Norris tells Dion about his absence from Indian work.
41 IAA Brief to the Special Joint Committee, Appendix 3 "Housing," *Minutes of Proceedings and Evidence*, 647-48.
42 Ibid., 648.
43 Ibid., 574.
44 Ibid., 575.

45 Ibid., 577.
46 Morris Schumiatcher, "The Buckskin Curtain," *The Beaver*, Outfit 290 (Autumn 1959), 12-15, particularly 14.
47 Dempsey, *Gentle Persuader*, 115.
48 NAC, RG 10, vol. 6811, file 470-3-6, pt. 2 (reel C-8534), *Calgary Albertan*, 19 April 1947
49 Ibid., *Lethbridge Herald*, 8 May 1947.
50 *Minutes of Proceedings and Evidence*, 21 April 1947, 545.
51 M656, John Laurie Papers, Glenbow Archives, f. 22, "The Indian Association of Alberta," by John Laurie, 29.
52 Hugh Keenleyside, *Memoirs of Hugh L. Keenleyside: On the Bridge of Time* (Toronto: McClelland and Stewart, 1982) 307. Keenleyside's approach to administering the DIA in the late 1940s very much reflected the desire to improve education and economic development in Indian communities, especially in northern Canada. His career is summarized in Shelagh Grant, "Hugh Llewellyn Keenleyside, Commissioner of the Northwest Territories, 1947-1950," *Arctic* 43, 1 (March 1990), 80-82.
53 M7655, James Gladstone Papers, Glenbow Archives, f. 329, John Laurie to James Gladstone 27 June 1947.
54 Ibid.
55 Special Joint Committee of the Senate and House of Commons Appointed to Consider the Indian Act, *Minutes of Proceedings and Evidence*, Fourth Report, 22 June 1948, 188.
56 Ibid., 189-90.
57 Johnson, *Helping Indians*, 43, 53, 54-55. McMurtry ("1946-1948 Special Joint Committee," 50) also suggests that the aim of the committee was the "assimilation" of Indian peoples.
58 Reta Rowan Papers, University of Edmonton Archives, 17/1/2-3, IAA Annual General Meeting Minutes, 1948, 2; IAA Brief to the Special Joint Committee.
59 M7655, James Gladstone Papers, Glenbow Archives, no file, John Laurie to James Gladstone, 22 October 1949.

Chapter 7: Political Pragmatics

1 M7655, James Gladstone Paper, Glenbow Archives, f. 322, John Laurie to James Gladstone, 4 July 1949.
2 Paul Tennant, *Aboriginal Peoples and Politics: The Indian Land Question in British Columbia, 1849-1989* (Vancouver: UBC Press, 1990) offers an excellent, detailed discussion of government interaction with BC Indian political associations. A general discussion of government-Indian political association interaction can be found in Richard Leuger, "A History of Indian Associations in Canada, 1870-1970" (MA thesis, Carleton University, 1977), 186-90. See also John F. Leslie, *A Historical Survey of Indian-Government Relations, 1940-1970* (Ottawa: Royal Commission Liaison Office, 1993).
3 See Sally Weaver, "The Joint Cabinet/National Indian Brotherhood Committee: A Unique Experiment in Pressure Group Relations," *Canadian Public Administration* 25, 2 (Summer 1982): 211-39 (quote from p. 212).
4 Reginald Whitaker, *The Government Party: Organizing and Financing the Liberal Party of Canada, 1930-1958* (Toronto: University of Toronto Press, 1977), 144-47.
5 Whitaker, *Government Party*, 167.
6 Denis Smith, *Rogue Tory: The Life and Legend of John G. Diefenbaker* (Toronto: Macfarlane, Walter and Ross, 1996), 156.
7 Smith, 179. During the federal election of 1949, Opposition leader Drew conducted a crusade against the civil service.
8 Smith, *Rogue Tory*, 201-17.
9 See Noel Dyck, *What Is the Indian "Problem": Tutelage and Resistance in Canadian Indian Administration* (Newfoundland: Institute of Social and Economic Research, 1991), 106-7. Dyck suggests that the implementation of programs to improve housing, roads, and basic community infrastructure was a product of the 1960s.
10 M656, John Laurie Papers, Glenbow Archives, no file, 1956 speech by Pickersgill to the Canadian Club of Ottawa, 28 March.

11 NAC, RG 10, vol. 8571, file 701/1-2-2-5, (reel C-14213), Alberta Field Staff Conferences, Calgary, 1949. See also M656, John Laurie Fonds, Glenbow Archives, file 23, Indian Affairs Policy Statement, 1956.
12 NAC, RG 10, vol. 8424, file 701/21-3, (reel C-13836), memo from superintendent of welfare.
13 J.W. Pickersgill, *My Years with Louis St. Laurent: A Political Memoir* (Toronto: University of Toronto Press, 1975), 247-51.
14 According to John Leslie, impediments to the introduction of new Indian Act legislation included changes at the ministerial level, a federal election in 1949, and opposition from the Roman Catholic Church to proposed changes in the education provisions. See Leslie, *Historical Survey*, 13, n. 31.
15 House of Commons, *Debates*, 21 June 1950, 3938.
16 Ibid., 3963.
17 Ibid., 3938, Harris.
18 Ibid., 7 June 1950, 3332.
19 Ibid., 21 June 1950, 3940.
20 Hugh Dempsey, *The Gentle Persuader: A Biography of James Gladstone, Indian Senator* (Saskatoon: Western Producer Prairie Books, 1986), 127; see also M7155, IAA Papers, Glenbow Archives, no file, Indian Association of Alberta meeting minutes, 1950; John Laurie, "General Meeting, 1950" *Canadian Cattlemen*, July 1950.
21 M7655, James Gladstone Papers, Glenbow Archives, no file, 10 July 1950, John Laurie to James Gladstone.
22 Hugh Dempsey, private collection, *Calgary Albertan*, 18 August 1950.
23 See Douglas Sanders, "The Queen's Promises," in *Law and Justice in a New Land: Essays in Western Canadian Legal History*, ed. Louis A Knafla (Calgary: Carswell, 1986), 101-27.
24 Personal communication with Ruth Gorman, 5 July 1992.
25 Ibid. Laurie did not want Gorman to mention issues related to trust accounts or enfranchisement for fear it would cause more harm than good.
26 M7155, IAA Papers, Glenbow Archives, no file, Indian Association of Alberta meeting minutes, Paget Hall, 10 August 1950.
27 Ibid., John Laurie in an open letter to Parliamentarians, 7 September 1950.
28 Ibid.
29 Ibid.
30 Here enfranchisement means to take away all special rights and status as Indian people under the law.
31 M7655, James Gladstone Papers, Glenbow Archives, no file, 30 August 1950, John Laurie to James Gladstone. Laurie expresses the Hobbema residents' fear in his letter to President James Gladstone.
32 John Laurie, "In Honor Bound," *Canadian Cattlemen*, November 1950.
33 M7655, James Gladstone Papers, Glenbow Archives, no file, John Laurie to James Gladstone, 10 July 1950.
34 M656, John Laurie Papers, Glenbow Archives, file 4, section of a speech presumably written by John Laurie.
35 Dempsey, *Gentle Persuader*, 129.
36 M656, John Laurie Papers, Glenbow Archives, file 4, discussion of Ottawa conference; John Laurie, "Ottawa Conference," *Canadian Cattlemen*, May 1951.
37 M7155, IAA Papers, Glenbow Archives, no file, IAA memo on Ottawa Conference.
38 M656, John Laurie Papers, Glenbow Archives, file 3, John Laurie memo to Don Brown, 20 April 1951.
39 M7655, IAA Papers, Glenbow Archives, file 328, John Laurie to James Gladstone, 15 May 1951.
40 Ibid., 26 January 1951.
41 Leslie, *Historical Survey*, 14-15.
42 John Laurie, "Ottawa Conference," *Canadian Cattlemen*, May 1951.
43 M7655, IAA Papers, Glenbow Archives, file, 323, James Gladstone to Minister Harris, n.d.
44 Ibid.
45 Leslie, *Historical Survey*, 18-19.

46 Michael G. Lacy, "The United States and American Indians: Political Relations," in *American Indian Policy in the Twentieth Century*, ed. Vine Deloria Jr. (Norman: University of Oklahoma Press, 1985), 83-104; another valuable article discussing special interest groups and their effectiveness is A. Paul Pross, "Governing Under Pressure: The Special Interest Group – Summary of Discussion," in *Canadian Public Administration* 25, 2 (summer 1982): 170-82. Pross discusses research indicating that the Canadian state actively co-opts those elements of society that it can, while actively destroying those that it cannot (181).

47 Lacy, "United States and American Indians," 85.

48 Ibid., 86.

49 Leslie, *Historical Survey*, 18-19.

50 NAC, vol. 8476, file 1/24-2-1 pt. 1 (reel C-138138), D. McKay to John Laurie, 8 February 1952.

51 NAC, vol. 8476, file 1/24-2-1 pt. 3, (reel C-13813), Laval Fortier, memo to Director of Indian Affairs, 7 July 1955.

52 Richard Daniel, "The Spirit and Terms of Treaty Eight," in *The Spirit of the Alberta Indian Treaties*, ed. Richard Price (Edmonton: Pica Pica Press, 1987), 54. An extensive literature deals with Indian economies in the fur trade era and their resource use in the western provincial north. I do not intend to summarize this information here. See Kerry Abel, *Drum Songs: Glimpses of Dene History* (Montreal: McGill-Queen's Press, 1993), chaps. 7 to 9; A.J. Ray, *Indians in the Fur Trade: Their Role As Trappers, Hunters, and Middlemen in the Lands Southwest of Hudson Bay, 1660-1870.* (Toronto: University of Toronto Press, 1974); Frank Tough, *As Their Natural Resources Fail: Native Peoples and the Economic History of Northern Manitoba, 1870-1930* (Vancouver: UBC Press, 1996).

53 Daniel, "Spirit and Terms of Treaty Eight," 55.

54 Gordon Burrell, Robert Young, and Richard Price, eds., *Indian Treaties and the Law* (Edmonton: Indian Association of Alberta, 1975), 47-48.

55 Ibid., 48.

56 David Knoll, "Treaty and Aboriginal Hunting and Fishing Rights," *Canadian Native Law Reporter* 1 (1979): 3.

57 Government correspondence found in NAC, RG 10, vol. 10414, box 48, is a record of the significance of hunting and fishing in the Edmonton Agency in the late 1930s and into the 1940s. Provincial big game and trapping licences were handed out to Indians through the Indian Agent. For Saddle Lake, see NAC, RG 10, vol. 6733, file 420-2-2 (reel C-08095), where the registration of traplines in 1943 indicates that that agency still relied upon trapping for Aboriginal income (even though, by that year, hunting and trapping were already in decline and only the spring "rat" hunt was still pursued).

58 NAC, RG 10, vol. 6733, f. 420-2-2 (reel C-08095), J.L. Grew to D.J. Allan, 14 August 1943.

59 Ibid., f. 420-2-1, H.W. McGill to Minister Tanner, 18 February 1939.

60 See ibid., f. 420-2-5, telegram from T.R.L. McInnes to Agent Lewis, Fort Chipewyan, 8 April 1937; Agent Head to the Secretary of Indian Affairs, 9 February 1938; Agent Head to Secretary of Indian Affairs, 30 December 1937.

61 See NAC, RG 10, vol. 6733, f. 420-2-2, Inspector Christianson to Dr. McGill, 10 March 1934. Christianson emphasized the importance of creating preserves. In negotiating with the province of Alberta, he requested "that certain sections of that Northern country be left entirely to Indians and halfbreeds."

62 NAC, RG 10, vol. 6733, f. 420-2 5, Indian Agent L'Heureux reporting to Department of Indian Affairs, 16 September 1938, Lesser Slave Lake Agency; see also 16 September 1938, Fort Vermilion Band Report, Agent L'Heureux. In these reports Indian leaders petitioned the government for separate game preserves for Indian hunters and trappers, respectively.

63 See NAC, RG 10, vol. 6733, f. 420-2-2 1, Indian Agent Laight to the Secretary of Indian Affairs, date illegible: "The usual method is for an Indian Agent or Farming Instructor to give the Indian a note certifying that he is a Treaty Indian and living on any Indian reserve in the Agency, the Indian then presents the note to any person appointed as a Game Licence Vendor who issues the Indian a license free of all charges."

64 NAC, RG 10, vol. 6734, f. 420-2-1-1, W.B. Skead, Fur Supervisor Indian Affairs Branch, to M. McCrimmon, Indian Affairs Branch Reserves and Trusts, 18 May 1947. See also RG 10,

vol. 6733, file 420-2-2, Director McGill to E.S. Huestis, Alberta Game Commissioner, 14 October 1942.

65 NAC, RG 10, vol. 6733, f. 420-2-2 1, Minster of Agriculture to Dr. Charles Camsell, Deputy Minister of Mines and Resources, 3 February 1940; see also RG 10, vol. 6733, f. 420-2-2 2, E.S. Huestis to the Department of Indian Affairs, 19 August 1942.

66 Frank Tough, "Indian Hunting Rights, Natural Resources Transfer Agreements and Legal Opinions from the Department of Justice," Documents Section, *Native Studies Review* 10, 2 (1995): 119.

67 Tough, "Indian Hunting Rights," 138.

68 See NAC, RG 10, vol. 6733, f. 420-2 5, Memo to the Deputy Minister of Justice, 13 January 1932, stating: "there does not appear to be any real inconsistency between the provisions of the Migratory Birds Convention Act and the stipulations with respect to hunting rights contained in the treaties applicable to the Province of Saskatchewan vez. treaties nos. 2, 4, 5, 6, 8 and 10." Clearly, there was no perceived conflict between the treaties and the act. For a more detailed analysis see Dan Gottesman, "Native Hunting and the Migratory Birds Convention Act: Historical, Political and Ideological Perspectives," *Journal of Canadian Studies* 18, 3 (Fall 1983): 69.

69 NAC, RG 10, vol. 6733, f. 420-2 5, summary of provincial game regulations and correspondence in Indian Affairs files. Trapline registration was initiated in 1934.

70 Ibid., f. 420-2-2, J.L Grew to D.J. Allan, 11 January 1944. See also Director McGill to Deputy Minister of Mines and Resources, 19 June 1944 re: trapline fees.

71 NAC, RG 10, vol. 6733, f. 420-2-2, Agent Iredale to C.P. Schmidt, 29 September 1942.

72 M656, John Laurie Fonds, Glenbow Archives, f. 3, M.J. Edwards to Tom Kaquitts, 18 January 1949.

73 NAC, RG 10, vol. 6733, f. 420-2-2, Agent Iredale to C.P. Schmidt, 29 September 1942.

74 M7655, James Gladstone Papers, Glenbow Archives, file 322, Reuben Bull to James Gladstone, 1 November 1949.

75 Arthur J. Ray, *The Canadian Fur Trade in the Industrial Age* (Toronto: University of Toronto Press, 1990), 227.

76 As early as 1940, Malcolm Norris was advising IAA members on hunting and trapping rights, and hunting and trapping issues were regularly raised at IAA meetings. Until the late 1940s, however, the IAA seemed primarily concerned with gaining social welfare benefits for Indian peoples.

77 M7655, James Gladstone Papers, Glenbow Archives, file 328, John Laurie to James Gladstone, 31 March 1952. See also John Laurie to James Gladstone, 12 August 1951.

78 M7655, James Gladstone Papers, Glenbow Archives, file 327, James Gladstone to John Laurie, 9 July 1949.

79 Ibid., file 322, Reuben Bull to James Gladstone, 1 November 1949.

80 M656, John Laurie Papers, Glenbow Archives, file 7, E.S. Huestis to John Laurie, 17 March 1950.

81 Ibid., G.H. Gooderham to Major D.M. McKay, 19 March 1950.

82 M7655, James Gladstone Papers, Glenbow Archives, file 323, John Laurie to James Gladstone, 19 March 1950.

83 Reta Rowan Papers, University of Alberta Archives, file 17-1-1-37, Police Magistrate John Thomson to Neil Primrose, 17 June 1950.

84 M7655, James Gladstone Papers, Glenbow Archives, file 328, John Laurie to Minister Tanner, 6 March 1952. Interestingly, Tanner was an early member of the Friends of the Indians Society in Edmonton.

85 Ibid., John Laurie to James Gladstone, 5 March 1952.

86 M7655, James Gladstone Papers, Glenbow Archives, file 329, John Laurie to Hugh Conn, Superintendent, Fur and Game, Indian Affairs Branch, 7 March 1953.

87 M100, Blackmore Papers, Glenbow Archives, file 129, P.C. 2150 – April 28 1949, under authority of Section 34 of the Fisheries Act, 1932.

88 M656, John Laurie Papers, Glenbow Archives, f. 7, IAA agenda draft for meeting with Alberta government officials, 1949; M100 John Blackmore Papers, Glenbow Archives, f. 129, John Laurie to John Blackmore, 1949.

89 Reta Rowan Papers, University of Alberta Archives, file 17-1-1-37, J. Pickersgill to D.S. Harkness, 1 June 1955.

90 Ibid.

91 See M7655, James Gladstone Papers, Glenbow Archives, file 329, John Laurie to Victoria McHugh, 31 May 1954. Victoria McHugh was voted treasurer in 1954. Her comments on Treaty 7 and related issues are published in Treaty 7 Elders and Tribal Council with Walter Hildebrandt, Sarah Carter, and Dorothy First Rider, *The True Spirit and Original Intent of Treaty 7* (Montreal: McGill-Queen's University Press, 1996).

92 Personal communication with Hugh Dempsey, 20 February 1995. Clarence McHugh's election is not easily documented, but it is noted in the correspondence between James Gladstone and Laval Fortier, Deputy Minister of Citizenship and Immigration, M7655, file 324, August 1954.

93 Personal communication with Harold Cardinal, 20 February 1997.

94 M7655, James Gladstone Papers, Glenbow Archives, file 329, John Laurie to James Gladstone, 2 September 1954; see also Donald B. Smith, "A Good Samaritan," in *City-makers: Calgarians after the Frontier*, ed. Max Foran and Sheilagh Jameson (Calgary: The Historical Society of Alberta, 1987), 271.

95 See Dianne Meili, *Those Who Know: Profiles of Alberta's Native Elders* (Edmonton: NeWest Press, 1991), 79-88.

96 See M7155, IAA Papers, Glenbow Archives, no file, IAA Annual meeting minutes, 1956.

97 Douglas Sanders, "The Queen's Promises," in *Law and Justice in a New Land: Essays in Western Canadian Legal History*, ed. Louis A. Knafla (Calgary: Carswell, 1986), 127.

98 *Calgary Herald*, 17 January 1957.

99 Reta Rowan Papers, University of Alberta Archives, file 17-1-1-34, Sam Currie, as spokesman for the Montana Band, to Reta Rowan, 14 August 1955.

100 M656, John Laurie Papers, Glenbow Archives, no file, John Laurie to Reta Rowan, 26 May 1955.

101 M7655, James Gladstone Papers, Glenbow Archives, file 329, John Laurie to James Gladstone, 28 March 1954.

102 M656, John Laurie Papers, Glenbow Archives, file 14, Canadian Bar Association Civil Liberties Section Report of the Committee on Legal Status and Civil Rights of the Canadian Indian; see also Sanders, "The Queen's Promises," 119.

103 *Calgary Herald*, 19 January 1957, and 17 January 1957.

104 Sanders, "The Queen's Promises," 121; M656, John Laurie Papers, Glenbow Archives, file 5, newsclipping showing Indians signing petition, no source.

105 M656, John Laurie Papers, Glenbow Archives, file 5, Ruth Gorman to John Laurie, n.d. In this letter Gorman reveals the contents of the petition to Laurie.

106 Ibid., Doug Harkness to John Laurie, 22 January 1957.

107 Leon Anthony, "Indian People Are Given Right to Vote 30 Years Ago," *Calgary Native News*, 2 September 1993, 5.

108 Jack Pickersgill, *My Years with Louis St. Laurent: A Political Memoir* (Toronto: University of Toronto Press, 1975), 249.

109 Reta Rowan Papers, University of Alberta Archives, file 35, Ruth Gorman to Reta Rowan, February 1957.

110 Sanders, "The Queen's Promises," 126.

111 Reta Rowan Papers, University of Alberta Archives, file 35, 20 March 1957, letter suggesting possible candidates for the council.

112 See *Indian News* 3, 1 (June 1958); see also Hugh Dempsey, *Gentle Persuader*, for a more complete discussion of Gladstone and his rise to the position of senator.

113 M 7155, IAA Papers, Glenbow Archives, no file, IAA Annual Meeting Minutes, June 1958.

Chapter 8: Political Visions

1 NAC, RG 10, vol. 8477, file 1/24-2-1, pt. 5, John Samson, IAA General Meeting minutes, 1962.

2 Quoted in Waubageshig, ed., *The Only Good Indian: Essays by Canadian Indians* (Toronto: New Press, 1970), 4.

3 See Denis Smith, *Rogue Tory: The Life and Legend of John G. Diefenbaker* (Toronto: Macfarlane, Walter and Ross, 1996), 341-47; see also Robert Bothwell, Ian Drummond, and John English, *Canada Since 1945* (Toronto: University of Toronto Press, 1989), 188-89.

4 Margaret Conrad, "Not a Feminist But ... : The Political Career of Ellen Louks Fairclough, Canada's First Female Federal Cabinet Minister," *Journal of Canadian Studies* 31, 2 (Summer 1996): 5-28.

5 *Indian News* 3, 1 (June 1958).

6 NAC, RG 10, vol. 8477, f. 1/24-2-1, pt. 5, Ellen Fairclough to IAA President Howard Beebe, 1959.

7 NAC, RG 10, vol. 8477, f. 1/24-2-1, pt. 5. This volume contains the correspondence between Fairclough and the IAA.

8 Hugh Dempsey, *The Gentle Persuader: A Biography of James Gladstone, Indian Senator* (Saskatoon: Western Producer Prairie Books, 1986), 161.

9 Ibid., 166; see also *Indian News* 3, 1 (June 1958), which contains an article on Gladstone's appointment to the Senate.

10 Dempsey, *Gentle Persuader*, 177.

11 M7155, IAA Fonds, Glenbow Archives, no file, 29 September 1956, James Gladstone to David Crowchild.

12 *Calgary Albertan*, 10 April 1959, Glenbow Clipping file.

13 John F. Leslie, "A Historical Survey of Indian-Government Relations, 1940-1970," paper prepared for the Royal Commission Liaison Office, 1993, 34.

14 Leslie, "Historical Survey," 38.

15 Sally Weaver, *Making Canadian Indian Policy: The Hidden Agenda, 1968-1970* (Toronto: University of Toronto Press, 1981), 25-27. For more detail, please note that Weaver's first chapter succinctly summarizes changes in the DIA for this time period.

16 Leslie, "Historical Survey," Annex E. See also Paul Tennant, *Aboriginal Peoples and Politics: The Indian Land Question in British Columbia, 1849-1989* (Vancouver: UBC Press, 1990), 139.

17 NAC, RG 10, vol. 9037, Minutes of the first National Indian Advisory Board meeting, 1966, 19.

18 Weaver, *Canadian Indian Policy*, 44.

19 Ibid., 46-47.

20 Ibid., 30-31. See also Harold Cardinal, *The Unjust Society: The Tragedy of Canada's Indians* (Edmonton: Hurtig, 1969) 104; NAC, RG 10, vol. 9037, Minutes of the first National Indian Advisory Board meeting, 1966, 15-21.

21 Edgar J. Dosman, *Indians: The Urban Dilemma* (Toronto: McClelland and Stewart, 1972) 20, 29-30.

22 Ibid., 26.

23 Weaver, *Canadian Indian Policy*, 48-49. For analysis and discussion of the nature of Indian leadership and politics in the post-1969 period, see Menno Boldt, *Surviving as Indians: The Challenge of Self-Government* (Toronto: University of Toronto Press, 1993). Boldt's work identifies the major developments in DIA policy and issues confronting Aboriginal leadership between 1969 and the late 1980s.

24 NAC, RG10, vol. 8477, f. 1/24-2-1, pt. 5, IAA annual meeting minutes, 1960, 1, Mr. Beebe to IAA members.

25 Ibid., 1961, 1 , Mr. Steinhauer to IAA members.

26 Ibid., 1964, 2.

27 Ibid.

28 Cardinal, *Unjust Society*, 104.

29 IAA, Constitution and By-Laws, 1963, as held in the National Library of Canada.

30 *Edmonton Journal*, 09/06/68

31 Ibid., 09/06/68.

32 *Calgary Herald*, 06/12/68

33 Cardinal, *Unjust Society* , 114.

34 *Edmonton Journal*, 15 November 1969.

35 More detailed discussions of the National Indian Brotherhood and funding of Indian organizations during this time period can be found in Cardinal, *Unjust Society*; Peter

McFarlane, "Aboriginal Leadership," in *Visions of the Heart: Canadian Aboriginal Issues*, ed. D.A. Long and Olive Dickason (Toronto: Harcourt Brace, 1996), 117-145; Richard R. H. Lueger, "A History of Indian Associations in Canada: 1870-1970" (MA thesis, Ottawa: Carleton University), 1977.

36 William Wuttunee, *Ruffled Feathers: Indians in Canadian Society* (Calgary: Bell Books, 1971) 5-6.

37 Ibid., 7.

38 Ibid., 1-2.

39 Joe Sawchuk, *The Dynamics of Native Politics: the Alberta Métis Experience* (Saskatoon: Purich Publishing, 1998), 60-61.

40 Lueger, "Indian Associations in Canada," 206.

41 Sally Weaver, "The Hawthorn Report: Its Use in Making Canadian Indian Policy," in *Anthropology, Public Policy, and Native Peoples in Canada*, ed. Noel Dyck and James B. Waldram (Montreal: McGill-Queen's Press, 1993), 75-98, 77.

42 Weaver, *Canadian Indian Policy*, 79-80.

43 Ibid., 87-89.

44 Ibid., 109.

45 *Edmonton Journal*, 28/06/68.

46 *Calgary Herald*, 8/11/68.

47 *Lethbridge Herald*, 28/02/69.

48 Canada, Statement of the Government of Canada on Indian Policy, 1969 (Ottawa: Queen's Printer, 1969), 5.

49 Ibid., 11.

50 *Edmonton Journal*, 15/11/1969.

51 Wuttunee, *Ruffled Feathers*, 58; Murray Dobbin, *Preston Manning and the Reform Party* (Toronto: James Lorimer, 1991), 39; Maria Campbell, personal communication, 3 June 2001.

52 Weaver, *Canadian Indian Policy*, 183-84.

53 Dobbin, *Preston Manning and the Reform Party*, 46.

54 Harold Cardinal, *The Rebirth of Canada's Indians* (Edmonton: Hurtig, 1977), 184.

55 Menno Boldt, *Surviving as Indians: The Challenge of Self-Government* (Toronto: University of Toronto Press, 1993), 79. In his article on political relations between the United States and American Indians, Michael G. Lacy astutely notes that co-optation, whereby the power holders (government) intentionally extend some form of political participation to actors who pose a threat to them, is not necessarily a negative process focused only upon neutralizing the threat. He suggests that co-optation may have certain benefits, including legitimizing the activities of both the power holders and those whom they seek to co-opt. I believe that this applies to the situation of Indian organizations in Canada in so far as their participation in the Canadian political process has advanced their causes and given them new powers and new voices within the state system. See Michael G. Lacy, "A Model of Cooptation Applied to the Political Relations of the United States and American Indians," *Social Science Journal* 19, 3 (July 1982): 23-36.

Chapter 9: "Nînâkastêwimâkêwin"

1 Speech delivered at the Saskatchewan Indian Federated College, 1990. Tape held in SIFC library.

2 Robert Allen Warrior, *Tribal Secrets: Recovering American Indian Intellectual Traditions* (Minneapolis: University of Minnesota Press, 1995), xvi.

3 Paul Tennant, "Native Indian Political Organizations in British Columbia, 1900-1969," *BC Studies* 55 (Autumn 1982): 8. See also Peter Kulchyski, "A Considerable Unrest: F.O. Loft and the League of Indians," *Native Studies Review* 4, 1 and 2 (1988): 95-117.

4 Norma Sluman and Jean Goodwill, *John Tootoosis: A Biography of a Cree Leader* (Winnipeg: Pemmican Publications, 1984) 172.

5 Hugh Dempsey, *The Gentle Persuader: A Biography of James Gladstone, Indian Senator* (Saskatoon: Western Producer Prairie Books, 1986), 108-9.

6 John Tootoosis, "Modern Indian Societies," speech given at the Plains Cree Conference,

Fort Qu'appelle, October 1975. *Proceedings of the Plains Cree Conference* (Regina: Canadian Plains Research Centre, University of Regina 1979), 76-77.

7 Saskatchewan Archives Board, Adrian Hope interview with Murray Dobbin, tape no. IH-381/381A, transcript disc 92, 1976.

8 Ibid.

9 Ibid. See also Reta Rowan Papers, University of Alberta Archives, file 17/1/1-5, Friends of the Indian meeting minutes, 14 March 1945.

10 Personal communication with Maria Campbell, Batoche, Saskatchewan, 16 June 2000.

11 M7155, IAA Papers, Glenbow Archives, 1944 Memorial, 1.

12 Ibid., Memorial, 2.

13 Reta Rowan Papers, University of Alberta Archives, file 17/1/1-57, membership lists.

14 Ibid., file 17/1/1-1, contains cards outlining the aims of the Friends.

15 "Michel Band Is Enfranchised," *Indian News* 3, 1 (June 1958). See also William I.C. Wuttunee, *Ruffled Feathers: Indians in Canadian Society* (Calgary: Bell Books, 1971), 120.

16 NAC, RG 18, vol. 2487, no file. Court documents related to Yellowmud Blanket's alleged "theft," 1884.

17 Personal communication with Neal McLeod, Regina, Saskatchewan, April 1998. Eric Tootoosis of Poundmaker First Nation, in sharing oral history of his reserve with McLeod, tells of the battle of Cutknife Hill (where Colonel Otter attacked Poundmaker and his people) and how Poundmaker urged the warriors to restrain themselves.

18 The events of 1885 in relation to the people of Poundmaker's community are perhaps best presented by Sluman and Goodwill, *John Tootoosis*.

19 Tootoosis, *Proceedings*, 76.

20 Canada, Special Joint Committee of the Senate and the House of Commons Appointed to Examine and Consider the Indian Act, Minutes of Proceedings and Evidence, Thursday, 8 May 1947, 948.

21 A1179, Saskatchewan Archives tape. Murray Dobbin interview with John B. Tootoosis.

22 NAC, RG 29, vol. 2916, f. 851-1-A671-, pt. 1 (B), W.L. Falconer to Minister of Indian Affairs, 31 July 1947.

23 Murray Dobbin, private papers, Malcolm Norris to John B. Tootoosis, 8 July 1944, letter in author's collection.

24 Saskatchewan Archives Board, Murray Dobbin interview with John Tootoosis, Tape 1179

25 Sluman and Goodwill, *Tootoosis*, 177-78.

26 Murray Dobbin, private papers, John Laurie to G.H. Castleden, 26 February 1945. Copy in author's collection.

27 R834, f. 37, Saskatchewan Archives, John Tootoosis in the Report on the Indian Meeting at Duck Lake, Saskatchewan, 10 January 1946.

28 Ibid., John Tootoosis in meeting minutes from the Barry Hotel, February 1946.

29 Glenbow Archives, M656, box 1, file 3, John Tootoosis to Frank Cardinal, 1 September 1953.

30 Speech delivered at the Saskatchewan Indian Federated College, 1990. Tape held in SIFC library.

31 Albert Lightning, *Proceedings of the Plains Cree Conference*, (Regina: Canadian Plains Research Centre, University of Regina, 1979), 117-18.

Chapter 10: Final Thoughts

1 Katherine Graham, Carolyn Dittburner, and Frances Abele, *Soliloquy and Dialogue: Overview of Major Trends in Public Policy Relating to Aboriginal Peoples, 1965-1992*, vol. 1 (Ottawa: Royal Commission on Aboriginal Peoples, 1996), 330.

Bibliography

Primary Sources

Interviews

Maria Campbell, June 2000
Harold Cardinal, February 1997
Sheldon Cardinal, November 1996
Gordon Crowchild, September 1996
Stan Cuthand, spring 1995
Hugh Dempsey, March 1995; March, September 1996
Pauline Dempsey, March, September 1996
Cynthia Downe, December 1994
Ruth Gorman, July 1992
Dorothy Gowan, August 1995
Aylmer Liesemer, December 1985, interviewed by D.B. Smith
Neal McLeod, April 1998
Muriel Manywounds, October 1996
Willie Norris, March 1995
Jim Tootoosis, September 1996

Archival Sources

Glenbow Archives, Calgary
Alberta Federation of Home and School Association Papers
George H. Gooderham Papers
James Gladstone Papers
John Laurie Papers
Joseph Dion Papers
James Brady Papers
Indian Association of Alberta Papers
Lucien M. and Jane R. Hanks Papers
Hobbema Agency Papers
United Farmers of Alberta Papers
John H. Blackmore Papers

Saskatchewan Archives Board
Oral History collection

University of Alberta Archives, Edmonton
Reta Rowan Papers

University of Calgary Special Collections, Calgary
John Laurie Papers

Private Papers
Hugh Dempsey, private papers
Murray Dobbin, private papers
Cynthia Downe, private papers
D.B. Smith, private papers

National Archives of Canada, Ottawa
Record Group 10, Indian Affairs
Record Group 14, Records of Parliament

National Archives, Washington D.C.
Record Group 75, Bureau of Indian Affairs

Government Publications

Alberta. Native Affairs. *A Guide to Native Communities in Alberta*. 1986.

Canada. House of Commons. *Debates*. June 1944, October 1945, December 1945, April 1946, May 1946, February 1947, June 1947, July 1947, April 1948, November 1949, December 1949, April 1953.

–. House of Commons. *Sessional Papers*. Annual Reports for Indian Affairs, 1939-1959.

–. Special Committee on Reconstruction and Re-establishment. *Minutes of Proceedings and Evidence*. Ottawa: 1944.

–. Special Joint Committee of the Senate and the House of Commons Appointed to Examine and Consider the Indian Act. *Minutes of Proceedings and Evidence*. Ottawa: 1946-1949.

–. Special Joint Committee of the Senate and the House of Commons on Indian Affairs. *Minutes of Proceedings and Evidence*. Ottawa: 1960-1961.

–. *Employment and Income*. Ottawa: April 1945.

–. *Statement of the Government of Canada on Indian Policy, 1969*. Ottawa: 1969.

Unpublished Manuscripts

Cuthand, Stan. "A Sacred Treaty." Unpublished paper in author's possession, Saskatoon, 1997.

Gowen, Dorothy M. "Morley Memories." Unpublished paper in author's possession, Calgary, June 1991.

Murdoch, Rauncie. "The Union of Saskatchewan Indians." Unpublished paper in author's possession. Saskatoon, March 1995.

Newspapers and Magazines

Selected clippings contained in government files and the Glenbow Archives clipping files are from the following news sources:

Brantford Expositor
Calgary Albertan
Calgary Herald
Canadian Cattlemen
Edmonton Bulletin
Lethbridge Herald
Newsweek
Regina Post
Saturday Night
St. John Telegraph Journal
Tekawennake
Vancouver Sun
Windspeaker

Secondary Sources

Abel, Kerry. *Drum Songs: Glimpses of Dene History*. Montreal: McGill-Queen's University Press, 1993.

Ahenakew, Edward. *Voices of the Plains Cree*. Toronto: McClelland and Stewart, 1973.

Arima, Eugene Y. *Blackfeet and Palefaces*. Ottawa: Golden Dog Press, 1995.

Ashley, C.A., ed. *Reconstruction in Canada*. Toronto: University of Toronto Press, 1943.

Barbalet, J.M. *Citizenship: Rights, Struggle and Class Inequality*. Milton Keynes: Open University Press, 1988.

Barr, John J. "The Impact of Oil on Alberta: Retrospect and Prospect." In *The Making of the Modern West: Western Canada since 1945*, ed. A.W. Rasporich, 97-103. Calgary: University of Calgary Press, 1984.

Barron, F.L. "A Summary of Federal Indian policy in the Canadian West, 1867-1984." *Native Studies Review* 1, 1 (1984): 28-38.

–. "The Indian Pass System in the Canadian West, 1882-1935." *Prairie Forum* 13, 1 (1987): 25-42.

Boldt, Menno. *Surviving As Indians: The Challenge of Self-Government*. Toronto: University of Toronto Press, 1993.

Bothwell, Robert, Ian Drummond, and John English. *Canada, 1900-1945*. Toronto: University of Toronto Press, 1987.

–. *Canada since 1945*. Rev. ed. Toronto: University of Toronto Press, 1989.

Brewis, T.N. *Canadian Economic Policy*. Toronto: Macmillan, 1961.

Burrell, Gordon, Robert Young, Richard Price, eds., *Indian Treaties and the Law*. Edmonton: Indian Association of Alberta, 1975.

Callihoo, Victoria. "The Iroquois in Alberta." *Alberta Historical Review* 7, 2 (Spring 1959): 17-18.

Cardinal, Harold. *The Unjust Society: The Tragedy of Canada's Indians*. Edmonton: Hurtig Publishers, 1969.

Caves, Richard E., and Richard H. Holton. *The Canadian Economy: Prospect and Retrospect*. Cambridge: Harvard University Press, 1961.

Clastres, Pierre. *Society against the State*. New York: Zone Books, 1989.

Comaroff, John, and Jean Comaroff. *Ethnography and the Historical Imagination*. Oxford: Westview Press, 1992.

Conrad, Margaret. "Not a Feminist But ... : The Political Career of Ellen Louks Fairclough, Canada's First Female Federal Cabinet Minister." *Journal of Canadian Studies* 31, 2 (Summer 1996): 5-28.

Conrad, Margaret, and Julie Landau. "Dorise Nielsen, 1902-1980: A Tribute." *Atlantis* 6, 2 (1981): 138-46.

Cook-Lynn, Elizabeth. "American Indian Intellectualism and the New Indian History." In *Natives and Academics: Researching and Writing about American Indians*, ed. Devon A. Mihesuah. 111-38. Lincoln: University of Nebraska Press, 1998.

Coutts, Dean H.T. "Presentation of John Lee Laurie." *New Trail* 14, 3 (1957).

Creighton, Donald. *The Forked Road: Canada 1939-1957*. Toronto: McClelland and Stewart, 1976.

Cuthand, Stan. "The Native Peoples of the Prairie Provinces in the 1920s and 1930s." In *One Century Later: Western Canadian Indian Reserve Indians Since Treaty 7*, ed. Donald B. Smith and Ian A.L. Getty, 31-42. Vancouver: UBC Press, 1978.

Dacks, Gurston. "From Consensus to Competition: Social Democracy and Political Culture in Alberta." In *Socialism and Democracy in Alberta: Essays in Honor of Grant Notley*, ed. Larry Pratt, 186-204. Edmonton: NeWest Press, 1986.

Dalheim, K., and M. Kerr, eds. *Calahoo Trails*. Calahoo Women's Institute, 1976.

Daniel, Richard. "The Spirit and Terms of Treaty Eight." In *The Spirit of the Alberta Indian Treaties*, ed. Richard Price, 47-100. Edmonton: Pica Pica Press, 1987.

Dempsey, Hugh A. *Tailfeathers*. Art Series No. 2. Calgary: Glenbow-Alberta Institute, 1970.

–. *The Gentle Persuader: A Biography of James Gladstone, Indian Senator*. Saskatoon: Western Producer Prairie Books, 1986.

–. *Treaty Seven: Treaty Research Report*. Ottawa: Treaties and Historical Research Centre, 1987.

–. *Indian Tribes of Alberta*. Calgary: Glenbow Museum 1988.

Dempsey, James. "The Indians and World War One." *Alberta History* 31, 3 (Summer 1983): 1-8.

–. "Problems of Western Canadian Indian War Veterans after World War One." *Native Studies Review* 5, 2 (1989): 1-18.

–. "Alberta's Indians and the Second World War." In *For King and Country: Alberta in the Second World War*, ed. K.W. Tingley, 36-52. Edmonton: Provincial Museum of Alberta, 1995.

Dickason, Olive Patricia. *Canada's First Nations: A History of Founding Peoples from Earliest Times*. Toronto: McClelland and Stewart, 1992.

Dickerson, Mark O., and Thomas Flanagan. *An Introduction to Government and Politics: A Conceptual Approach*. Third ed. Scarborough: Nelson Canada, 1990.

Dion, Joe. *My Tribe, the Crees*. Calgary: Glenbow-Alberta Institute, 1996.

Dobbin, Murray. *One and a Half Men: The Story of Jim Brady and Malcolm Norris, Metis Patriots of the Twentieth Century*. Vancouver: New Star Books, 1981.

–. *Preston Manning and the Reform Party*. Toronto: James Lorimer, 1991.

Dosman, Edgar J. *Indians: The Urban Dilemma*. Toronto: McClelland and Stewart, 1971.

Drucker, Philip. *The Native Brotherhoods: Modern Intertribal Organizations on the Northwest Coast*. Bureau of American Ethnology, Smithsonian Institution Bulletin No. 168. Washington: Government Printing Office, 1958.

Dyck, Noel. "An Opportunity Lost: The Initiative of the Reserve Agricultural Program in the Prairie West." In *1885 and After: Native Society in Transition*, ed. F. Laurie Barron and J.B. Waldram, 121-38. Regina: Canadian Plains Research Centre.

–. *What Is the Indian 'Problem': Tutelage and Resistance in Canadian Indian Administration*. Newfoundland: Institute of Social and Economic Research, 1991.

–. "Tutelage, Resistance, and Co-optation in Canadian Indian Administration." In *The Canadian Review of Sociology and Anthropology* 34 (August 1997): 333-48.

–, ed. *Indigenous Peoples and the Nation-State: Fourth World Politics in Canada, Australia and Norway*. St. John's: Institute of Social and Economic Research, 1985.

Fairclough, Ellen Louks. *Saturday's Child: Memoirs of Canada's First Female Cabinet Minister*. Toronto: University of Toronto Press, 1995.

Finkel, Alvin. *The Social Credit Phenomenon in Alberta*. Toronto: University of Toronto Press, 1989.

–. "Populism and Gender: The UFA and Social Credit Experiences." *Journal of Canadian Studies* 27, 4 (Winter 1992-93): 76-94.

Fiske, Jo-Anne. "Gender and Politics in a Carrier Indian Community." PhD diss., University of British Columbia, 1989.

Fleras, Augie, and Jean Leonard Elliot. *The Nations Within: Aboriginal-State Relations in Canada, the United States, and New Zealand*. Toronto: Oxford University Press, 1992.

Foran, Max. "Calgary, Calgarians and the Northern Movement of the Oil Frontier, 1950-1970." In *The Making of the Modern West: Western Canada since 1945*, ed. A.W. Rasporich, 115-32. Calgary: University of Calgary Press, 1984.

Foucault, Michel. *The Archeology of Knowledge*. New York: Pantheon Books, 1972.

Fox, Richard G., "For a Nearly New Culture History." In *Recapturing Anthropology*, ed. Richard G. Fox, 93-113. Santa Fe: School of American Research Press, 1991.

Francis. D.R., and H. Ganzevoort, eds. *The Dirty Thirties in Prairie Canada*. Vancouver: Tantalus Research Ltd. 1980.

Franks, C.E.S. *The Parliament of Canada*. Toronto: University of Toronto Press, 1987.

Frideres, James. "Government Policies and Programs Relating to People of Indian Ancestry in Alberta." In *The Dynamics of Government Programs for Urban Indians in the Prairie Provinces*, ed. Raymond Breton and Gail Grant, 321-74. Montreal: The Institute for Research on Public Policy, 1984.

–. *Native Peoples in Canada: Contemporary Conflicts*. Scarborough: Prentice Hall, 1993.

Fumoleau, René. *As Long as This Land Shall Last: A History of Treaty 8 and Treaty 11*. Toronto: McClelland and Stewart, 1975.

Gaffen, Fred. *Forgotten Soldiers*. Penticton: Theytus Books, 1985.

Galois, R.M. "The Indian Rights Association." *Native Studies Review* 8, 2 (1992): 1-34.

Gibbins, Roger. "Regionalism in Decline: 1940 to the Present." In *Riel to Reform: A History of Protest in Western Canada*, ed. George Melnyk, 215-33. Saskatoon: Fifth House Publishers, 1992.

Gillies, James, and Jean Pigott. "Participation in the Legislative Process." *Canadian Public Administration* 25, 2 (Summer 1982): 254-64.

Goddard, John. *Last Stand of the Lubicon Cree*. Toronto: Douglas and McIntyre, 1991.

Gottesman, Dan. "Native Hunting and the Migratory Birds Convention Act: Historical, Political and Ideological Perspectives." *Journal of Canadian Studies* 8, 3 (Fall 1983): 67-89.

Graham, Katherine, Carolyn Dittburner, and Frances Abele. *Soliloquy and Dialogue: Overview of Major Trends in Public Policy Relating to Aboriginal Peoples, 1965-1992*. Royal Commission on Aboriginal Peoples. Vol. 1, *Public Policy and Aboriginal Peoples, 1965-1992*. Ottawa: Canada Communications Group, 1996.

Grant, Shelagh. "Hugh Llewellyn Keenleyside, Commissioner of the Northwest Territories, 1947-1950." *Arctic* 43, 1 (March 1990): 80-82.

Grant, S.D. "Indian Affairs Under Duncan Campbell Scott: The Plains Cree of Saskatchewan, 1913-1931." *Journal of Canadian Studies* 18, 3 (Autumn 1983): 21-39.

Gray, John Morgan. *Fun Tomorrow*. Toronto: Macmillan, 1978.

Greene, B.M., ed. *Who's Who in Canada, 1945-1946*. Toronto: International Press Ltd, 1946.

Guest, Dennis. *The Emergence of Social Security in Canada*. 2nd. ed. Vancouver: UBC Press, 1985.

Guillemin, Jean. "The Politics of National Integration: A Comparison of United States and Canadian Indian Administrations." *Social Problems* 25, 3, 9 (1978): 319-32.

Hall, Anthony J. "Indian Treaties." In *The 1997 Canadian Encyclopedia*, CD ROM. Toronto: McClelland and Stewart, 1996.

Hall, D.J. "Clifford Sifton and Canadian Indian Administration, 1896-1905." *Prairie Forum* 22, 1-2 (1977): 127-51.

Harper, Allan G. "Canada's Indian Administration: Basic Concepts and Objectives." *Americana Indigena* 5, 2 (April 1945): 120-32.

–. "Canada's Indian Administration: The 'Indian Act.'" *Americana Indigena* 6, 4 (1946): 297-314.

–. "Canada's Indian Administration: The Treaty System." *Americana Indigena* 7, 2 (April 1947): 128-48.

Hawthorn, H.B., ed. *A Survey of the Contemporary Indians of Canada*. Vol. 2, *Economic, Political, Educational Needs and Policies*. Ottawa: Indian Affairs Branch, 1967.

Heywood, Andrew. *Political Ideas and Concepts: An Introduction*. London: Macmillan Press, 1994.

Huizinga, J. *De Wetenschap Der Geschiedenis*. Haarlem: H.D. Tjeenk Willink en Zoon N.V., 1937.

Hunt, Lynn, ed. *The New Cultural History*. Berkeley: University of California Press, 1989.

The Indians Speak to Canada: A Series of Broadcasts sponsored by the CBC in cooperation with the Indian Affairs Branch, Department of Mines and Resources. Ottawa, 1937.

Isaac, Thomas. *Aboriginal Law: Cases, Materials and Commentary*. Saskatoon: Purich Publishing, 1995

Jenness, Diamond. "Canada's Indian Policy Yesterday. What of Today?" *Canadian Journal of Economics and Political Science* 20, 1 (February 1954): 95-100.

Jobson, Valerie K. "The Blackfoot Farming Experiment." MA thesis, University of Calgary, 1990.

Johnson, Ian V.B. *Helping Indians to Help Themselves: The 1951 Indian Act Consultation Process*. Ottawa: Indian and Northern Affairs, Treaties and Historical Research Centre, 1984.

Keenleyside, Hugh L. *Memoirs of Hugh L. Keenleyside: On the Bridge of Time*. Toronto: McClelland and Stewart, 1982.

Knoll, D. "Treaty and Aboriginal Hunting Rights." *Canadian Native Law Reporter* 1 (1979): 1-29.

Kulchyski, Peter. "A Considerable Unrest: F.O. Loft and the League of Indians." *Native Studies Review* 4, 1 and 2 (1988): 95-117.

Lacy, Michael G. "A Model of Cooptation Applied to the Political Relations of the United States and American Indians." *Social Science Journal* 19, 3 (July 1982): 23-36.

. "The United States and American Indians: Political Relations." In *American Indian Policy in the Twentieth Century*, ed. Vine Deloria Jr., 83-104. Norman: University of Oklahoma Press, 1985.

Laliberte, Ronald F. "The Canadian State and Native Migrant Labour in Southern Alberta's Sugar Beet Industry." MA thesis, University of Saskatchewan, 1994.

Laurie, John. "One of the Greatest Indians Ever Born in Alberta." *Camsell Arrow* 9, 3 (September/October 1955): 9-11.

Leslie, John F. *A Historical Survey of Indian-Government Relations, 1940-1970*. Ottawa: Royal Commission Liaison Office, 1993.

Leslie, John F., and Ron Maguire. *The Historical Development of the Indian Act*. Ottawa: Indian and Northern Affairs, Treaties and Historical Research Centre, 1978.

Leuger, Richard R.H. "A History of Indian Associations in Canada, 1870-1970." MA thesis, Carleton University, 1977.

Long, David Alan. "Trials of the Spirit: The Native Social Movement in Canada." In *Visions of the Heart: Canadian Aboriginal Issues*, ed. David Alan Long and Olive Patricia Dickason, 377-96. Toronto: Harcourt and Brace, 1996.

Lupul, David. "The Bobtail Land Surrender." *Alberta History* 26, 1 (Winter 1978): 29-39.

MacEwan, J.W. Grant. *Portraits from the Plains*. Toronto: McGraw-Hill, 1971.

McFarlane, Peter. *Brotherhood to Nationhood: George Manuel and the Making of the Modern Indian Movement*. Toronto: Between the Lines, 1993.

–. "Aboriginal Leadership." In *Visions of the Heart: Canadian Aboriginal Issues*, ed. David Alan Long and Olive Patricia Dickason, 117-45. Toronto: Harcourt and Brace, 1996.

McIlwraith, T.F., and C.T. Loram, eds. *The North American Indian Today*. Toronto: University of Toronto Press, 1943.

MacInnes, T.R.I. "History of Indian Administration in Canada." *Canadian Journal of Economics and Political Science* 12 (February 1946): 387-404.

McMurtry, Jim. "The 1946-48 Special Joint Committee on the Indian Act and Educational Policy." MA thesis, University of Alberta, 1985.

McNeil, K. *Indian Hunting and Fishing Rights in the Prairie Provinces of Canada*. Saskatoon: Native Law Centre, University of Saskatchewan, 1983.

Meili, Dianne. *Those Who Know: Profiles of Alberta's Native Elders*. Edmonton: NeWest Press, 1991.

Meijer Drees, Laurie. "The League of Nations and the Six Nations of Grand River." *Native Studies Review* 10, 1 (1995): 75-88.

Miller, J.R. *Skyscrapers Hide the Heavens*. Toronto: University of Toronto Press, 1982.

–. *Shingwauk's Vision: A History of Native Residential Schools*. Toronto: University of Toronto Press, 1996.

Miller, J.R., ed. *Sweet Promises: A Reader on Indian-White Relations in Canada*. Toronto: University of Toronto Press, 1991.

Milloy, J.S. *A Historical Overview of Indian-Government Relations, 1755-1940*. Ottawa: Indian and Northern Affairs, 1992.

Mitchell, Darcy Anne. "The Allied Tribes of British Columbia: A Study in Pressure Group Behaviour." MA thesis, University of British Columbia, 1973.

Mitchell, Marybelle. *From Talking Chiefs to a Native Corporative Elite: The Birth of Class and Nationalism among Canadian Inuit*. Montreal: McGill-Queen's University Press, 1996.

Monod, David. "The End of Agrarianism: The Fight for Farm Parity in Alberta and Saskatchewan, 1935-48." *Labour/Le Travail* 16 (Fall 1985): 117-43.

Morris, Alexander. *The Treaties of Canada with the Indians*. Saskatoon: Fifth House Publishers, 1991.

Notzke, Claudia. *Indian Reserves in Canada: Development Problems of the Stoney and Peigan Reserves in Alberta*. Marburg/Lahn: Universitat Marburg, 1985.

–. "Indian Land in Southern Alberta." In *A Cultural Geography of North American Indians*, ed. Thomas E. Ross and Tyrel G. Moore, 107-26. Boulder: Westview Press, 1987.

–. *Aboriginal People and Natural Resources in Canada*. North York: Captus Press, 1994.

O'Donnell, Jaqueline P. "The Native Brotherhood of British Columbia 1931-1950: A New Phase in Native Political Organization." MA thesis, University of British Columbia, 1985.

Palmer, Howard, with Tamara Palmer. *Alberta: A New History*. Edmonton: Hurtig Publishers, 1990.

Patterson, E. Palmer II. "Andrew Paull (1922-1959): Finding a Voice for the New Indian." *Western Canadian Journal of Anthropology* 6, 2 (1976): 63-82.

–. "Andrew Paull and the Early History of British Columbia Indian Organizations." In *One Century Later: Western Canadian Reserve Indians since Treaty Seven*, ed. Ian A.L. Getty and D.B. Smith, 43-54. Vancouver: UBC Press, 1978.

Pettipas, Katherine. *Severing the Ties that Bind: Government Repression of Indigenous Religious Ceremonies on the Prairies*. Winnipeg: University of Manitoba Press, 1994.

Pickersgill, J.W. *The Liberal Party*. Toronto: McClelland and Stewart, 1962.

–. *My Years with Louis St. Laurent: A Political Memoir*. Toronto: University of Toronto Press, 1975.

Pitsula, James M. "The CCF Government and the Formation of the Union of Saskatchewan Indians." *Prairie Forum* 19, 2 (Fall 1994): 131-52.

–. "The Saskatchewan CCF Government and Treaty Indians, 1944-1964." *Canadian Historical Review* 75, 1 (1994): 21-52.

Pope, Richard K. "North American Indian Nationalism and the Decline of Sacred Authenticity." *Canadian Journal of Native Studies* 2 (1985): 253-59.

Ponting, J. Rick, and Roger Gibbins. *Out of Irrelevance: A Socio-political Introduction to Indian Affairs in Canada*. Toronto: Butterworths, 1980.

Pross, A. Paul. "Governing under Pressure: The Special Interest Group – Summary of Discussion." *Canadian Public Administration* 25, 2 (Summer 1982): 170-82.

Prucha, Francis Paul. *The Indians in American Society*. Berkeley: University of California Press, 1985.

Ray, Arthur. *The Canadian Fur Trade in the Industrial Age*. Toronto: University of Toronto Press, 1990.

–. *I Have Lived Here since the World Began*. Toronto: Lester Publishing, 1996.

Rex v. *Commanda*. *Canadian Native Law Reporter* 5 (1987).

Rostkowski, Joelle. "The Redman's Appeal for Justice." In *Indians and Europe*, ed. Christian Feest, 1-4. Aachen: Herodot, 1987.

Russell, Dale. *Eighteenth-Century Western Cree and Their Neighbours*. Mercury Series Paper 143, p. 187. Ottawa: Canadian Museum of Civilization, 1991.

Sanders, Douglas. "The Queen's Promises." In *Law and Justice in a New Land: Essays in Western Canadian Legal History*, ed. Louis A. Knafla, 101-27. Calgary: Carswell, 1986.

Sawchuk, Joe. *The Dynamics of Native Politics: The Alberta Métis Experience*. Saskatoon: Purich Publishing, 1998.

Schumiatcher, Maurice (Morris). "The Buckskin Curtain." *The Beaver* Outfit 290 (Autumn 1959): 12-15.

Scott, Duncan Campbell. *The Administration of Indian Affairs in Canada*. Toronto: Canadian Institute of International Affairs, 1931.

Sluman, Norma, and Jean Goodwill. *John Tootoosis: A Biography of a Cree Leader*. Ottawa: Golden Dog Press, 1982.

Smith, Denis. *Rogue Tory: The Life and Legend of John G. Diefenbaker*. Toronto: Macfarlane, Walter and Ross, 1995.

Smith, Donald B. *Long Lance: The True Story of an Impostor*. Toronto: Macmillan, 1982.

–. "The Original Peoples of Alberta." In *Peoples of Alberta: Portraits of Cultural Diversity*, ed. Howard and Tamara Palmer, 50-83. Saskatoon: Western Producer Prairie Books, 1985.

– "A Good Samaritan: John Laurie." In *Citymakers: Calgarians after the Frontier*, ed. Max Foran and Sheilagh S. Jameson, 263-74. Calgary: Historical Society of Alberta, 1987.

–. "Now We Talk – You Listen." *Rotunda* (Fall 1990): 48.

–. "Fred Loft." In *Encyclopedia of North American Indians*, ed. Frederick E. Hoxi, 344-45. New York: Houghton Mifflin, 1996.
Smith, Peter J. "Urban Development Trends in the Prairie Provinces." In *The Making of the Modern West: Western Canada since 1945*, ed. A.W. Rasporich, 133-43. Calgary: University of Calgary Press, 1984.
Snow, John. *These Mountains Are Our Sacred Places*. Toronto: Samuel Stevens, 1977.
Taylor, John Leonard. *Canadian Indian Policy During the Interwar Years, 1918-1939*. Ottawa: Department of Indian Affairs, 1984.
–. *Treaty Six – Treaty Research Report*. Ottawa: Treaties and Historical Research Centre, 1985.
Tennant, Paul. "Native Indian Political Organizations in British Columbia, 1900-1969: A Response to Internal Colonialism." *BC Studies* 55 (Autumn 1982): 3-49.
–. *Aboriginal Peoples and Politics*. Vancouver: UBC Press, 1990.
Tester, Frank James, and Peter Kulchyski. *Tammarniit (Mistakes): Inuit Relocation in the Eastern Arctic, 1939-63*. Vancouver: UBC Press, 1994.
Thomas, Robert K. "Pan-Indianism." In *The Emergent Native Americans: A Reader in Culture Contact*, ed. Deward E. Walker Jr., 739-46. Boston: Little, Brown and Co. 1972.
Titley, E. Brian. *A Narrow Vision: Duncan Campbell Scott and the Administration of Indian Affairs in Canada*. Vancouver: UBC Press, 1986.
Tobias, John L. "Protection, Civilization, Assimilation: An Outline History of Canada's Indian Policy." In *As Long as the Sun Shines and Water Flows*, ed. Ian A.L. Getty and Antoine Lussier, 39-55. Vancouver: UBC Press, 1983.
–. "The Origins of the Treaty Rights Movement in Saskatchewan." In *1885 and After: Native Society in Transition*, ed. F. Laurie Barron and J.B. Waldram, 241-52. Regina: Canadian Plains Research Centre, 1986.
Tootoosis, John. "Modern Indian Societies." Speech given at the Plains Cree Conference, Fort Qu'appelle, October 1975. In *Proceedings of the Plains Cree Conference*. Regina: Canadian Plains Research Centre, University of Regina, 1979.
Tough, Frank. "Indian Hunting Rights, Natural Resources Transfer Agreements and Legal Opinions from the Department of Justice." *Native Studies Review* 10, 2 (1995): 119-40.
Treaties and Historical Research Centre. *Indian Acts and Ammendments, 1868-1950*. Ottawa: 1981.
–. *Contemporary Indian Legislation, 1951-1978*. Ottawa: 1981.
Treaty Seven Elders and Tribal Council with Sarah Carter, Walter Hildebrandt, and Dorothy First Rider. *The True Spirit and Original Intent of Treaty 7*. Montreal: McGill-Queen's University Press, 1996.
Upton, L.F.S. "The Origins of Canadian Indian Policy." *Journal of Canadian Studies* 8, 4 (November 1973): 51-61.
Veach, Richard. *Canada and the League of Nations*. Toronto: University of Toronto Press, 1975.
Warrior, Robert Allen. *Tribal Secrets: Recovering American Indian Intellectual Traditions*. Minneapolis: University of Minnesota Press, 1995.
Waubageshig, ed. *The Only Good Indian: Essays by Canadian Indians*. Toronto: New Press, 1970.
Weaselfat, Frances, and the Indian Association of Alberta. *Our Legacy: 50 Years in Unity 1943-1993*. Indian Association of Alberta 50th Annual Assembly and Anniversary Commemoration brochure, September 1993.
Weaver, Sally. *Making Canadian Indian Policy: The Hidden Agenda, 1968-1970*. Toronto: University of Toronto Press, 1981.
–. "The Joint Cabinet/National Indian Brotherhood Committee: A Unique Experiment in Pressure Group Relations." *Canadian Public Administration* 25, 2 (Summer 1982): 211-39.
–. "Federal Policy-making for Métis and Non-Status Indians in the Context of Native Policy." *Canadian Ethnic Studies* 27, 2 (1985): 80-102.
–. "The Hawthorn Report: Its Use in the Making of Canadian Indian Policy." In *Anthropology, Public Policy, and Native Peoples in Canada*, ed. Noel Dyck and James B. Waldram, 75-93. Montreal: McGill-Queen's University Press, 1993.

Whitaker, Reginald. *The Government Party: Organizing and Financing the Liberal Party of Canada, 1930-58*. Toronto: University of Toronto Press, 1977.

Whiteside, Don. *Efforts to Develop Aboriginal Political Associations in Canada, 1850-1965*. Ottawa: Aboriginal Institute of Canada, 1974.

Wuttunee, William I.C. *Ruffled Feathers: Indians in Canadian Society*. Calgary: Bell Books, 1971.

Index

Note: IAA stands for the Indian Association of Alberta; "m" indicates a map; "p" indicates a photograph

Printed and bound in Canada by Friesens

Set in Stone by Brenda and Neil West, BN Typographics West

Copy editor: Joanne Richardson

Proofreader: Lorne Madgett

Indexer: Patricia Buchanan

Cartographer: Eric Leinberger